DRAFTED

A Memoir of the '60's

Also by Heywood Gould

BOOKS

Green Light For Murder
The Serial Killer's Daughter
Leading Lady
Double Bang
Cocktail
Fort Apache, The Bronx
Glitterburn
One Dead Debutante
Corporation Freak
Sir Christopher Wren: Renaissance
Headaches and Health
Complete Book of Camping
The Fabulous UCLA Bruins

SCREENPLAYS

Rolling Thunder (Starring: William Devane and Tommy Lee Jones)
The Boys From Brazil (Starring: Gregory Peck and Laurence Olivier)
Fort Apache, The Bronx (Starring: Paul Newman, Danny Aiello, Rachel Ticotin)
Cocktail (Starring: Tom Cruise, Bryan Brown, Elizabeth Shue)
Streets of Gold (Starring: Klaus Maria Brandauer, Wesley Snipes)
One Good Cop (Starring: Michael Keaton, Rene Russo)
Written & Directed by Heywood Gould
Trial By Jury (Starring: William Hurt, Gabriel Byrne, Armand Assante) Written & Directed by Heywood Gould
Mistrial (Starring: Bill Pullman, Robert Loggia)
Written & Directed by Heywood Gould
Double Bang (Starring: William Baldwin, Jon Seda)
Written, Directed & Produced by Heywood Gould

TELEVISION

The Equalizer
NYPD
Hazard's People
Dog and Cat

PLAYS

Frank Merriwell
Dracula

HEYWOOD GOULD

DRAFTED

A Memoir of the '60's

Tolmitch Press
New York

DRAFTED, Memoir of the '60's

FIRST EDITION

Published by Tolmitch Press
New York

http://www.tolmitchebooks.com
http://www.heywoodgould.com

Hardcover ISBN: 978-1-63760-520-2
Paperback ISBN: 978-1-63760-534-9
EBook: 978-1-63760-533-2

Printed in the United States of America

Book jacket designed by Laurie Elvove

Tolmitch Press
New York

To Patricia

"...BEFORE THE PEACENIKS SHOW UP..."

New York, February 4, 1966

Life couldn't be better.

I'm a twenty-three-year-old Brooklyn boy working at my dream job—reporter for the New York Post.

I'm wealthy on $95 a week. Rent, $53 a month, gas, 24 cents a gallon, subway,15 cents. A mountain of pork fried rice goes for $1.80 in Chinatown. Veal parmigiana hero, full loaf, and a large cream soda, $2.75 at Whitey's Pizzeria. Movies are a buck, Rheingold on tap, a quarter... I'm training to be a heavy drinker.

Now all that is about to change. After five years of student deferments, doctors' notes, psychiatric exemptions, marriage proposals, offers of asylum from Canada and Sweden, conversion to Quakerism and a plot to blow up the draft board and become a folk hero, I've run out of options. I'm about to be inducted into the United States Army.

8:30 a.m. I'm outside Selective Service Headquarters, 39 Whitehall Street, downtown Manhattan, across from Battery Park. A Revolutionary War cannon points toward the Hudson, a rusty remnant of the battery that protected the harbor from British warships. A chill breeze whistles. A hundred anxious boys wait for the door to open. Some have sandwiches packed by their mothers. Extra socks and underwear from their dads. My father gave me a pair of scuffs. "I'm sure they haven't changed the showers since I was in," he said, "Better wear these so you won't get a splinter or pick up some toe crud."

The building is besieged every day by anti-war demonstrators. Broken pickets are scattered on the sidewalk. Scraps of ripped signs, tatters of a torn American flag. Two sailors on their knees scrub at a spot on the sidewalk where someone painted "HELL NO WE WON'T GO!" in red, white and blue. Across the street the Bowling Green subway plaza is covered with black paint and graffiti. There is a thick chain across the station entrance. Sanitation guys are hosing down the street and sweeping up the broken bottles, food bags, newspapers and the discarded clothes of the people who stripped naked in the freezing rain to protest the war.

On the ground a pamphlet from the War Resister's League, "STOP THE WAR". An article by "Anonymous" offers hints on how to beat the draft. By now I'm enough of an expert to know that "Anonymous" is either misinformed or an FBI agent. Drink a gallon of Coke the night before your physical, it says, to turn your urine brown and raise its sugar content. I know people who did it and nothing happened except they puked on the bus to Fort Dix. Smoke hundreds of Camels, dipped in ink. Might cause black spots to form on your lungs, might even kill you but won't keep you out of the Army because they don't give chest X-rays at the physicals. Eat a special "diarrhea menu" of Heinz beans, Hershey bars, peanut butter and cherries to cause constant bowel movements that will eventually produce the hemorrhoids that guarantee a 4F. I have friends who eat that way every day and they're in great shape. The only thing left for me is an act of civil disobedience. Like Gandhi and Martin Luther King Jr. I've heard stories of kids who refused to get on the bus. Do I have the guts to do that? My father was a decorated combat engineer during World War II. Every male and some females in my family served in World War II. They felt a patriotic obligation. Will I be betraying them by defying the country they love? My father felt he had to prove his courage against the accusation that Jews were cowards and slackers. He speaks gratefully of officers and friends who defended him against anti-semites in the ranks. Will he worry that I'm acting like a coward and a slacker?

Two Shore Patrol cops stand guard at the door checking draft cards against a list. Another shouts, "Get in and form a line against the wall."

A Marine Sergeant gives me a funny look. I'm scruffy, bloodshot, with nicotine fingers, and at least four years on everyone else. There's another older guy, gray ponytail, fatigue jacket. He ducks behind a fat kid as the Sergeant passes.

Excited talk in the ranks.

"They make you do fifty pushups. I can't even do two."

"My cousin got meningitis and almost died..."

One kid volunteered for the paratroops. "You get special treatment," he says. "Plus sixteen dollars jump pay."

Ponytail pops up. "You're too short for the program." He's got a military tattoo on his forearm. Southern accent, booze reeking off his clothes.

Another kid and his friend are going on the "buddy" plan so they get to serve together.

"That's just a come on," Ponytail says. "They'll put you where they need you."

"But they signed a contract..."

"And you signed your rights away. You're under the Uniformed Military Code of Justice, brother, which means they can do anything they want to you and you can't do squat about it..."

Ponytail turns to the wall as another Marine walks by. "Have your papers ready for inspection, Gentlemen..." Then turns back.

"Don't let 'em shame you into bein' a good soldier, brothers," he says. "Get yourself two left feet in the drills. Do pussy pushups. Fire wild over the targets. Don't scream "Kill!" in bayonet practice. Don't fall on the dummy grenade. Run away when the DI drops it. Report to the infirmary... Sprained ankles, blisters. Slam the butt of your rifle on your foot. That'll raise a bruise and put you out of commission. They have to keep you for at least a day 'cause they don't wanna pay disability. They'll recycle you through Basic. They count on your pride. Don't improve. Stay outta the infantry. Don't let them put your ass in the grass."

An Army Sergeant comes running down the hall followed by three MPs. He stops in front of Ponytail, neck veins bulging, "You back again?"

"It's a public building," Ponytail says. "I have a right to express my views."

The Sergeant goes eyeball to eyeball with him, fists clenched white at his side. "Remember what I told you yesterday?"

Ponytail glares back. "You can't arrest me, I'm a civilian… If you want to eject me you'll have to get Federal Marshals."

The Sergeant hits Ponytail in the chin with the heel of his hand and cracks his head against the wall. Grabs his wrist and tries to twist his arm behind his back, but Ponytail breaks free and stumbles away, shouting, "I am an honorably discharged veteran of the United States Army…"

An MP puts him in a headlock. The other two grab his arms. They carry him kicking and screaming down the corridor. "They have your bodies, don't give them your minds," he shouts. "Resist, brothers. Don't die for their money…"

Then he's gone behind a slamming door. We wait in an uneasy silence as the same Sergeant comes back, jamming his shirt back down his pants. "Gentlemen, please take seats in the auditorium. We wanna get you squared away and on the buses before the peaceniks show up."

WORDS WOULDN'T COME

Brooklyn, 1944

Heart thumping in his ears. Rain spattering against the window. Open umbrellas outside the door. Yellow raincoat smell. Mommy kneeling to buckle his boots. Coffee smell and the pot making bubbles on the stove. Aunt Rae in the kitchen dropping a sugar lump into her cup with a cigarette burning between her fingers.

His army was under the bedspread. Toy soldiers in green uniforms with helmets. Aiming rifles, moving cannons, crouching, running. Jeeps with soldiers behind the wheel and tanks with drivers sticking their heads out. The "Japs" had yellow uniforms and yellow caps. Their faces were yellow, too, with black lines where their eyes should be. His soldiers knocked them down and chased them under the pillow until they were all lying on the ground like in the movie.

The nice Mommy smell. "How'd you do last night, sweetheart?" Patting the bed and feeling his tushy. "Dry as a bone. Good for you." The nice warm of her hand as she slid his slippers over his feet. Her dress with all the colors. Silver pins sparkling in her brown hair. The radio noise in the kitchen as Aunt Rae turned the dial. Then the happy music and the man with the happy voice, "Welcome to the Breakfast Club." Mommy made her mad noise. "Can you put on CBS, Rae?" In the bathroom, she lifted him over the toilet seat. "Do you want to stand up?" He shivered and the pee came out hot all over the toilet seat. "Good boy," Mommy said. And pushed his pee pee down with her finger so it would splash in the water.

Aunt Rae came in with her crying face. "Can we have one morning without war news?"

Mommy made a shush with her finger to her lips. "Look Rae, our big boy made pee pee right in the toilet.

Aunt Rae's face got smiley and her eyes were shining. "He's ready to join the Army with Daddy and Uncle Bernie and Uncle Sam."

He hit his feet together and saluted like the soldiers in the movie to make them laugh.

Aunt Rae pinched his cheeks with her fingers so hard… "Could you just eat that face…"

Mommy had the tiny spoon. "Open wide for your vitamins…" It tasted bad like medicine. The cold orange juice burned his mouth. Mommy took the brown strings off the banana. She poured some of her coffee into his milk and put a spoonful of sugar to make it sweet.

Talking and door slamming. And the house was quiet. He shouldered his rifle and marched down the long dark hallway, past the kitchen where the candle burned for Grandpa Harry. Stop at the sideboard to salute the pictures of Daddy and Uncle Bernie in their uniforms. And Uncle Sammy with his army friends in front of a big tank. Into the room with the Bubbe smell. Bubbe in her long white sleeping dress. "Did you make Number Two, sweetheart?"

Bubbe put the wooden Number Two box by the toilet so he could climb up by himself on his own seat. He squeezed so hard his tushy hurt, but nothing came out.

"We'll try later," Bubbe said.

In the bedroom she took the cover off her sewing machine. "Bring my fabric," she said.

It was on her big chair by the window where she sat and talked to Grandpa Harry when he came down from the sky. He liked the turning wheel sound. Needle bouncing up and down. Bubbe wetting her lips and singing "lu lu lu…"

The doorbell rang and Bubbe put the cover on the sewing machine. "That's Mr. Wolf. Get the pishke…"

The pishke was his special job. It was a glass jar wrapped in blue and white with writing like in Bubbe's newspaper. It had coins at the bottom, nickels, dimes and a few pennies. Bubbe told him to hide it in a different place every night so the evil spirits couldn't find it and steal the money from our people in Palestine. This time he had put it under Aunt Rae's bed behind her big black shoes.

He marched back down the hallway and stood on tippy toes to turn the brass knob. Mr. Wolfe was standing there in his big brown coat and hat. He saluted and Mr. Wolfe saluted back. "Reporting for duty," Mr. Wolfe said.

Mr. Wolfe took off his hat and looked different with just a little white hair on the side of his head and brown spots with little hairs growing out of them. He took a leather bag off his shoulder and dropped it on the kitchen table. "Oy... Small money is heavy coins. Big money is paper, light like a feather so the rich people shouldn't strain themselves, God forbid."

Bubbe came in wearing the green dress with the different flowers on it with some of Mommy's red color on her cheeks. "Nice garment," Mr. Wolfe said.

"Made it myself," Bubbe said. She poured steaming water that turned red in the glass. "He hides the pishke in a different place every night," she said.

Mr. Wolfe patted his head. "Smart boy, a regular espion. Tell me what this money is for."

"For our people in Palestine to have their own country," he said.

Bubbe clapped her hands. "Two years old, would you believe it?"

"A smart boy is better than gold," Mr. Wolfe said. "We should only live long enough, God willing to see what he become, he should have good health." He poured the coins into his big bag and gave him the empty pishke. "Fill it up, Soldier. Everybody who comes has to put a penny in the pishke for our people in Palestine."

At supper Mommy put the big yellow book in the big armchair at the table and let him climb onto it. "Make believe you're Old King Cole." He banged his knife and fork.

"Who was Old King Cole?" Aunt Rae asked.

"A merry old soul," he said and everybody laughed.

The bedroom door flew open so hard that the coats flew off the hooks. A man in a soldier's uniform came in with Mommy behind him. "Hey killer, wake up…" He had a red ring on his little finger and a silver watch. His hands had the burning cigarette smell. His black hair was shiny like pictures in a magazine. There was a red line on his face and a big hole with the top of his ear sticking out.

"You know who this is?" Mommy asked.

"Uncle Sammy, mommy's big brother," he said. He tried to touch the hole in Uncle Sammy's ear. "Did you fall down?" he asked.

"No, something fell on me…"

"Does it hurt?"

"Only when I laugh, buddy… How'd he know me?"

"From the photo," Mommy said. "Show Uncle Sammy…" She carried him to the picture on the sideboard.

"Uncle Sammy," he said, pointing to the smiling soldiers at the tank.

Uncle Sammy made a crying noise. "Oh Jesus, Stella… my crew."

Mommy took the picture away. "Sorry Sam, it was the only photo we had and I wanted him to see his uncle."

"Sure, sure," Uncle Sammy said. "Big kid, look at the mitts on him. Like Papa."

In the morning Leo the super helped Uncle Sammy move Mommy's bed. "I'm going to sleep with Aunt Rae," Mommy said. "And Uncle Sammy will stay here with you."

Uncle Sammy opened his big green sack and took out a little brown bag with a zipper. "Wanna see my loot, buddy?" he asked. He showed him the coins with a man's face. "I got these off a Kraut…" A gold watch like Grandpa Harry's. "This too. Same day, different Kraut. A Captain, I got his Luger in my bag…"

At supper he climbed on the arm chair to be Old King Cole, but Uncle Sammy lifted him out of it—"c'mon buddy, sit next to me," and put the yellow book on the chair next to him. "This was my papa's chair, your

Grandpa Harry," he said. "Sat here every night with his shot of schnapps. Got any schnapps, Mama?" he called into the kitchen.

"I saved for you, Sam," Bubbe called back and brought out a bottle.

Bubbe kissed Uncle Sammy right on his boo boo. "Does it bother you, Sam?" she asked.

"Only when I pass a mirror, Mama," Uncle Sammy said.

Uncle Sammy had the bad smell like the burning stuff mommy put on his mosquito bites. There was black hair on his arms. Black hair sticking out of his undershirt. Little bubbles coming out of his mouth. He wanted to touch Uncle Sammy's boo boo but Mommy made "shush," and whispered, "let him sleep, he's very tired..."

"Did Uncle Sammy hurt himself fighting in the war?" he asked.

"Yes he hurt himself," Mommy said. "So the Army let him come home to get better."

"Did his friends come home, too?" he asked.

"They all came home," Mommy said.

Bubbe gave him soup with saltines. She blew on the spoon, but it burned his tongue. The doorbell rang and Bubbe said, "Go, let in my customers." He marched down the hall and opened the door. Mrs. Rubin and Mrs. Mendera came in—pinching his cheeks—"such a sweet face..."

"Get the pishke, bubbelah" Bubbe said.

This time he had hidden it under the pillow on Bubbe's chair. He put it on the table next to the dish with Bubbe's hard candies.

"Tell Mrs. Mendera what the pishke is for," Bubbe said.

"For our people in Palestine to have their own country," he said.

"Such a smart boy," Mrs. Mendera said. She hopped on the stool and Bubbe knelt to look at her skirt.

Uncle Sammy came out in his green bathrobe. "What's this Macy's basement?"

"Congratulations on your quick recovery, Sammy," Mrs. Mendera said. "We're hoping my Victor will be discharged soon..."

"Tell him to get his ear shot off, that'll get him home early," Uncle Sammy said. "He took Bubbe's arm. "C'mon Mama, get up…"

"I'm just fixing a hem for Mrs. Mendera," Bubbe said.

He pulled Bubbe under her arms. "Get up, Mama," he said.

Mrs. Mendera got down off the stool and picked up her shoes. "I'll come back later. Welcome home, Sam…"

Everybody was talking loud and mad. He watched Uncle Sammy through the glass door, walking fast around the big room. "My mother's not getting on her knees for anybody," he said.

"She likes to work," Mommy said. "Otherwise she'd sit around doing nothing."

There was a loud noise like a glass breaking.

"Be quiet, you'll wake the baby," Mommy said.

"And what's with that pishke racket?"

"Not necessarily a racket," Mommy said.

"What are you talkin' about, it's the same con game they had before the war…"

"So what if it is or it isn't," Mommy said. "He's a nice old man. Keeps Mama company…"

"I'm gone for three years. I come back and she's still sewing shmattes. Nothing's changed except now I'm a one-eared freak…"

"Who says you're a freak?" Mommy said.

"Walk down the street with me, you'll see," Uncle Sammy said.

Uncle Sammy was sleeping on top of the bed with all his clothes on. The red hole in his ear felt hard, not like skin. The bell rang and he ran down the hall to tell Mr. Wolfe: "My Uncle Sammy was hurt in his ear and came home to get better."

"He's a brave soldier," Mr. Wolfe said. "You must be very proud of him."

In the bedroom Uncle Sammy was blowing smoke circles from a cigarette. "Hey buddy, wanna keep me company while I shave?"

"Mr. Wolfe is here," he said. He took the pishke out of Uncle Sammy's green bag where he had hidden it the day before.

"What's that doin' there?" Uncle Sammy said.

"It's for our people in Palestine to have their own country," he said.

Uncle Sammy pulled the pishke out of his hands so hard the blue and white paper came off. He opened the door and the coats fell off again. He walked fast through the big room. In the kitchen Mr. Wolfe was standing up. "This is an honor…"

Uncle Sammy shook the pishke at him. "You got a little kid doin' your dirty work?"

Mr. Wolfe looked at Bubbe. "Dirty work?"

"Sam, this is a good cause, "Bubbe said.

"It's the same con game they were working before the war, mama," Sam said. "He pockets half of what he gets and splits the other half with the crooks who send him out…"

"I don't take a penny," Mr. Wolfe said. "It all goes to the Jewish Agency. I get lunch and carfare." He took out a paper. "Here is my accreditation…"

Uncle Sammy pushed the paper away. "I can get one of them at Woolworth's."

"We have fifty-three people collecting all over Brooklyn," Mr. Wolfe said. "The money goes into an account at Rothschild Bank here in Tel Aviv."

"You tryin' to tell me the Rothschilds are in on this?" Uncle Sammy said. "They might be, they're crooks, too…" He pushed the pishke across the table. "Get out and take this with you…"

Mr. Wolfe smiled at him with a crying face. "Can't I leave it for the boy?"

"He doesn't want it," Uncle Sammy said. He threw the pishke so hard at Mr. Wolfe that some coins fell out, and yelled loud: "Get out now you old goniff before I throw you out."

Bubbe sat down with her head on the table. "Oy Sam, what are you doing?"

There were two pennies on the floor. He picked them up and ran down the hall to give them to Mr. Wolfe, but the door was closing. He tried to call, but the words wouldn't come.

"I TOLD THE TRUTH"

February 1963

"My friend did the queer act," Jerry, the embalmer says. "Put a little polish on his nails, like he tried to scrape it off. Splashed on his mother's old lady perfume. Checked off 'bed wetting,' on the form, which got him in to see the shrink. And when the shrink asked if he was attracted to men he acted like he was tryin' to cover it up..."

"Is that what you did?" I ask.

"I tolya, it was my friend. I got out on my asthma..."

Benny, the bongo player in the Figaro Cafe with his radical girlfriend, tall and scornful, long blonde hair braided into plaits.

"I did the *jibaro* number. Puerto Rican hick. No spicky ingleese man..."

"Are you going to resist?" his girlfriend asks me.

"Dodge is the better word," I say.

"In other words, pay a corrupt doctor to fabricate a medical condition. Claim drug addiction or homosexuality..."

"Anything that works..."

"You realize you're reinforcing establishment stereotypes of alternative lifestyles..."

"It hadn't occurred to me..."

"Lying and faking strengthens the status quo. It exposes flaws in the system that they can correct. You consider yourself a radical I'm sure, but you're really a pawn of the forces you oppose."

Benny is talking to a kid with greasy hair at the next table. "My boy's goin' for his physical tomorrow."

"Put a penny in your mouth," the kid says. "It'll raise your temperature and turn your tongue green…"

I decide to stay out all night and get wrecked. "Go home, baby," Benny tells his sulking girlfriend, "I'm gonna hang with my boy." We go into a liquor store on Sixth Avenue. Old Black clerk in a gray smock. "Quart of Gallo Port," Benny says. "My boy's goin' for his Army physical tomorrow. Gonna show up drunk and disorderly…"

"That won't keep you out," the clerk says. "What you gotta do is keep askin' for your gun. Where's my gun? Do I get my gun today? Is this where I get my gun?"

"Is that what you did?" I ask.

"I was with the 92nd… 370 CT… Colored troops…" He shows us a plaque on the wall behind the register. A patch with a buffalo's head and two medals. "The Germans put some guy on a loudspeaker, sayin' why are you boys fightin' for your slave masters? Sounded just like a Harlem boy…"

At dawn Benny is holding my head as I puke in a trash can on Waverly Place. I chug three cups of coffee loaded with sugar at the Cube Steak Diner right by the subway and decide to walk downtown. "I'm goin' to a warm bed and a big hello," Benny says.

Lower Manhattan is deserted, a few cabs speeding by, headlights diffusing in the mist, winos freezing on benches in Battery Park. Lights go on in the Selective Service building. Guys in Army overcoats come out of the subway and run up the steps.

Then the kids. Coupla hundred coming from all over. Dropped off by car or truck. Straggling out of the subway.

A guy in a green uniform at the door yells "Down the hall…"

It's a large room with picnic tables. A crewcut in a khaki shirt and sharply creased blue trousers with a red stripe claps loudly. "Take a form and a sharp pencil. Find a seat. Answer all the questions. Print clearly and legibly."

Some kids leave out questions. Some are sent back to fill out the form all over again. "Can't read your excellent penmanship. Print in block letters..." When the forms are completed Crewcut comes back and leads us out into the hallway. "Form a line. One man looking at the back of the head of the man directly in front of him..."

We shuffle into a large room the size of a gym. Medics: young Black guys in crisp white uniforms. Doctors: old white guys in frayed white coats watching bleakly at tables.

Another form and a stubby pencil. An endless column of diseases, I've only had chicken pox. I check off a few of the mental disorders: problems in school, psychiatric treatment, feelings of persecution, anger; "homosexual feelings" will be my secret to the grave. Can't even force myself to check "bed-wetting," although Jerry, the embalmer, says it will get me out. "Alcohol and illegal drug use" are manly disorders. A medic checks my form and hands it back, "uh huh..."

"Strip to your shorts and shoes," Crewcut says. "Guard your belongings..."

I've never seen such a grotesque profusion of male flesh. Fat and mortified, muscular and arrogant, slight and timid. Red pustules on white flab, flaring acne clusters, sores, Rorschach bruises, black stains on brown skin. Wiry black hair like a coat of fur from the ankles to the nape. Red tufts and freckles. Sparse mustaches, one bald kid, white scalp gleaming, head down like he knows he's going to get ragged to death. The muscle guys have slicked back pomps, the shrimps are cowlicked or unkempt as if why waste the effort. The muscle guys strut and show off. The shrimps look at their shoes, hoping nobody will notice them. I try to rank myself in this procession. Tall, but slouched and narrow-shouldered. Skinny arms: I can lift a two hundred pound cadaver, but you'd never know it. Thousands of sit-ups haven't put one cut in my gut. Push-ups and pull-ups have failed to raise a bump in my biceps. Should have worn my father's billowy boxers. The "tighty-whiteys" were a big mistake. I don't have a ball bulge because I'm one short, but nobody knows that.

We pass an eye chart. "Cover your right eye and read the first line..." One wiseguy gets the letters wrong. "Use both eyes," the doctor says. Still misreads it. "Read one letter," the Doctor says. "H", says the kid. "Okay, move on..." The kid protests, "but there is no 'H' on the chart." The doctor waves him on. "How do you know?"

Hearing test. A doctor says "turn around..." We turn... Okay, next..." Stethoscopes are pressed to our chests. "Deep breath... Breathe out." Pin lights shined in our eyes, ears and noses. A tongue depressor is thrust so deep, we gag. "Say Ahhh..."

A doctor with a tiny hammer points to a chair. He taps a knee. The kid in front of me shudders and his foot shoots up. I clench my knee so it won't move. The doctor taps me on the head with the hammer. "Get up. You waiting for the second feature?"

A doctor at the last table shouts, "Drop your drawers. "A kid walks up to him. He lifts the kid's dick with his finger and looks under it. Thrusts his hand under a kid's right testicle and orders, "Cough." Then moves to the left. "Cough."

"What's this, a fuckin' hand job?" somebody whispers. Nervous giggling in the ranks.

When it's my turn he flicks my dick for a quick look. Puts his hand under my right testicle, looking me in the eye. Nothing there so he pushes harder against my groin. "Cough..." Then the left ball. "Cough..." Checks my form. "When did you have chicken pox?" he asks. "Third grade," I say. He writes on my form... "Ascended testicle..." I try to correct him. "That's from orchitis..."

He waves me on. "I didn't ask for a second opinion."

We walk into another empty room. A doctor commands:

"Drop your drawers. Lean over and press the wall with both hands. Now reach back and spread your cheeks... C'mon, spread 'em!"

He walks up and down the line looking up everybody's ass.

"Lose somethin' Doc?" someone asks.

More giggling.

We're sent into a room with rusty troughs along the walls. A medic hands out vials. "Piss in the vial, shake off into the tub and bring the specimen outside to the desk."

Another moment of truth as we check out the line of pissing penises. Dark ropes, purple veined monstrosities, fragile pink wands. It's amazing that they are all the same organ. At least I know where I stand. I won't draw jibes, won't be called "needle dick the bug fucker," which tormented one kid on the basketball team.

The windows are wide open, to kill the smell. Hard to piss when you're shivering. Some kids complain "I can't do it," and the medic turns on a sputtering faucet. "Don't need a lot, just cover the bottom of the vial."

The medic at the desk hands me a tiny dipstick. "Stick it in your specimen. Show it to me." He hardly looks. "Dump it in the sink."

We're back were we came in. "Get dressed, you're done," Crewcut says. Most of the kids are sent down the hall toward the door, but a medic checks my form and points the other way. "Third office on the right."

Handful of kids against the wall. Who's playing junkie? Or queer? As I get closer I hear, "How many times a week?" "Is there a police report...?" "Don't give me the letter, send it to your draft board."

My turn to go into a small office. Another old man with two brown moles, each sprouting a hair. Looks at my form. Then at me.

"Didn't get a lot of sleep last night Mr. Gould." German accent like a movie Nazi. "Nervous about coming here?"

"Yes."

"So did you take anything last night to calm down?"

"Wine," I say.

"What kind of wine do you drink?"

"Italian Swiss Colony, Gallo Port, Night Train..."

A small smile. "Oh, a connoisseur..."

He's not writing, a bad sign. "And did you take a drug?" he asks.

"Marijuana..."

"Anything else?"

"Last night? No..."

"Some other night?"

"Sometimes I take Romilar…"

Now he's writing. "The cough syrup?"

"I take the tablets. Fifteen or twenty."

He's nodding as he writes like I'm confirming his diagnosis.

"Anything else?"

"Benzedrine, Dexedrine."

He cocks his head, suspiciously. "They have different effects than marijuana and alcohol."

Is he trying to trap me? These shrinks never know when you're telling the truth.

My voice breaks. "You asked what I take, I told you…"

He's writing on the bottom of my form. "Many of the other boys do more or less what you do," he says, "but they don't admit it. Why do you?"

"I just filled out the form."

"Do you think you could go long periods of time without drinking or taking drugs?"

"I don't know," I say.

"But if drugs were available you would take them."

"Yes."

More writing. He looks up as if he's surprised I'm still there. "You can go," he says.

Outside, Bowling Green is bustling with the Wall Street lunchtime crowd. Cold winter sun. It's barely noon, but it feels like I was in there for hours.

Three weeks later I get a letter from the Selective Service System. I've been reclassified "1Y," which means only to be drafted in case of national emergency. Later that night I see Benny outside the Figaro.

"I'm out, man. I'm free…"

He slaps me five "All right brother! What did you pull?"

"Nothing," I say. "I told the truth."

PORKY THE KOSHER PIG

Brooklyn, 1952

Mrs. Schiller wanted everybody to stand up and say "present" when she called their names. Mrs. Jaffe in second grade had let him say "here." That was hard, too, but he could push it out from his belly. "HEEERE."

He said "here" the first day of third grade and Mrs. Schiller called him up to her desk.

"Did you hear what I said, young man? You will say 'present' in my classroom. 'Here' is a rude response and can have different meanings."

"But so can 'present,'" he said. "Like birthday present."

Mrs. Schiller put a red check mark next to his name in her book. "We don't talk back in my classroom. That's one demerit. If you get two more your mother will have to come for a conference. Now go back to your desk."

Then she started taking attendance. When he heard his name he gripped the sides of his desk so hard his fingers hurt. Eddie Madison and Billy Solvek turned so she couldn't see and stuck out their tongues, imitating him.

Mrs. Schiller repeated his name without looking up from her book.

His lips felt like they were glued together. He squeezed and squinted and the word exploded in a drizzle of spittle. "PUH PRESENT!"

The first few days there had been giggles, which Mrs. Schiller silenced -"quiet please." But now the kids ignored his morning ordeal. Except for Eddie and Billy. At recess they came up to him faces contorted-and imitated Porky Pig in the cartoons, "pdeet, pdeet, pdeet'" and spit it in his face-THAT'S ALL FOLKS!'" After school they were waiting outside. He tried to run past them, but they chased him down the street, hitting him with their lunch boxes and screeching "Pdeet, pdeet, Porky the kosher pig..." Mrs. Esposito saw them. "What you doin' to that nice boy? Big bullies, shame on you..." She walked him all the way to the building. "You go home with my grandson Anthony from now on. Wait for him tomorrow in the schoolyard."

Next day he stood in the shadows by the baskets so he could walk away if Anthony didn't recognize him. Anthony was the toughest fifth grader—he even beat up sixth graders—and all the kids wanted to be his friend. He came out laughing with some girls and called, "hey c'mere..." He had black hair and dark skin and real muscles in his arms. His voice was hoarse and deep like a grown up. "Where'd these punks jump ya. At the corner?" Put his arm around his shoulders. "C'mon, we'll ambush'em."

They turned down Tenth Avenue and saw Eddie and Billy hiding behind cars. Anthony ran up and punched Billy in the back with a thump so hard he fell flat on his face. "Now it's two against two," Anthony said. "You take Billy..."

Billy scrambled to his feet, eyes scrunched up like he wanted to cry. Anthony nudged him. "Dump him. Kick his ass."

He had never hit a kid, but now he would have to because Anthony was watching. He made a fist and took a step, his heart pounding. Billy's leg buckled as he stumbled away. "Look at the chicken," Anthony said. "He can't even run he's so scared of you." But he knew it was Anthony he was scared of.

At dinner Mommy was looking at him and he knew Mrs. Esposito had told her.

"You walked home with Anthony Esposito, today," she said.

"The super's son?" Dad said. "Isn't he a few years older?"

"He protected you from those boys, didn't he?"

"No, we were just walking home."

"Do they chase you every day?"

"Not every day..."

"Make fun of you?"

"Sometimes."

"What do they say?"

"Call me Porky the kosher Pig..."

"Nine-year-old Catholic kids, "what do they know from kosher?"

"Probably hear it at home," Dad said. "Sit around the dinner table laughing at the stuttering Jewboy..."

"Oh God..." Mommy hugged him so hard to her he could feel her bosoms and squirmed away. "You see, if you solve your... problem... those boys won't bother you anymore. That's why you should go to that speech therapy class."

"I don't need a class."

"There's nothing wrong with it. Make believe it's like a cold or sore throat and the teacher is like the doctor."

She was always telling him to make believe things. That never worked.

The speech class was in the kindergarten classroom after lunch. All the kids who had no friends and walked home alone were sitting in a circle on the little chairs. None of the tough guys or the good ballplayers. The teacher, Mrs. Chesler, was young like Eileen, his next door neighbor, who was in high school. She sat on the floor with her skirt spread out and made each of them sing the ABC song. "When you come to the first letter of your name stop singing and say it," she said. Two of the kids did it. "Let's give them a round of applause," the teacher said and they clapped. And the kids grinned like it was the greatest thing.

"Your turn," Mrs. Chesler said to him.

"I can't sing," he said.

"It's an easy song," she said. "You can do it."

"I don't wanna," he said.

Then she got mad—"you're a bad example for the other pupils who want to get better." And made him sit outside.

Next day he played hooky from the class and hid in the back stairway, looking out the window at the fifth graders playing dodge ball in the schoolyard. Anthony threw the ball so hard they all ran away from him.

At supper Mom asked him: "How was speech class?" He said "good," but she looked at him like she knew he was lying.

"Mrs. Chesler says you're so bright your brain works faster than your tongue…"

"That's a stupid reason," he said.

"Why won't you let people help you?"

"I'll get better myself," he said. "I'm not going to that class…"

"Don't raise your voice to your mother," Dad said. "You'll go to the class if she says so…"

Tears boiled in his eyes. He punched the table so hard the table plates shook and Aaron's cup of chocolate pudding fell on the floor. "No I won't," he yelled. "I won't go." He jumped up and ran into his room and slammed the door. Now they would say, you scared your brother. They would say it was all his fault.

Mommy usually knocked when he had a tantrum, but this time she and Dad came in and sat on his bed.

"We have two problems to solve," Dad said. "One is those boys…"

"If you tell me their names I'll get Mrs. Schiller to talk to their mothers," Mom said.

"No…!" He pulled at his hair so hard a few strands came off in his hand.

Dad slapped his hand away hard. "Stop doing that and listen."

He was gulping tears and couldn't talk.

"Alright, alright, calm down," Mommy said. "I won't tell Mrs. Schiller if you go to Mrs. Chesler's class. Okay? Is that a bargain?"

"Okay…"

But he burned with hatred at the trick they had played on him and lay awake thinking of how he would wait a few more years and then join the Army and never see them again.

At lunch, Mrs. Chesler was sitting alone in her classroom. "You can eat while we talk, it's okay." She smiled at his sandwich: cream cheese and cucumber and tomato on pumpernickel. "What, no lox?" She reached under her blouse and pulled up a Jewish star on a chain. "I'm sorry I got you in trouble with your mother," she said. "But you got me in trouble, too, with the principal by cutting class so we're even, okay?"

"Okay," he said.

"See, they think Speech Therapy is a lot of baloney. They want you to go on stuttering forever just to prove they're right. The bullies who called you porky the kosher pig want you to be afraid and not fight back."

She pulled him to her closer and whispered, her warm breath tickling in his ear. "They think we're weak and afraid because we're Jewish. We'll show them."

Her soft lips brushed his cheek as she sat back. "You know, sometimes when you get mad you feel that you can do anything," she said. "Soldiers in combat get mad and forget their fear. Do you think you could do that?"

"Yes," he said, hoping she would come close and whisper in his ear again.

"Tomorrow morning when Mrs. Schiller is taking attendance think about how she wants you to fail. Stare right at her... And those bullies, too. Think how they want you to be afraid and run away so they can make fun of you. Get mad and forget your fear like a soldier. Say "present!" loud and clear right in their faces. Don't just say the puh sound. Say the p and the r together...Pruh...Can you do that?"

"Yes," he said. And surprised himself by saying "Pruh..."

"Good..." She tucked the Jewish star back under her blouse. "Open the door for the other kids."

That night he made believe he was at his desk as Mrs. Schiller called the names. He jumped out of bed and said "Present..." over and over.

In the morning Mommy said, "You were talking in your sleep last night. Did you have a bad dream?"

He just shook his head. He wanted her to feel bad and worry about him.

The class lined up in the hall waiting for Mrs. Schiller to open her door. Billy was play punching with some of the kids, and didn't look at him. Mrs. Schiller stepped out. "Alright, everybody settle down." She looked down at them as they walked in. Tapped James O'Connor on the arm with her fat red pencil. "Your nails are filthy, young man. Wash your hands and face before you come into my classroom." Her shoes clomped on the floor as she walked back to her desk. She took out her attendance book and started calling names. When she got to Frank Marinara he knew he was next.

He jumped up and shouted.

"Present!"

Some of the kids giggled, but it was okay because they thought he was being funny. Mrs. Schiller didn't look up from her book. "You don't have to shout," she said. "Say it again. Quietly this time…"

She knew it was harder that way. She wanted him to stutter. Billy and Eddie turned with their mean screwed up faces.

Get mad like the soldier. Say the Puh and arr sound together… Pruh…

It came out of his mouth like a soft puff of air. "Present…"

Mrs. Schiller looked over her glasses at him. "Now you'll never have to worry about that word again."

"LIKE A DUCK TO WATER"

June 1960

At seventeen I am a shameless liar and petty thief. I am smart enough to win an $800 scholarship for high scores on the State Board of Regents exams. Accepted to the University of Wisconsin, I choose Brooklyn College. I tell my parents it's because I don't want to leave home, but the real reason is Brooklyn College is free, which means I can pocket the scholarship money and secretly book passage on a freighter to Europe.

My plan is to stick around just long enough to get the 2S student draft deferment and cash the scholarship. Then I'm off to Paris to live in a garret and write novels that will change the world.

James Joyce is my model. I copy his credo out of *Portrait of the Artist as a Young Man*:

"I will not serve that in which I no longer believe whether it call itself home, my fatherland or my church..."

My fifth grade teacher said I was a "troublemaker." At Brooklyn Technical High School they said I was "deliberately obstructive."

All because I would not serve.

Joyce vowed: *"I will try to express myself in some mode of life or art as freely as I can using for my defence the only arms I allow myself to use, silence, exile, and cunning."*

Yes again! They called it lying, cheating and stealing, but it was silence, exile and cunning. I knew it all along.

Joyce left Dublin, determined to "forge the consciousness of my race in the smithy of my soul." The only forging I've done so far is my mother's name on notes to my teachers, but once I get away from Brooklyn the inspiration will come. I'll be cool, doomed and irresistible like Jean Paul Belmondo in *Breathless*. I'll sit in a cafe with a cognac and a Gauloise. A French girl, dark hair, violet eyes, smooth long legs will drape her arm around my shoulder, snuggle her soft cheek against mine.

It's the two-month hiatus between high school and college. Nothing to do or think about. I smoke marijuana every night, chasing the morning malaise with a cherry Coke and an egg salad sandwich. "You look like a raccoon," my mother says.

I close my savings account at $180. 25. That plus the $800 should give me enough for a year in Paris, plenty of time to become a famous writer. I won't be eighteen until December so I'll have to wait to get my draft card. Then I'll have to stay in school just long enough to get my deferment before I can put my plan into operation.

I get a job as a bicycle delivery boy at Bohack's Supermarket on Seventh Avenue near the Prospect Expressway. We're paid the minimum wage, a dollar an hour, plus tips. The store manager, Phil, is trim and bald, starched white shirt and red tie. He wears an officer's gold ID bracelet, engraved with his name, rank and serial number and spends most of his time laughing with the housewives. Dennis is the floor manager in charge of the delivery boys. He was in the first Marine wave to land on Tarawa and has an angry red trench in the side of his face where a Japanese bullet grazed his jaw, shattering his cheekbone. My first day on the job, he turns on me. "Whaddya lookin' at?" He starts calling me "Mr. Gold." When I correct him—"my name is Gould"—he says "sorry Mr. Gold."

Four of us work from four p.m. to closing. There are three new bikes with "Bohacks" painted in red on the sides of the bins. Dennis gives me a rusty old Schwinn with a shopping cart basket hooked to its handle bars. With fifty pounds of groceries in the basket it's almost impossible to handle. As I ride it fully loaded up the hill toward Prospect Park, items fall out of the bags and I have to stop, put down the kickstand and run down the hill to retrieve them. Once a dozen eggs falls out. I run into a corner grocery and buy a replacement.

Dennis sells the good tippers to the boys, taking half of what they make. He sends me to the old ladies who give me a dime out of their purses. Makes me stay late and mop the floors, flatten the cartons and tie them together with twine. Stuff the garbage into black iron trash barrels and roll them out into the alley. Sometimes he stands behind me, hands poised, daring me to complain. One day, in front of the other kids, he blows a gust of Rheingold in my face and says. "Why are you working here, Mr. Gold? You're just taking a job away from some kid who really needs the money."

After two weeks of this I cut work and spend the next few days in Leo's Billiards on 14th Street.

My mother is slicing a salami in the kitchen. "You're not going to work are you?"

"I didn't wanna tell you," I say. "I was fired."

"You were not fired. Phil says you haven't been at work for a week. Dennis had to make the deliveries."

There's some grim satisfaction in that. "I quit," I say. "Wasn't making enough."

"You just decided to quit without telling anybody?"

"For God's sake, Ma, it's a fuckin' delivery job!"

"Don't curse at me!" She comes at me swinging the salami. I try to duck, but she catches me in the ear. "Don't open your filthy mouth to me."

That night, my father isn't surprised. "This is a lesson, for you. Always get in good with the sergeants…"

"Phil likes you," my mother says. "He says you can come back if you make up with Dennis."

"No way I'm makin' up with him," I say.

"Why are you so mad at him?"

"He gave me all the crappy jobs. Kept calling me Mr. Gold."

My mother's anguished look. "You can't spend the whole summer, sleeping late and staying out all night," she says.

"He can work at the chapel," my father says.

"Not in the morgue," she says.

"Just as a receptionist, directing people. He won't touch a body."

My father is the manager of the Riverside Memorial Chapel the largest Jewish funeral home in Brooklyn. A Bronx kid, son of Galician immigrants, he had to leave Cooper Union during the depression when my grandfather's sheet metal shop shut down. My mom was a bookkeeper for a small department store called Solomon and Birnbaum and a secret organizer for the Office Workers Union. They met at a May Day Parade in '37. "Your father took his hat off so I could see his beautiful head of hair," my mom told me.

Soon after they met my dad was set to go off to Spain with the Lincoln Brigade to fight the fascists, but my mom said she wouldn't wait for him to come back so he stayed and they were married. My dad wore a tailcoat, my mom an elegant gray dress and a dark hat with a veil, slanted rakishly over her eye. "I was five-eight, tall for a girl," she says. "Your father was the only man I knew who was taller than me so I could wear heels when we went out…" I have the wallet-sized version of their wedding picture. My father does have a mountain of hair, building in curly gleaming ridges. My mom is flushed, laughing at something he just said. Even as a kid I am confused at how this happy couple became the two people screaming in bitter frustration in the kitchen. My father crying, "Stella, for God's sake." My mother leaning against the stove arms folded, biting her lip.

In the third grade I throw up after lunch and the teacher sends me home. I find my father on top of my mother on the living room sofa. My mother shrieks "Benny!" and pushes him off her onto the floor. I run into my room, assailed by anxious feelings. Trying to blink away the memory of my mom, dress hiked up over her thighs, panties around her knees.

World War II was my dad's big moment. He graduated OCS a Lieutenant in the Engineers. Commanded a detention camp of

Japanese POWs. Won a medal for building bowling alleys for the troops in the Philippines and has a photo of General MacArthur shaking his hand. His postwar setbacks are told and retold like Bible tales. He was one of the first to see the potential in embroidery, but couldn't get a bank loan, and a year later, embroidery became the hottest thing in fashion. Borrowed money from an army buddy to go into leather accessories, handbags, wallets and belts. When the business started to take off, the buddy wouldn't give him an extension on the loan. He had to sell his share to a man named Murray, who is now a millionaire. He had trouble finding a job because of his left-wing past. Finally was hired at Riverside by a lodge brother in the Knights of the Pythias who admired his war record. He has worked himself up from monument salesman to manager, but is mortified at being in the funeral business. When people ask him what he does he says: "I play third base for the Cubs..." Or: "I'm the wine steward in the Woman's House of Detention."

I put on my black high school graduation suit and drive to work with my father.

Riverside Memorial Chapel is on a large circular drive that feeds into Prospect Park and the Parade Grounds baseball diamonds where the Dodgers still hold tryouts every year, even though they've moved to L.A. It has three floors with fifteen "reposing" rooms, most of them full every night. Mamanna, the floor manager, is waiting in the lobby. Seems like a young guy but he's got a big gut, fleshy nose and a shock of white hair.

"Give him the tour," my father says.

Mamanna takes me downstairs to the morgue. He stops to light a cigarette. "You're the boss's son, which means you're gonna have to work harder and be better than everybody else," he says. He opens the door and steps back to see how I react.

There are three cadavers on the white embalming tables. Slack jaws, sightless eyes. An elderly woman, her breasts drooping over the sides of the table. A younger woman, trim, mouse- grey patches showing through the henna, red surgical scars like pencil lines across her breastless chest.

I am transfixed by an old man with an enormous penis. "Blood flows to the dick when you die," Mamanna says. "You'll look like that, too. Bad news is you'll be dead."

Mamanna picks up a hollow metal spear attached to a plastic tube. "This is called a trocar," he says. "Aspirates the blood and guts out of the cavity and replaces them with embalming fluid." He stabs the trocar through the abdomen of the elderly female. Bloody pink liquid bubbles into a large plastic vat.

A gray suit is hanging from a hook on the door. "Help me dress this guy," Mananna says. There are dark blue argyle socks and billowy white boxers in a Safeway shopping bag. A pair of shiny black shoes.

"Nobody's gonna see underwear." I say.

"Family always sends a complete outfit," he says. "They'll check to see it's all on him…"

The old man's eyes and mouth are sewn shut. I pick him up under the chest while Mamanna slips his arms through the sleeves of the blue dress shirt and ties a Windsor knot in his red Countess Mara tie. Lift him under the knees so Mamanna can slip the boxers over his withered blue-veined legs. His skin is stony cold.

"He's heavier than he looks," I say.

"Cause he's got a coupla gallons of fluid in him."

The feet are unbending, pointing up, toenails gray and jagged. Mamanna trims them with clippers. Rolls the socks over the toes and unrolls them up to the ankles. Few flicks of a comb to get wisps of hair off the forehead.

"Is it true your hair and nails keep growing when you're dead?" I ask.

"Afterspark," says Mammana. "Like a car bucking after you turn it off."

He wheels in a dark mahogany casket on a cart with red plush curtains. We lift the old man into the casket, step back to check that everything is on straight, and close the lid.

Upstairs, my father comes out of his tiny office off the lobby. "How'd he do?"

"Like a duck to water," Mamanna says.

"I JUST MARRIED ARTURO, THE BUS BOY"

June 1965

Stories out of Ottawa and Stockholm show American boys applying for political asylum to avoid the draft. They are welcomed by prominent politicians. Photographed with beautiful actresses.

"KGB operation," 'Joe the Russian,' a chess hustler says. "They are trying to entice more young men for a big propaganda coup."

He is setting up his board in the Cafe Figaro on Bleecker Street, smoking a Parliament down to the nub then lighting another from the burning filter

"Now they are useful for publicity," he says. "But when their novelty fades they are a nuisance. Foreigners taking jobs and women away from the local boys?"

"The war will be over by then," I say.

"War ends when someone surrenders. Who will surrender here, Johnson? First American President to lose a war? I don't think so. Viet Cong? A guerrilla doesn't have to win major battles. Send a little girl on a bicycle past an American jeep. She throws a grenade and kills three soldiers. They blow her to pieces. Big victory both ways for the guerrilla. Dead soldiers and limp body of little girl with crying parents supplied for the occasion. They can do that for years. Russians finance them, help with intelligence, spread propaganda about Yankee Imperialists. Mobilize the world against the war, force stupid Johnson to draft more mama's boys like you…"

Does he think I'm chicken? He laughs at my expression. "I say

31

this with the utmost respect. You are not a brainless *muzhik* who runs to the front with a rusty rifle for the greater glory of Comrade Stalin or Secretary McNamara. Under the Tsars you could only bribe your way out. Under the Soviets, it was the army or the gulag. Democracy gives many advantages to the bourgeoisie. Student exemptions, National Guard, emotional problems… physical disability?"

"I have one testicle," I say.

"So did Hitler…And Napoleon. You are in good company… So… What is left?"

"LBJ hasn't lifted the marriage exemption," I say.

"And he won't. He wants to wage his private war in the shadows, not anger the populace by taking husbands from the bosoms of their happy families. So we will get you married and you'll be safe…" He waves to Hilda, the waitress. "Hilda darling, will you marry my handsome friend to keep him out of the Army?"

"Too late," she says. "I just married Arturo, the bus boy."

"YOU'RE ALWAY GONNA FEEL SLIMY ABOUT SOMETHIN'"

September 1960

It's hard to stay awake in the overheated classrooms of Brooklyn College. Luckily, the freshman survey courses are given in lecture halls and I can snooze undetected in the top row. At 5:30 I change into my suit and black shoes and take the 41 bus to Parkside Avenue. A convivial group has gathered in my father's office. He's pouring Haig & Haig scotch into paper cones from the water cooler.

This solves one mystery. My father always has a shot of from a bottle in the sideboard when he comes home, and my mother complains: "Benny, how can get you so drunk on one drink." It's really his fourth or fifth.

He's happy at the chapel. He enjoys being the boss. The men laugh at his jokes, accept his judgement, obey his orders. He changed his name from Benjamin to Bernard after the war and the men call him "Bernie," but he's still "Benny" in the family.

My mother doesn't like the men. "They cover up for each other when they go out with other women. They can't look me in the eye…" I realize she suspects my father as well.

From 6 to 9 p.m. I stand in the lobby and direct visitors to the bereaved. I have a list of the families, but the names are so similar— "Glickman or Gluckman, Bernstein or Bronstein"—that sometimes I send them to the wrong room. "That's not Cy Tashman…" …Or they make a startling discovery. "I didn't know Sylvia was dead, I just saw her last week in Waldbaum's…"

At 9:30 I make an announcement: "Visiting hours are over, the chapel will be closing in fifteen minutes." Jewish law requires that the deceased never be left alone so the families hire pious, elderly men as "watchers" to sit and pray through the night. They arrive tieless and unshaven in shabby suits, prayer books and shawls in embroidered bags. To them we're all unbelievers. They scowl in the shadows as people come out, laughing or making dates. Won't even acknowledge the family, but go right to work, rocking and chanting prayers.

Sometimes a mourner will linger by the casket. I move up discreetly—"visiting hours are over"—and they mumble apologies on their way out. But one night a watcher named Mr. Zaltz takes a swipe at me with his prayer book. "You're not allowed to speak to a mourner unless he speaks to you."

"But I have to turn off the lights."

"So you'll turn and he'll be in the dark and he'll leave. You're a Jewish boy, you should know the law..." He squeezes my wrist with surprising force. "It's a *shandeh* what goes on here at night. They have Italyenas and Irishers working here, defiling Jewish bodies. I found a policeman on the sofa. Shoes off, gun on a chair, sleeping in the same room as the departed..."

"The cops don't understand."

"If you don't know the law the sin is still the same. I'm coming here twenty-five years. The *goyim* drank... Police, too. They even brought women. But they never did it in a room with a soul whose fate has not been decided..."

From 10 to midnight I take a Chevy 30 panel truck out on "removals" to collect bodies from the hospitals. This is illegal, I'm not a licensed undertaker. Charley Price the night manager, a white-haired, pink-faced Irish guy gives me six dollars to bribe the morgue attendants to release the bodies. "Two bucks apiece, not a penny more," he says.

I'm accompanied by Marshall, the night porter, a wiry Black man in his fifties from the tobacco fields of South Carolina. Fastidious as an ancient Hebrew, Marshall refuses to touch a cadaver. He watches, arms folded, as I mummy-wrap two sheets around the deceased. When all the flesh is covered he lifts it gingerly under the feet and helps me drop it into a body bag. At the chapel he helps pull the bag out of the truck onto a gurney and wheel it into the morgue, but won't touch the body; I have to brace it against the embalming table and wrestle it onto the slab. Sometimes the legs slip and the body starts to list. I have to drop it or it'll fall on top of me. I look down into the eyes. If it's a man the gaze is indifferent... "I'm fat, so what?" But if it's a woman I see hurt and reproof... "I was fat and rejected all my life and now you do this to me?" Sometimes the look is so pitiful I say, "I'm sorry..." out loud in the empty morgue. The gaze seems to soften and the body yields enough to get it back up on the slab. I pat the hand in thanks.

I'm driving illegally. A chauffeur's license is required to drive the hearses, panel trucks and flower cars. Plus you have to be twenty-one and pass a special written exam and road test.

"Rizzo will get you a Chauffeur's license," Mamanna says.

Rizzo is a limo driver with connections way above his station. He is short and wide with huge hands. His hairline begins above his eyebrows, and he's got a nose like a cartoon hippo.

"It'll run you forty bucks, Baby Gould," he says. "I'll front it for you."

We drive over the Manhattan Bridge. On the way Rizzo tells me the story of his life in staccato bursts... "Eight kids... I'm the baby... My father only had enough gas left in the tank to make a dwarf..."

He details his sexual conquests, smacking his thick lips as if he's tasting the women. "Married broads are the best. Fast and furious and they ain't curious..."

There are lines out the door at the DMV. Only one window for chauffeur's license applicants and there are at least a hundred guys ahead of me.

Rizzo pulls me away. "Lines are for the schmucks..." And disappears.

He comes back with a form. "Fill this out." Takes it and disappears again.

A few minutes later he is back. "Let's get your picture took..."

The photographer is a little guy in a plaid bow tie, eyes bulging behind horn-rimmed glasses. "You look like Jeff Chandler, are you related?" he asks me. "A Jewish kid from Brooklyn, too, and now he's a Hollywood star... Nice country, America..."

My license shows up in the mail five days later. I take forty dollars out of the bank. Rizzo shakes his head and takes a twenty. "Don't ever let anybody lay out money for you, 'cause they'll always lie about how much you owe 'em..."

Jews don't bury on Saturday so Sunday is a major funeral day, fifteen to twenty in a six- hour period. There are two chapels: the "large," for expensive funerals, is ornate with chandeliers, plush benches and a picture window in front of a man-made glade of bushes and potted ferns; the "small," for the poor people, is a bare room with a curtained wall. Funerals last fifteen minutes. Rabbis are picked for their ability to rush through the prayers. Eulogists are discouraged. "They didn't say three words to the guy when he was alive, all of sudden he's their best friend," Mamanna says.

After the funerals Rizzo and I load the truck with *shiva* benches, short-legged wooden stools that the mourners will sit on for seven days. "These old Jews go nuts if they don't have enough benches," Rizzo say. "They think God's gonna punish them if they don't get a splinter up their ass while they're fightin' over papa's money."

The order is for five benches, but he only takes three out of the truck. A haggard man, nose running, eyes red-rimmed runs out, agitated. "We have to have five benches for the immediate family."

Rizzo pats his arm. "Let me see what I can do." He brings the two extra benches into house and comes back waving a five dollar bill.

"Works every time."

I borrow my father's '56 Mercury. It's a big eight and can fly. The Brooklyn Bridge at two a.m. is a great proving ground. But one night I get a speeding ticket. Next day I'm telling everybody how this motorcycle cop came out of nowhere. Rizzo shakes his head.

"Didn't nobody ever tell ya how to beat a ticket?"

He gives me a copy of the NYPD house organ, *Spring 3100*, a magazine distributed only to cops. "Put this on your rear window," he says. "Keep your license in a little plastic envelope with a tensky folded up behind it. The cop'll see the magazine. You slip him the ten..." He snaps his finger. "Bingo, you're outta there."

No one can be buried without a valid death certificate, issued either by the attending physician or the Medical Examiner. The Board of Health is very strict about correct cause of death and has been known to disallow a death certificate, causing a delay in burial. Religious Jews and Catholics object to autopsies, causing more costly complications.

But Rizzo has "fixed" Katz, a clerk on the night shift. "Wait'll there's nobody around. Go to the cage and tell him you're Rizzo's friend from Riverside. Slip him the certificate with a deuce under it."

I do exactly as ordered. Katz, his face shadowed by a green visor, stamps the certificate without even looking at it and slides it back minus the two dollars.

It occurs to me that we might be helping somebody get away with murder.

Rizzo agrees. "Never thought of that." And laughs. "We could shake that guy down for plenty..."

In November, I get a draft questionnaire, a month in advance of my eighteenth birthday. I fill in "full time student." In a month I'll get my deferment. At the end of the semester they'll send my scholarship check. Lately I've been riding my bike to the piers under the Brooklyn Bridge where freighters set sail for far off places. In seven months I'll be on one.

Meanwhile, I'm seeing Brooklyn from behind the wheel of a Chevy 30 panel truck. Every night I go to cluttered apartments in shabby neighborhoods where a very old person has quietly passed among his/her souvenirs. I walk into stuffy bedrooms, past stiffly posed sepias of the old country, wedding pictures, military photos. On a rumpled bed, a crumpled person in a cotton nightgown or striped pajamas. A trail of spittle on the sheets... Urine or blood... A crust of dried shit.

Sometimes there's a relative around to tell the story of the body in the bed. Gertie's husband was killed at Anzio in '44 and she never left the apartment. Sam's girlfriend went to California during the war and met some guy. He never married and was in and out of VA alcoholic wards. Eli brought that "Filipina" home with him. It killed his mother. So now he's dead and she never bought a family plot and his kids don't care so his brother Seymour is gonna cremate him.

I venture into Brooklyn's vast, uncharted interior. To forgotten Jewish nursing homes in encroaching Black neighborhoods. The splintered steps creak. The warped screen door squeals. On the porch skeletons turn.

Who's he here for?

The deceased is covered by a threadbare gray sheet. A friend sits by the window, nodding and licking cracked lips. They hand me a small valise and a shopping bag filled with used sundries. I belt it onto the stretcher on top of the body. As the gurney bumps down the steps, a lung collapses and air whooshes out with a "WHOOO..."

Rizzo hates making removals in Brownsville, the oldest Jewish neighborhood in Brooklyn. "This area's goin' to the coloreds," he says. "Only the old Jews who are too poor to move." Our first stop is a four-story walk up on Blake Avenue. We climb over tattered stair carpets to the top floor. The super lets us in, then takes off downstairs. In a second we know why. Rizzo holds his nose. "It's a floater."

A "floater" is someone who's been dead for days, maybe weeks. People who die alone lay undiscovered, their death scent oozing out from under the door, obscured by cooking smells, gas leaks and general funk. Eventually, the uncashed Social Security checks in the mailbox sound the alarm. A relative is found, but doesn't have a key so the cops arrive with crowbars. The doctor who's been treating her for forty years scribbles a death certificate. Finally, we show up, black suits and body bags our badges of office.

The now familiar sweet stench wafts out of the bedroom. A shriveled old woman is lost in the bedclothes. Her arms are so brittle I'm afraid they might break off.

"Could happen," Rizzo says. "My uncle was takin' his socks off one night and his big toe came off in his hand, I swear to God."

He opens the drawers... Empty... "See how the clothes are all messed up," he says. "Somebody was searchin'. Super maybe. Cops... Neighbor coulda snuck in... Don't put it past the doctor, neither. Somebody had a good payday. "He shows me the indentation on a left ring finger. The faded circle on a left wrist where a watch had been. The total absence of jewelry. "Did ya ever see one of these old broads without a little pin or brooch on their dress?"

We wrap the body in a sheet and a blanket, but the odor comes right through the leather body bag. Rizzo lights a cigarillo to kill the smell. At the second landing he can't take it anymore. "Let go," he tells me. He drops the gurney and watches it bounce down the steps. A door opens and closes as it rattles by. On the next landing an old man in a black vest steps out. "God will punish you for this," he says. The door slams and the locks click.

Back in the car Rizzo takes out a silver flask. "Nice huh? My girlfriend Sylvia gave it to me. Her husband's a dentist. Office is in the house downstairs so we gotta pick our spots. I see her when he goes golfin' and last year when he was in the hospital with a hernia..." He takes a gulping swig. "Get your draft notice yet?"

"I'm not eighteen."

"Five and a half years I was in," he says. "I told the CO, you waitin' til all the Japs are dead before you let me out? Mamanna was on Guadalcanal. Thirty-one, looks like he's fifty, right? My buddy paid a guy to back a truck over his foot in boot camp and he got a medical.

My cousin jumped off his fire escape after Pearl Harbor and broke his leg. Got out on a 4F. Spent the war bangin' the broads and sellin' phony gas coupons..."

"A lot of kids from the neighborhood are enlisting," I say. "They told me the draft board already filled its quota so I might not get called at all."

Rizzo snorts. "The only quota they got is to take everybody. You wanna stay out 'cause once you're in you're their fuckin' slave. Shit food, wrecks your stomach. Cast iron shoes. You got one foot larger than the other, you're outta luck..."

"I'm going to get a student deferment."

"They'll get you when you graduate. "You ain't no hillbilly, you can read and write. They need a smart Jewboy to be Company Clerk." He lowers his voice and looks around, although it's just the two of us in the car. "Tell me when you get your notice. I got a doctor who'll make you 4F. Cost 'ya coupla hundred. "

I think of all the stories I've heard: my father's photo with MacArthur, my grandfather who did double shifts at the Brooklyn Navy Yard building Destroyers. Cousin Milton, who got shell-shocked on D-day and could only work in the Post Office sorting letters.

"I'd feel slimy getting out that way," I say.

"Don't let that stop you," Rizzo says. "You're always gonna feel slimy about somethin'."

"IT'S CHOPIN"

There was an old upright piano against the wall in his room. Mom played it sometimes, clucking her tongue and starting over again when she made a mistake. He would pick little tunes out of it until he got bored. Once Mom brought Dad in to watch him from the doorway. "Sounds like Satie," Dad said.

"Do you want to take lessons?" Mom asked.

"No," he said.

"Well, just try a few with Mrs. Ratner on the first floor. If you don't get interested we'll stop."

Mrs. Ratner was an old lady with an accent so thick sometimes he couldn't understand her. Her hair was black like shoe polish with a part on the side. She had thick legs in brown stockings and wore a plain black dress with ruffled sleeves and a large green pin in the shape of the sun surrounded by golden rays. Her living room was almost empty except for an itchy sofa and a few kitchen chairs. A grand piano was in the middle of the room. He would hear her playing whenever he passed.

"Do you like music?" Mrs. Ratner asked him.

"He only listens to rock and roll," Mom said.

"That's good music, popular music," Mrs. Ratner said. She pointed to the piano. "Sit... Play..."

"I don't know how," he said.

"Play a note and then try to play another that makes a melody."

He picked at the notes. Going up and down. Repeating some notes that sounded like a song.

"His hand already almost stretches to an octave," Mrs. Ratner said. She

patted his shoulder. "So now try to imagine what the notes will sound like before you play them and make a song."

He imagined a song like "Peggy Sue," and tried to figure it out.

"Did you hear what the notes would sound like in your mind?" Mrs. Ratner asked

"Yeah, but a few of the notes were wrong," he said.

"So now sing a melody first, then try to play it…"

"I can't sing."

"Oh for God's sake, just hum a few notes," Mom said.

He sang the first few words of "Why Do Fools Fall In Love—Why do birds sing so gay/Lovers await the break of day…" He hated the way his voice was high like a girl's and made the words sound stupid.

"Now play what you sang," Mrs. Ratner said. He played one note then figured out the others.

"He has a good ear and that you can't teach," Mrs. Ratner said to Mom. "He'll have to practice at least an hour a day in the beginning. Will you practice every day?" she asked him.

Mom poked him before he could answer. "Tell Mrs. Ratner you'll practice."

"I'll practice," he said.

"You should be honored Mrs. Ratner accepted you," Mom said when they got upstairs. "She was a famous teacher in Europe before the war."

"But my PAL team practices after school," he said.

"It'll only be an hour. You can go to the schoolyard when you're finished."

"But the coach will bench me…"

Mom rubbed her forehead so hard he couldn't look. "Alright, I'll make you a deal. You can practice with your team, but you also have to practice piano after supper. That means no TV…"

That night he heard them arguing in the kitchen. "She says he has a good ear," Mom said. "He could be a prodigy."

"Prodigies start when they're three," Dad said.

"Not on piano. They need time for their hands and wrists to grow

42

stronger. She says his hand already can reach an octave..."

"She just wants the three bucks..."

"Are you kidding, they're lining up outside her door. She only takes advanced pupils going into the Conservatory."

An old man came to tune the piano. "Did you buy this or did they pay you to take it away?" he asked Mom. Pointed to him. "This the next Horowitz?"

The first lessons were easy. He only had to learn all the notes and draw them on a piece of music paper. It took ten minutes and then he could creep down the hall and peek around the corner where they were watching Milton Berle in the living room. Next lesson he had to play the notes on the piano for Mrs. Ratner. That was easy, too, and only took ten minutes. But she made him stay the whole hour, telling stories about great composers and playing little pieces for him. Her tiny fingers flew over the keys. She closed her eyes and threw her head back, but still hit the right notes. Sometimes she would raise her hand and hold it for a few counts, then drop it gently on the key. When Mom came in she offered tea. He waited until she went back into the kitchen to whisper. "Can I go?"

"Not yet," Mom said.

"But I'll be late for practice."

"So tell the coach you were at your piano lesson," she whispered back. "I'll give you a note."

Mrs. Ratner came out with a tray. "You like butter cookies?" He watched the clock on the piano as she told stories about the Berlin Symphony and her husband, who was a great violinist. "Furtwangler wanted to make him concertmeister," she said. "They say he was a Nazi, but he loved his Jewish players." By the time he got to the schoolyard everybody was going home.

The lessons got harder. He had to learn the bass clef. Then play the major and minor scales with both hands. If he made a mistake with a note or the fingering Mrs. Ratner would wait until he played all the scales then make him play the bad one over again." She gave him Czerny's book of études. "Just play the notes don't worry about how fast," she said. But after two lessons she turned on a metronome and made him play to the beat, faster and faster. "This is only the beginning," she told Mom. "The work will get harder and he'll have to practice more..."

"He will," Mom said.

Upstairs he yelled at Mom. "You lied. You said only an hour."

"Maybe some days you'll have to take a little bit longer..."

"I told you the coach will bench me if I miss practice."

"Don't raise your voice to me." She rubbed her forehead. "Mrs. Ratner says you can become a really good pianist. Doesn't that mean anything to you?"

"You lied," he said.

Next lesson Mrs. Ratner gave him a song with easy notes. "So... Imagine that you are waking up Frère Jacques early in the morning," she said. "Wake up, wake up Frère Jacques, church bells are ringing. Feel the sun rise as you play. Make the church bells ring." She listened with her head back and her eyes closed. Mom came in and sat on the sofa while he was playing.

"Did you hear the church bells ring?" Mrs. Ratner asked.

He wanted to say no, but she looked so sad with her teary eyes that he nodded. "I did..."

"So did I," she said. "You made me hear them. This is another thing that cannot be taught," she said to Mom. She sat next to him. "Here is something you will play one day." She rolled up her ruffled sleeves. There were some green spots on her wrist, which looked like blurry numbers. She struck a chord and a chill went through him. The piano sounded different when she played it. At the end the notes still lingering in the air, Mom clapped lightly. "That was wonderful. Such a privilege..."

"Neh..." Mrs. Ratner waved her into silence. "So, what do you think this piece was about?" she asked him.

"An army marching into town after they won a battle," he said.

She nodded at Mom as if he had given the right answer. "This is Chopin's Polonaise," she said. "Would you like to play it one day?"

"It's too hard," he said.

"You can play it if you study. You can play it one day in a concert hall in

front of an audience. Would you like that?"

"I don't know."

Mrs. Ratner looked sad like he had hurt her feelings. "Let me show you something," she said. She went into her bedroom and brought out a photo in a leather frame. A man in a dark uniform with a white hat like the army pictures of Dad and Uncle Sammy. "This is my son, David. He's a captain in the British Navy," she said to Mom. "Would you believe, a captain"

"That's wonderful," Mom said.

"Wonderful," Mrs. Ratner said like she wasn't sure. "But when he was a young boy like you he was already giving recitals."

"You must have been very proud," Mom said.

"I taught in the only way I knew. Hours of practice and repetition. I was never happy with what he did. Always make corrections. Work, work, until your fingers were so sore you had to stop..." She closed her eyes like she was listening. "Like a butterfly coming out of the cocoon you could see his genius emerging..." She opened her eyes. "You know what happened to the Jewish people in Germany, don't you?" she asked him.

"The Nazis put them in concentration camps," he said.

"Yes. But before that we had such a good life devoted to music. When Hitler came to power we didn't understand what was happening. Even after the Nuremberg laws we didn't want to believe. Then it was too late to leave. But we heard we could send our children away and they would be safe in England. Kindertransport, you've heard of it?" she asked Mom.

"Yes," Mom said.

"So Maestro Furtwangler gave my husband a man in the Gestapo to call and he gave us a transit visa for our son. We put him on a train to Vienna. I gave the lady a note asking whoever got him to please let him continue his studies."

"What happened to you and your husband?" Mom asked.

"That's a story for another day," Mrs. Ratner said. "So my David was sent to an English family in Yorkshire. They raised him as their own son. Nine years he was away and they didn't respect my wishes. This boy of genius never touched a piano except to play simple hymns on the organ for

the church. Hymns your son can already play. When we were finally reunited it was too late. He hardly remembered his childhood. He was an English boy now, studying for the British Naval College."

"It's quite an accomplishment for a Jewish boy, "Mom said.

"Yes, yes, it's amazing, everybody says," Mrs. Ratner said. "He has a wife and a son almost your age," she said to him. She took a wrinkled snapshot out of her pocketbook. A blonde lady and a blonde boy in short pants. "My grandson," she said. "I never see him."

"Well, they're in England," Mom said.

"I went once to visit. Not even a piano in the house. He introduced me to his neighbor. This is my little Jewish mother, he said. My daughter-in-law was nicer. Showed me a room where I could stay as long as I wanted, she said. But I could see my son didn't want me there. I said if you want to see me come to Brooklyn. That was three years ago or more."

"They'll come when he has time," Mom said.

Mrs. Ratner patted her hand. "You don't have to console me, my dear. I'm trying to show you that it was my ambition, not my son's..." She smoothed his hair, which felt funny because it was what Mom always did. "You're just taking lessons to please your Mom, aren't you?" she said. "You can tell the truth, I won't be insulted..."

That night Mom was furious. "One thing I ask you to do," she said. "One little thing..."

"She told me to tell the truth," he said.

"Oh yes, and you never lie I suppose..."

"You lied," he said. "You promised I could stop if I wanted to..."

Over the weekend she didn't talk to him. On Monday when he came home to change into his sneakers she stood at the door of his room, glaring. The buzzer rang. His friends were waiting for him. "I should make you stay home," Mom said.

"You can't punish me," he said. "I didn't do anything wrong."

"Smart aleck," she said, her face all twisted up. "You think you're gonna be such a terrific basketball player? You're already worried the coach won't let you play..."

Downstairs his friend John was listening at Mrs. Ratner's door.
"Wow, that sounds like Liberace."
"It's Chopin," he said.

"I GUESS GENIUS DOESN'T HAVE TO BE CONSISTENT"

May 1961

I buy a cheap ten-inch album at the A&P. A short history of jazz from Dixieland to bop. Louis Armstrong to Bird and Diz. Basie, Goodman, Ella Fitzgerald, Django Reinhardt, Erroll Garner and Shorty Rogers, all for 49 cents. I play the Garner and Shorty Rogers over and over. Also Bird and Diz. But mostly Django playing "Sweet Georgia Brown."

Rock and Roll is like a high school crush; I wake up one morning and it's gone. The fantasy of being on stage at the Brooklyn Paramount in a sharp suit and pointy "french toe" shoes, doing "steps" and singing simple love songs in four-part harmony to shrieking teenyboppers suddenly holds no allure. I want to be in the jazz world I see on album covers. Musicians on a bandstand. Swirling abstractions. Sophisticated ladies. Rock and roll is a simple story. Jazz is complex, a cool surface with fire seething beneath. Musicians play together but seem in their own worlds. They let the tune determine the mood and can express anything from elation to despair. I am awed by their ability to improvise the most complex riffs on the spot. Their skill is greater than anything I could even fantasize about. But I can aspire to their defiant indifference as a way of facing the world.

I find a trove of old jazz records at the Brooklyn Public Library. Spin them on a turntable, put on earphones and get lost for hours. There's a light-skinned Black kid, skinny with owl eyes behind thick glasses, listening as well. Finally, he walks over. I quickly hide my

Benny Goodman Quartet under a stack of bop albums. (Swing is uncool, especially white swing.) "Can I have the Bird at Massey Hall record when you're done?" he asks. It takes a few more weeks for us to start greeting each other. There are no Black kids in my neighborhood and the ones in high school kept to themselves, even on the JV basketball team. After a few more weeks we start talking about the music. I don't mention my passion for Brubeck; I saw an interview with Miles Davis where he put him down along with Getz and Zoot Sims and the other "white guys." Even the Modern Jazz Quartet, four Black guys, is suspect because of their success in the white world. It's Monk and Mingus and Bird, Diz and Miles. Bill Evans is accepted because he plays with Miles.

A few more days and we walk out together. We talk politics to make sure we're on the same side. His name is Donald. He shakes my hand when I tell him I'm Jewish. "You're oppressed, too." One night I see him at the Washington Square fountain. We greet each other like old friends and join a group listening to Symphony Sid's all night jazz show on a tinny transistor. Jazz fans from all over the city, black and white, old and young, sharing esoteric knowledge, united in our scorn of the "folkies" strumming their guitars. They test me. I drop the right names. "Personnel is my boy's specialty," Donald says. They try to stump me, but I know who played with whom and can recite the whole band right down to the replacements on the various tunes. I've studied the bop drummers—Kenny Clarke, Art Blakey, Roy Haynes, Philly Joe Jones, Max Roach, even the lesser known guys like Gus Johnson, Art Taylor, Shadow Wilson—and can identify them by their drum tone and their fills.

One Monday night Donald and I go to Birdland for Symphony Sid's live broadcast. A midget in a red tuxedo takes tickets at the door. "C'mon in boys. No whiskey now, I'm trusting you." A buck and a quarter gets a seat in the "bullpen" by the stage. A dollar gets a coke at the bar. Sid talks like a hipster, but wears a salesman's checked suit and looks like my Uncle Louie, who is a broker in the Fulton Fish Market.

He sprinkles his jazz patter with Yiddish—"c'mon up and *shpiel* a *bissel, tatele*"—which everyone seems to understand and appreciate. We see the young stars from Art Blakey's Jazz Messengers, Lee Morgan, Benny Golson, Bobby Timmons. Musicians come out of the audience, unpacking their horns, and jam. We stay until closing. On the way out the midget stops me with a finger in my chest. "You lookin' at me funny, boy." I deny it, nervous around all these Black guys. He laughs and slaps me five. "Come back Wednesday for Basie," he calls.

Wednesday night we go uptown again. Sneak a skinny reefer in a doorway on 51st, one checking for cops while the other tokes... Same buck and a quarter, same buck for a coke. First show's at eight. It's early for the jazz crowd and we get seats in the first row on the bullpen right under the rhythm section. Count Basie smiles benignly down at us as he sits at the piano. He two fingers a minimal riff, the notes floating like wisps of gold. Bass comes in and picks up the beat. Freddie Green on guitar strums the rhythm. The drummer, Sonny Payne hunches over the high hat. The band, big guys in cream suits with red ties, files in and settles into their seats, looking bored. Horns go to lips as Basie plays his patented ending phrase. Then Sonny Payne does a thunderous fill and the band bursts out in perfect unison, brass shaking the room. The soloists step to the mike casually, as if it's no big deal and blow the audience into cheering ovations. Basie is imperturbable at the keyboard. Sonny Payne is a dervish at the drums without breaking a sweat. I close my eyes and the music inhabits my brain. I see patterns, feel emotions I can't describe. Set ends. Basie stands at the piano for applause. The band rises for a bow and walks off, some pausing to joke with a tall guy in a dark suit, who sits at the piano. A bass player and drummer play until Sarah Vaughan, lissome in a purple gown walks on singing, "All of me/Why not take all of me." We stay through two more sets, nursing our cokes, grinding our cigarettes out on the floor. No one hustles us for drinks, no one makes us leave. At closing Pee Wee jumps in front of some other awkward white guy. "Why you lookin' at me funny?" He slaps me five and I'm exalted to be part of the joke.

We head downtown, talking about who swings harder, Basie or Ellington, who scats better, Sarah or Ella. At dawn we steal the bread deliveries from the doorways of the super markets and go to the fountain to eat the warm rolls with light coffee and tons of sugar. "I can still hear Basie in my head," I say. "Marijuana intensifies the music," Donald says. "But Bird said he always played lousy when he was high," I say. Donald is puzzled. "But Bird was always high," he says. "I guess genius doesn't have to be consistent."

"DRIVE CAREFULLY"

April 1962

I've been seeing hairballs in my shoes, strands on my pillow. Tufts fluttering in the morning sun beams. Never thought much about it, but now I notice a twisted clump of hair in the shower drain.

Fuck! Am I'm going bald?

My grandfather, at seventy, has a thick black mop, which he wets down, parts and combs across his head. But my father is bald on top with a wave that he carefully arranges over his forehead. Gone is that terraced mountain of glistening curls seen in his wedding picture. "I lost my hair from wearing that steel pot in basic training," he tells me. Another reason to stay out of the army.

Check my passport photo. I've receded in six months. Angle the mirrors in the bathroom so I can see the back of my head. My scalp gleams through the sparseness,

My mother's reflection in the kitchen window standing behind me.

"What are you looking at?" I ask her.

"Nothing."

"I'm going bald, right?"

"Can't blame me for this," my father says. "The mother carries the baldness gene."

"They say bald men are the most virile," my mother says.

"But nobody gives them a chance to prove it," he says and they laugh. They hate each other, but they can come together to make fun of me.

I get a letter from Selective Service. "You are hereby ordered to report for physical examination on April 11, 8:30 a.m. at Selective Service headquarters, 39 Whitehall Street, where it will be determined if you qualify for military service."

Rizzo is in the basement washing the big Packard hearse. "Remember that doctor you said would give me a letter for the draft board?"

Rizzo checks the empty garage. "Schmuck! Keep your voice down. His name is Doctor S... It'll cost you two hundred."

Saturday night. We pick up three bodies at Coney Island General. Bob T. pushes me out of the driver's seat. "I can run faster than you drive, cowboy." He zooms down Ocean Parkway, swerving and cutting people off like a cabbie. Yelling at slowpokes, "Hit the curb Harry!" And girls, "Shake it up, baby, twist and shout." At Quentin Road and East Seventh he jumps a STOP sign. I hear a horn blaring, brakes shrieking. A car is bearing down on us. Yelling, "Bob!" I jump into the back just as it crashes into the driver's door. The truck is launched. Moonlight streams through the window. The tailgate flies open. Bodies fly off the gurneys, sheets flapping like sails. I start to slide after them but hook my foot under metal seat frame and feel something tear in my groin. The truck hits the street, hood first, then bounces back and rolls over on its side. It creaks and wobbles. Dust settles in a prickly mist.

"Hey Gould." Bob is stuck under the contorted steering column, the wheel pressing against his head, blood streaming down his face. "I think I'm fucked up..."

The bodies have slid out of the sheets and are splayed, naked, in the road.

People in bathrobes and slippers. "My God, what happened?"

"It's not that bad," I explain. "They were dead already."

"Dead already!"

The other car, a Nash Rambler is a smoking wreck in the middle of Quentin Road, its horn blaring. A girl is in the car behind the shattered windshield out cold, forehead on the dashboard. The driver, a kid, is on the curb, bloody hand holding a bloodstained towel to his head, crying, "it's my fault, it's my fault."

A police car comes up. The cops saunter out, looking irritated.

"Cops are always pissed off when they have to do their jobs," I tell somebody.

"I've noticed that," a cop says. He takes my arm. "Better sit in the radio car…"

Bob's got a bloodstained towel to his head. "This guy came right through the stop sign…"

More cop cars. A fire truck. The firemen spray foam under the crumpled hood of the Rambler. Reach in and shut off the horn. An ambulance screeches up. Young doctor, good Jewish boy I'm supposed to be… instead of the bum I am…

"What happened to the people on the road?" he asks me.

"They're already dead."

"We'll have to take them to the hospital," he says. "Establish cause of death…"

"You deaf? They're dead!"

"Go sit in the ambulance, you're in shock."

"I'm in shock because you're such a schmuck." I'm walking away. "You're going to get a cause of death on dead people…"

"That's usually how it's done. Better come, too, we'll check out that leg…"

I limp over to the Sergeant. "Let's skip all this aggravation," I tell him. "Just take the bodies to the funeral home. They'll end up there anyway."

"Where you from?"

"Riverside. Charley Price is the night manager. All the cops know him."

"Charley's good people but we can't let these stiffs lay out here forever…"

"We can have a car here in ten minutes, case closed," which is code for "there's money in this…" I call into the crowd. "Can I use a phone?" An old man in carpet slippers takes me into a kitchen. Sitting on a stool I feel a twinge in my groin. "You should get x-rays," he says.

Turns out I saved the day. If they had taken the bodies to the hospital the families would have been notified that their loved ones were found lying on the street. They would have done an autopsy, anathema to many Jews. There would have been complaints for sure. Some shyster would have smelled money so probably a lawsuit as well. "Mamanna says you're a real *shtarke* (strong guy)" my father tells me.

That's high praise, but what does it matter? What does anything matter? I'm going bald.

I always had an itchy head. My mother would yell, "stop scratching, you'll get your nails dirty." She'd poke through my scalp looking for lice. Yell through the bathroom door, "make sure to wash your hair," but I hated to get soap in my eyes so I would just wet it. Fuck! If I had only listened to her.

My father has a vibrating scalp massager in his medicine chest. You wear it like a glove. Turn on the motor and it makes your fingers vibrate. Feels good, but when I take it away precious strands are twined tightly around my fingers.

How can I become a famous writer if I'm bald? A quick survey of jacket photos reveals glossy coifs on all my idols. Hemingway, dark and gleaming with a mustache to match. Fitzgerald, alcoholic, semi-invalid, but with a thick, sandy head of hair. Faulkner, a salt and pepper thatch. John O'Hara and Irwin Shaw, thick and lustrous. James Joyce, neatly groomed, must have had regular haircuts. Leon Trotsky, a mountain of unruly curls. Mailer, wild and kinky. James Jones, nothing special, but it covers his head. Even the old guys, Sandburg, Bertrand Russell, Walt Whitman. You'd think Dostoevsky wouldn't care, but it looks like he might have had a comb over. Baudelaire goes with the tonsure, the Julius Caesar-Napoleon comb down. Kafka and Orwell, emaciated consumptives dead in their forties, but they sport healthy pompadours over haggard faces.

I search the 8th Street Bookstore and find Henry James, fat, bald and glowering. Try *Golden Bowl* and can't get through the first ten pages. John Dos Passos. Chrome dome rising over clipped sides. Hemingway called him "Baldy" (he would.) Looks like a high school history teacher, but he's a page turner, I go through the *USA Trilogy* in a weekend. Is he that good or do I love his books because he's bald? I'm am reassured when I read Sartre's judgement: "John Dos Passos is the greatest writer of our time." Sartre had hair.

There's a standoff in Berlin between American and Soviet tanks. They both back away the same distance so it wouldn't look like one had been punked by the other. The Russians put up a wall between the eastern and western zone. They're shooting people who try to escape. Everybody's talking about World War Three...

Yeah, but I'm bald.

Kennedy mobilizes the Reserves and the Air National Guard. In the *New York Post* Jack Anderson says, "The President has been smarting since the CIA backed invasion of Cuba was repelled." Columnist Max Lerner calls the Bay of Pigs "America's first military misadventure..."

What if war comes and I'm drafted? I'll have to wear one of those steel "pots." If I'm not killed right away I'll be a human cue ball by the time I get out.

Fifth frame at Park Circle Lanes. I'm in the pocket tonight, the pins are flying. Working on four strikes and calling "perfect game." Elise, the barmaid has stopped to watch. She's new and everybody's after her. Dark eyes and a secret smile. Maybe I still have enough hair to make a move. Feeling her eyes I lose focus and hit the one pin head on. Now I'm looking at the seven-ten, the impossible split. The guys are jeering, "perfect game, huh?" Trick is to graze the ten hard enough to launch it across the alley to knock over the seven. Speed up the approach and extend the back swing. Release between the middle and right arrow. I clip the ten pin a touch too full and it misses the seven, but then the ball bounces off the wall back onto the alley and rolls into the seven. They shove me, pound me on the back. "You gotta be fuckin' kiddin!"

Elise smiles. "This is your lucky night…"

Something's twisting inside my groin. Fuck! I head to the bench in agony. "I think I pulled something."

Back at the chapel I get a couple of aspirin from Charley Price. "Better take care of that, kid," he says, "you don't wanna fool around down there."

I'm like the baby who shrieks in outraged innocence at his first hunger pang. Except for skinned knees, bloody noses and sore throats that went away after I had my tonsils out I've never felt real pain in my life. Two more aspirin don't work. Two Anacin after that make me nauseous. No way to get comfortable. Lie on my back in the darkness, groin on fire, counting spasms instead of sheep. At dawn, I roll out of bed and almost fall over. My right testicle is the size of a baseball and hanging from thickened veins. I can't stand erect and have to monkey walk into the bathroom. Have to sit down to pee.

Can't let my mother know. I pull on my old high school jock and walk erect into the kitchen. "You're green," my mother says. "Too many cheeseburgers at the bowling alley last night," I say.

I sneak out while she's on the phone with my aunt. Make it down to Prospect Park Southwest just as the Coney Island bus is pulling away. Palm walk down the aisle. Everybody looks away like what kind of maniac is this?

Dr. S. is in a second floor office over a children's clothing store on Brighton Beach Avenue. A sign on the frosted door says "Ring Bell Once." The door opens a crack. A bent old guy, more hair coming out of his nose than on his head. Graying white shirt and red suspenders, holding up black gabardines. Keeps his foot in the door. "Mimi Rizzo from Riverside referred me," I say. "What's your problem?" he asks.

"My right testicle is the size of a bowling ball," I say. "That's a problem," he says.

It's the dingy office in the movies where the bad guy goes to get patched up after he's been shot by the cops. Three kids my age, hiding behind old copies of *Life* and *Look*. All here for the same reason? I sit back and rest my testicle on the edge of the chair. The doctor opens the door. "I'll take you now…"

The Doctor washes his hands at a stained porcelain sink. "So what happened?"

"I was in a car accident. Felt a strain. Bowling last night, it came back. Couldn't sleep. Then in the morning it was swollen and I could hardly walk."

"Drop your pants and undershorts."

He puts a thermometer in my mouth. Cups my ball in his hand. "Not as big as a bowling ball," he says. "A *bocce* ball maybe… Have you overexerted sexually in the past week or so?"

"I haven't had sex at all."

He fingers my scrotum. The pain shoots to the top of my head like a weight in a carnival strength machine… Ding!

"Personal relief is actually more strenuous than sex with a partner," he says.

The top of a bald head is actually more interesting than hair. Thick hair is boring. One look and you've seen it all. A bald head is an undiscovered country with its bumps and veins and odd discolorations. Little gray patches cropping up in random places like weeds in a vacant lot.

"You don't have to be embarrassed about this," he says. "Personal relief goes back to prehistoric times. There are cave paintings of Neanderthals with their dicks in their hands…"

This is a big joke to him.

"Okay, I had personal relief."

"Perfectly normal for a boy your age…" He shoves his hand under my ball and commands, "Cough."

I cough and cringe from the pain.

"Have you fallen awkwardly or lifted a heavy object?"

"I work at Riverside and move bodies," I say and wait for the joke.

"Dead weight," he says. "You have orchitis, essentially torsion of the testicles. You twisted something in the accident, then aggravated it bowling and overindulging in personal relief. Imagine trying to force water through a twisted hose. I'm going to give you a shot of penicillin to be safe. Your testicle should start to shrink in a day or two."

"When will it return to normal size?"

"Never. You have no blood supply to that testicle. When it begins to atrophy it will occasionally ascend into your scrotum like you had chicken pox. If you go to a high-class urologist he'll tell you need to have it surgically removed, but the truth is it'll disappear on its own. You can pull up your pants unless you like the breeze."

It hits me: I'll only have one ball.

Dr. S. peels off his latex gloves with a snap. "Look on the bright side," he says. "You're losing a gonad, but gaining a deferment. I'll write the draft board. It'll keep you out at least six months…"

Try to keep the tears out of my voice. "Can I still have sex?"

He smiles and pats me on the shoulder. "Yes, if you can convince some gullible female. You only use one testicle doing intercourse, anyway. Think of it as changing a flat. Now you're on the spare. Drive carefully."

"A JEW ALWAYS WANTS TO SHOW HOW SMART HE IS"

November 1960

State law requires all undertakers to serve an apprenticeship before they get a license. My colleagues are young men whose families own small funeral homes. They are Italian and Irish so Mamanna, gives them Jewish aliases to accommodate the clientele. Celiberti becomes "Krieger;" Aiello is "Altman;" McCadden answers to "Meyers." Mamanna calls himself "Mr. Morris."

But these names are too tame. The boys make up their own burlesque versions, calling to each other across a lobby crowded with mourners... "Mr. Shmatler, will you please take these people to the Gladstein room..." "Mr. Krapinsky, could you please direct these people..." "Be right there Mr. Plotzstein..." And then run into an alcove red-faced with suppressed laughter.

Still, there is some sacrilege even these pranksters won't commit. They'll wear skull caps, but won't say the short prayer for the dead. Because I am the only real Jew I'm elected.

On Sunday Aiello's mother cooks Italian dinner for the staff. A big pot of veal *pizzaiole* with meatballs and chunks of sausage. Baked ziti with eggplant and mozzarella. Broccoli rabe. We eat in white burial shrouds to keep the sauce off our shirts. I gorge myself between funerals, then run out to say the prayers. Scolari, the day manager, stands at the door with a box of Clorets. "For Chrissake don't go breathin' *pizzaiole* on the bereaved." I stand in the family room off the chapel keeping an appropriately grave face as Shmatler, Plotzstein and

Krapinsky lurk out of sight in the wings of the chapel, making faces, obscene gestures, even dropping their pants. I stare at them stony and unmoved. Before the ceremony I recite a short prayer, which the immediate family repeats after me. Then I rend their garments with a razor blade.

"Please repeat after me," I say to one man. "I'm going to cut your tie..."

"I'm going to cut your tie," he blubbers.

"No, just the prayer," I say.

"Just the prayer," he repeats.

"No the Hebrew part..."

"Say the prayer already," someone interrupts. "He's only the son-in-law."

I begin the prayer... *"Baruch atah adonai..."*

Aiello/Shmatler enters at the proper funereal pace. I know what he's going to do and steel myself.

"Eloheinu melech haolam..."

As Aiello passes he turns to me and opens his mouth. Out pops a lit cigarette. He closes his mouth and walks on. I bite hard on my lip and finish the prayer.

"Dayan ha emet..."

I'm on the road with Rizzo. First stop Coney Island General. There's a new morgue attendant, a Black guy in sparkling white with a shiny shaved head. Rizzo whispers, "We're in trouble now," and flashes a phony smile. "Hiya pal, what happened to Mr. Gendelman?"

The guy won't look from his paper work. "Retired."

Rizzo strains for affability. "Jeeze, I thought he was a young guy. Musta saved his pennies..."

"License please," the guy says.

Rizzo shoves the authorizations at him, the two dollars peeking over the top. "I left it in my other suit. C'mon, everybody knows me..."

The guy ignores the money. "I'm new here," he says. "Once I've seen the license I won't ask for it again."

It's a long drive to Jewish Chronic Disease Hospital. Rizzo takes a few hits at his flask. "What did I tell ya about them people holdin' a grudge? This guy would rather screw a white man than have a coupla extra bucks in his pocket..."

Schultz, the morgue attendant at Jewish Chronic, is a scowling dwarf in his eighties. He won't trade pleasantries and never helps take bodies off the slabs, but quickly pockets the two dollars. "Looks like Rumplefuckin'stiltskin," Rizzo whispers. "Lives in a hospital room next to the morgue. Betcha he's got a bundle stashed. Somebody's gonna hit that room one of these nights. He better not be there or it'll be Truth or Consequences for him..."

Schultz pulls open a drawer on a big, middle-aged man. Mound of fish white belly, crinkly gray hair on his chest. "Prick always puts the fat guys on the top row," Rizzo says as we dump the body onto the gurney.

On the way out Schultz hands us a shopping bag with the man's effects—baggy suit, scuffed shoes, stained underwear. The jacket is empty, the trouser pockets have been turned inside out. "No payday here," Rizzo says. "Guy drops dead, the cops search him, the ambulance guys take the change out of his pockets and leave the shorts where the poor bastard crapped himself." He searches the man's shoes... "Nuttin!" Shakes one sock out. Then the other... "Hey, here's somethin' they missed." A ticket has fallen out of the sock. "It's from Yonkers Raceway. The guy played the trifecta for Chrissake..."

"Maybe that's why his pockets were empty," I say. "He lost all his money."

Rizzo shakes his head at my ignorance. "A guy don't hide a losing ticket in his sock."

"Why didn't he just cash it at the track?"

"Maybe he was with some other people he owed money to and didn't want them to see." He puts the ticket in his pocket as he walks out. "Ah, it's probably worth nothin'..."

An hour later he's back. "Okay Baby Gould this is your lucky day for bein' in the right place. I did a little checking. We found a winning trifecta ticket. Handsome Teddy, Sayonara Baby and Dapple Dan…"

"How much did it pay?" I ask.

"What are you, a big fuckin' handicapper all of a sudden? It paid thirty-nine hundred for a two dollar bet, but this guy bet twenty…"

I do a quick calculation. "That's thirty nine G's!"

"Poor slob probably never won that much money in his life," Rizzo says. "First time something good happens he gets so excited he drops dead, that's the kinda world we live in. Don't think you're a full partner. I found it."

"We both did."

"Awright, awright, but I'm takin' the risk cashin' it. I'll give you ten percent." He hands me a folded twenty. "Here's a down payment. Don't drop no remarks."

On Sunday the morgue is the only quiet place to eat. I've got an eggplant parmigiana hero, full loaf. Bottle of Mission orange soda. This month's *Playboy*…

Two wide guys in drab suits come barging in. "You Ghoul?"

Detectives—they say the names so quickly I don't get them—from the something squad—I don't hear that either.

Look at me in disgust. "How the fuck can you eat in here?"

"He's a ghoul, that's how." Standing over me, cracking his knuckles. "Did you remove the body of Sherman Flinker from Jewish Chronic?"

"I don't remember the name…"

"Your partner says you found a winning trifecta ticket from Aqueduct."

Dumb trick. Saying the wrong track so I'll correct them and prove my guilt. "I didn't find anything," I say.

"Mr. Flinker's wife says he called her from the track all excited because he hit the trifecta. But she couldn't find the ticket in his effects…"

I use Rizzo's line. "We're the last people to see the body. Talk to the guys at the track or the ambulance driver or the morgue attendant."

The knuckle cracker gives me a light slap with a heavy hand on the back of the head. "We're talkin' to you, tough guy…"

"Ticket's useless to anybody but a member of the Flinker family," his artner says. "Anybody else tries to cash it is subject to arrest. In six months it'll expire…"

Knuckle cracker bumps me. "Better not go on a spending spree, Ghoul…" They go out laughing at their little joke… "Ba Fong Ghoul… Ghoul…"

Later, I see them watching from their car as I get in the truck with Rizzo.

"Act natural," he says. He watches in the rearview mirror. "They're tryin' to figure out a way to shake us down… Mr. Flinker, he should rest in peace, was a degenerate gambler."

"How do you know?"

Rizzo taps his head. "Who puts twenty bucks on three longshots? A guy who wants to get even in a hurry, that's who. I asked around. He owes every bookie in the neighborhood so he hides the ticket so nobody will know he won. I sold it for a buck fifty to Jerry Silone at the Caton Inn. He'll sell it back to the son-in-law. The son-in-law will cash it in and give Jerry twenty per cent. Case closed…"

He turns down Coney Island Avenue. If a guinea had dropped dead we'd be whackin' up thirty-nine large right now, the two of us. Just our luck we catch a pussy-whipped Jew who runs to call his wife."

I feel I have to defend the deceased. "Hitting the trifecta is a big deal after all."

"But a guinea wouldn't tell nobody," Rizzo says. "He'd buy a car and spend the money on a *gummare*. A guinea can keep a secret. A Jew always wants to show how smart he is."

TRAIFE

Brooklyn, 1954

On Sunday he went to the schoolyard with his basketball. All the kids were in church so he practiced his jump shot, making believe someone was guarding him. On his way home, he saw Mrs. Esposito struggling across the street with a huge black pot, a long loaf of Italian bread under her arm. "Do me a favor," she said, "take this bread before I drop it."

He eased it out from under her arm—"I'll take the pot, too," he said— and gave her his basketball to hold. The pot smelled like the pizza Dad got on Saturday night. The steel loop bit into his hand.

"Too heavy for you?" Mrs. Esposito asked and patted his head. "You think my daughter-in-law would send somebody to help me? Mama will do it, they say. What'll they do when Mama's not here anymore?"

Anthony, Leo the super's son, had two younger brothers, Junior and Danny, and an older sister, Lucy, in high school. His older brother, Bruno was in the Navy and came home on holidays. All of them lived in an apartment on the first floor. Mrs. Esposito lived across the street with Anthony's aunt and uncle and his three cousins. One cousin who was married with two little kids lived down the block. They were all crowded around the dining room table, laughing: "Hey Grandma, where were you, we're starvin? You playin' basketball now?" Leo was at the head of the table pouring red wine from a half gallon bottle into a water glass. "You wanna eat?" he asked. "Lucy get another chair for him."

"I have to ask my mother," he said

"Go ahead, we'll wait for you."

As he walked out he heard Mrs. Esposito—"He's a good boy."

Upstairs in 4A, Mom was setting the table. On Sundays Dad drove to the appetizing store on Flatbush Avenue and got lox and bagels and whitefish and cream cheese. Bubbe came to make pirogen and Grandpa Dave brought Barracini milk chocolate. The salty fish made his eyes feel blurry and dried out his mouth and the pirogen made his belly feel stuffed. The candy was good, but he always ate too much and couldn't go to the bathroom. "Leo invited me to eat with them," he said

Mommy got her worried look. "How'd that happen?"

"I helped Mrs. Esposito carry her pot across the street."

"I guess you have to be polite. Tell them your grandmother's coming and you can't stay long. Come back in an hour… Make sure you thank them."

Downstairs, they squeezed him next to Lucy so close he felt her leg. She was wearing a sleeveless blouse and he had a peek at her bra and the patch of stubble in her armpits. Caught the scent of her shampoo and imagined her silhouetted behind the glass door of the shower washing her hair. "Help your grandmother," Leo said and Lucy stood up, her bare arm brushing against his. They brought out more black pots of meatballs and sausage and chunks of veal, plates of roast chicken and broccoli, salad with bottles of French's dressing. Quarts of Meyer's 1890 cream and black cherry soda, which was a real treat because soda wasn't allowed in his house. Only cold water or seltzer, which burned his throat.

Anthony crammed ziti dripping with sauce into his mouth, chewing loudly. "Don't make noise when you eat, how many times I have to tell you?" his mother said

"Your mother let you eat sausage?" Mrs. Esposito asked him. "I don't wanna give you nothin' your mother wouldn't approve." He expected it to taste like the franks Mom made with baked beans, but it was spicy and made the sweat prickle out on his forehead. The meatballs and the veal came apart under his fork. There were chunks of cooked tomato in the sauce and something that looked like Mom's stuffed cabbage.

"Look how he can eat and so skinny…"

Mrs. Esposito smiled at him, her eyes glistening. "It all goes to his brain. That's why he's so smart."

"But he ain't a punk,"Anthony said "You shoulda seen him dump Billy Sladek…"

That wasn't what had happened at all. Yet Anthony was smiling proudly like he really believed it.

Leo poked him. "Make a muscle."

He flexed his arm and Leo tapped his bicep… "Hard as a rock."

There was nothing there. Leo and Anthony were just trying to make him look like a tough guy. And Lucy was looking at him in admiration.

Mrs. Esposito brought out two quarts of Breyers three-flavor brick ice cream and a box of Stella D'Oro assorted cookies. There was black coffee for the grownups. The kids got milk.

He got up to take his plate into the kitchen.

"Sit down, where ya goin' with that?" Leo said. "That's woman's work."

The girls smiled and didn't seem to mind. Lucy took his plate.

Leo lit a little black cigar. "Wanna watch the football game?"

"Better go home, your mother's waitin' for you," Mrs. Esposito said.

"Thank you for having me," he said.

"Come again," Mrs. Esposito said "You're a good boy, your mother can be proud."

But she wouldn't be, she'd be mad. In the elevator he thought he might as well go outside and hang around until nighttime, he was going to be punished anyway. It would be worse because Bubbe was there. Mommy was always nervous and in a bad mood when she came.

The foyer was dark as he opened the door, the smoke from the fried pirogen hanging in the air. He heard Bubbe in the kitchen:

"He's running around with the Italyenas like a vilde chaya."

He knew vilde chaya meant wild animal because that's what Bubbe always called him.

"Eating traife, you'll see, one day he'll bring home a shikse."

Traife was pork like the sausage on pizza or the shrimp they had in Chinese restaurants. This word, shikse, was new to him.

"There are a lot of activities he could go to at the temple," Aunt Rae

said,

"It's two miles away for God's sake, Rae," Mom said. "Do me a favor, stay out of this."

Everybody was sitting in the darkness. The remains of the meal were on the dining room table. A piece of lox, brown around the edges, bagel ends, a mound of cream cheese sooty with black crumbs. A coffee cup with a cigarette floating in the grounds.

Dad and Grandpa Dave were on the couch, a bottle of whiskey on the coffee table. Uncle Bernie was in a dark corner with a cup of coffee.

"Oh boy, are you gonna get it," he said.

"Better go right to your room," Dad said

Mom came out of the kitchen and grabbed his arm. "I told you to be back in an hour…"

"I was eating," he said.

"Took you three hours?"

"They had a lot of food."

"Grandma saved you some pirogen."

"But I'm full…"

"Just eat a couple and a piece of strudel." She pushed him toward the kitchen and whispered, "don't tell her you ate downstairs…"

Bubbe was at the stove flipping the fried dough filled with sweet cheese. Swollen ankles sticking out over the top of her thick shoes. Sparse hair, bald like a man. Brown warts on her chin. Cold blue eyes behind the gold-rimmed glasses.

"So look who decided to come," she said.

"He was playing basketball with his friends," Mommy said.

"So late? Their parents let them play like this on Sunday?" She pokes at his shirt. "What's this, tomato sauce? Did you eat with your friends?"

Mommy pulled him back. "They invited him, Mama. He couldn't say no."

"Was the old lady cooking?" Dad called. "I love that stuffed pig skin. It's like Sicilian stuffed cabbage."

"OH COOL," SHE SAYS

March 1961

I get a letter from Selective Service. I've been classified "2S," deferred from military service until I graduate. They enclose my draft card with "2S," the magic number. "This is your official identification. You must carry it with you at all times."

My mother opens a letter from the State Department. "What's this, a passport application?"

I wanted to wait as long as possible before I told her so I wouldn't have to suffer that worried look, those anxious questions. "I thought I'd go to Paris for the summer," I say. "I can get a year's language credit if I take the summer course at the Alliance Francaise."

She's dunking Lorna Doones in her coffee. "How are you going to live?"

"I'll use the scholarship money and what I saved from my salary. There's a German boat, the Bremen. It's a hundred and eighty dollars to Cherbourg. Then I can take the boat train to Paris…" I make up a date. I'll be home on the fourteenth."

She gives me the searching look that usually uncovers a lie. "Well, I guess you have to," she says.

My friend Lenny Frankel from the freshman basketball team picks me up after work in his father's '56 Buick Regal—lime green with a white top. We split a "tre bag" of marijuana, three dollars for a pay envelope of mostly seeds and twigs. The twigs poke through the rolling paper and the seeds pop and crackle. After a few tokes I have a stabbing headache.

We go to Dubrows Cafeteria on Kings Highway, famous for cheese blintzes and hot girls, "no dogs allowed," Lenny says. Impalas and Corvettes and Bonnevilles are double-parked. Guys are combing their pomps, flashing watches and fancy lighters. It's a windy night and the girls are inside. Heavy eye makeup, high color on the cheeks, tight sweaters and clingy blouses. Bold and chatty in miniskirts and boots.

Lenny's my expert on women. "They give you a blip like on radar," he says. "If you're talkin' to them sometimes they look down to check your dick. Some guys put a wad of toilet paper in their shorts, you know like falsies. If they leave their coats open, it means they wanna show off their tits. Stare at their asses as they walk by. They'll feel your eyes. If they reach back to fix their slacks they're uptight. If they shake their asses even more they're ready... Eager don't get beaver so be cool like you could care less."

Lenny's the star of the team. Gangly, big nose, kinky hair, he'll be on the varsity next year. Girls call him over. A few stand up to open their coats. "They're blippin' tonight," he says. "I got a dick check and a secret smile." Zero for me. It's a simple world where clothes and cars and keywords rule. My black suit isn't appreciated here. Neither are my gnomic jokes. Standing in a cold sweat of utter rejection I decide I don't belong in Brooklyn anymore.

After work I take the "D" train to West 4th Street. I love the Village. It's all mixed up between stores and apartments, not like Brooklyn where there is one shopping street and everything else is houses. The people stroll, some arm in arm, laughing and chatting. Not like Brooklyn people, rushing around with their heads down, always upset about something. They wear the clothes I see in the New Yorker advertisements, not like my neighborhood where it's either suits and plain dresses or work clothes. They have yappy little dogs, instead of surly Brooklyn mutts. Their hair is longer. A lot of beards. I walk the streets for hours, looking through the cafe windows at groups in animated conversation, books and magazines on the tables, men leaning forward, women throwing their heads back and laughing. Everybody looks like my vision of a writer or an artist.

I wander to the fountain in Washington Square Park, past the folksingers, bongo drummers, poets reciting, old people arguing politics. Pass the Washington Square Arch, designed by Stanford White, a Gay Nineties socialite, famous for drugging and raping teenage girls. Now dope dealers cluster around it determined to continue his tradition. Unsmiling desperadoes they stand under the inscription *"Let us raise a standard to which the wise and honest can repair"* selling "beat" marijuana, which they call "Village Green," made of a few stalks of the real thing mixed with the crushed leaves and twigs of the park's elm trees. Whispering men flit in and out of the darkness, faces glowing ghastly white. For a buck they'll squeeze a "taste" of amphetamine from an eye dropper onto your tongue. Junkies mingle at the benches, sucking cigarettes, waiting for their "conneeze."

A group of Puerto Rican kids from the Bronx play congas, gourds and cowbells at the fountain. I sit a few feet away playing along on a pot from my mother's kitchen. Struck with the fingertips the pot makes a metallic ring that is crisp and resonant and provides a bongo embellishment to the relentless rhythm of the congas. I'm taking a chance. They're a tight clique and don't like people to mess up their beat. But one night one of them slides over to make room for me. "Cool sound. I'm Benny," he says. We slap fives and I have a new place to hang out.

"They do some serious dopin' down here," Benny tells me. I've smoked reefer. Got high enough to get the giggles and go for a "slice." Here the joints keep passing until I feel myself getting nervous about what people think of me. Trying to read their expressions when I make a joke. Worrying that I'm acting like a schmuck in front of the girls. One night I drink a pint of Night Train, share a spliff—pot wrapped loosely in a newspaper page—and swallow a handful of Romilar cough tablets. Suddenly, the noise and the lights are unbearable. I find a quiet bench in the dark. Space winds howl in my ears. The deceased fly by me in their shrouds, their hospital gowns, their sad pajamas. Bloodshot eyes staring in reproach. White maggots crawling like bloated slugs on chalk white flesh. I cling to the slimy walls of my sanity. Trying to reassure myself. "This will end soon..."

Midnight and the subway is packed like rush hour. People going to night jobs, or snoozing on their way home. Drunks quarreling in slow motion. A man in a tuxedo and a woman in a white gown, party tinsel sparkling in her blonde hair are slow dancing in the middle of the car. I'm afraid if I talk to them they'll vanish and then I'll know they aren't real. The drugs ebb to a last few drops of euphoria. I exult. What a city! What a life! Hot bile rises in my throat and I puke between the cars.

In the park, the air is charged with expectation. Only a few months before the folksingers had been denied permits to play at the fountain and dragged off to paddy wagons if they resisted. Now, a thousand people are marching in protest down Fifth Avenue, singing folk songs and chanting, "The Park is for the People." A freckled redhead in a calico granny dress reaches out to me. "Come join us..." I link arms with her and fake the lyrics to "This Land Is My Land," which I've never heard before. Police cars and paddy wagons are coming down the side streets. Motorcycle cops ride alongside the marchers. Huge police horses clop out of carriers.

"Fill their jails," the redhead cries. The people around her pick up the chant. "Fill their jails/Fill their jails..."

"Gandhi said we must resist them with love and forbearance," the redhead calls. Somebody starts chanting "Resist/Resist..." A cop with a bullhorn stands under the arch shouting, but his words get lost in the wind. A flying wedge of cops moves up the street, tearing down signs, whacking people with billy clubs and dragging them into paddy wagons. I try to run away, but the redhead grips my arm even tighter, screaming "fill their jails." Mounted cops gallop into the crowd, swinging their clubs like polo mallets. They're singling out the Black guys for arrest and mistreatment, but anyone who resists gets whacked as well. An old man is sitting on the curb with a bloody towel to his head, his Scotch terriers climbing on his shoulders to lick his face. "This is what they did when we were on strike in the '30s," he says. "They would ride their horses right through the picket lines."

Next day there are pictures of cops dragging women by the hair. The police call it a "beatnik riot," and say they acted after residents complained about noise and harassment in the park. The marchers come back, their ranks swelled by civil rights groups and old lefties— and me looking for the redhead. The cops turn out in force, but Mayor Wagner calls them off, and we march to the fountain in triumph. Now the park is packed every night. Orators, conga drummers, dancers, tourists. It's a lukewarm melting pot, blacks and whites feeling each other out. Interracial couples are safe at the fountain, but if they venture onto the side streets of Little Italy they risk a beating from the locals.

On my way to the subway one night the redhead runs by in a crowd of "folkies," long hair, tie dyes, guitars. "Hey, we're going to the ferry..." She takes my hand—"c'mon."—and I follow her down Sixth Avenue. "What's that pot for?" she asks me. "It's my drum," I say and do a roll. "Oh, cool," she says.

Below Canal the streets are deserted. We run downtown past the Stock Exchange. "Wall Street, enemy territory," someone shouts. A kid throws a rock through a shoemaker's window and everybody cheers.

"But shoemakers aren't the enemy," I say.

"They are down here," he says.

We run through Battery Park onto the Staten Island Ferry. At this hour it's mostly night workers coming and going. Some in their job uniforms, some carrying lunch boxes. They glare at this festive group of heedless kids, singing folk songs, passing wine, openly, defiantly kissing and groping.

There's a chill in the morning breeze. The red head shivers and moves closer to me. I wonder if I should put my arm around her.

"What's your art?" she asks.

"I'm a writer," I say.

"Oh cool," she says.

THERE HAS TO BE A BETTER WAY

October 1962

Headline in *The New York Times:* KENNEDY READY FOR SOVIET STANDOFF. A U2 spy plane has discovered Soviet missile sites in Cuba. JFK accuses the Russians of violating the Monroe Doctrine and demands the Soviets remove their missiles. Khrushchev refuses until we remove our missiles from Turkey and Italy. *The New York Post* calls it an "eyeball to eyeball confrontation." Kennedy has ordered a naval blockade with orders to fire on any Soviet ship that tries to land in Cuba.

Another notice from the Draft Board. "You are hereby ordered to report..."

I go back to Dr. S. "Your missing testicle won't work this time," he says. "There was some risk that your injury would be aggravated in active duty, causing a service-connected disability. But now you'll go into your physical fully healed."

"With one ball?"

"Won't stop you from shooting Russians. Just aim slightly to the right to compensate."

"What if we sink one of their ships?" I ask.

"Then we'll have to let them sink one of ours. Don't worry, it's just an excuse to spend more money on bombs."

"I'm not worrying about war, I'm worrying about baldness."

He considers this. "You are not afraid of dying in combat?"

"I'm afraid all my hair will fall out from wearing a helmet."

"It's an obsession. Keeps you awake at night. Thoughts of

suicide."

I follow his lead. "What's the point of living if you're bald, balless and barren?"

"Infertile," he corrects. "Let me refer you to a psychologist. This gambit just might do the trick."

October. 13, 1962

Kennedy has thrown a cordon of battleships around Cuba and turned back a Soviet freighter. RED SHIPS FACE SEARCH OR SINKING, says the *Daily News*. There's a story that the Russians shot down one of our spy planes, but we're denying it. A lot of speculation about who's going to "blink" first.

Dr. S.'s psychologist, Dr. F. "is booked for the next two months," his secretary says.

"It's urgent that I see him," I say. "I'm taking my Army physical next week..."

"November third," she says. "And if you're a minute late he won't reschedule."

After work we go to the Caton Inn, a bar on Coney Island Avenue, down the block from Riverside and across from the 74th Precinct. Burly bodies milling in the dark. Jukebox blasting Hit Parade tunes. Off-duty cops, getting loudly plastered at one end, big .38's bulging off their belts or peeking out of their jackets in shoulder holsters. Mob guys in back. Not the kind with fancy suits and Caddies double parked, but working class hoods in windbreakers who peddle swag and break legs. A few *gummare*, mistresses, sulking in their apricot sours, lipstick stained cigarettes piling up in the ashtrays. The cops are having a beery good time, the wise guys are sullen whiskey drinkers, going into dark corners for brief conversations, coming back to the bar, waving their glasses. "Hey Skipper..."

Bob chugs Rheingold on tap, Jimmy G. orders a Canadian Club and Ginger. I fall back on my father's drink. "Haig & Haig on the rocks." The bartender is darkly tan, gray at the temples, white on white shirt rolled over massive forearms, ruby pinky ring, suit pants and shiny shoes like he just shed his jacket and loosened his tie to tend bar. He ignores my order and pours out of a bottle of Three Feathers American Whiskey, daring me to complain. Feels like I swallowed a lit match, I'm dizzy after one sip. I step back and tilt the glass when nobody is looking, spilling a little on the floor. "I'll play a tune," I say. Make believe I'm checking the playlist and pour the rest of the booze behind the jukebox.

Bob T. yells, "Hey Skipper, gimme me another." Drapes his arm around me. "Wanna see a trick?" Hands me a kitchen match. "Betcha I can light this with a fart. Just hold it under my ass." He bends over and emits a volcanic fart right in my face. I'm standing in a cloud of flatulence, holding the unlit match and Jimmy G. is hysterical laughing. "A trick I learned in the Army," Bob says. "We called it skunking." Waggles his glass. "Hey Skip, whaddya say?"

He tells stories about his cab driving days. Drunken women paying for their ride with oral sex. "This blonde says to me, I'm broke, willya take it out in trade? Queers too"—he lisps in imitation—"I spent all my money in the bar. Is there another way I can pay the fare?"

I'm astonished at this admission. "You let a guy blow you?"

"Don't look at 'em and don't let em touch you," he says. "They do a better job than some broads."

"Don't knock it 'til you try it," Jimmy says.

"Hey Skip," Bob yells.

"They don't like it when strangers call them by their neighborhood names," I say.

"Ah whaddya worryin' about?" He puts a twenty in the bar. "Keep throwin' these around and I can call him anything I want."

"He doesn't need your twenty," I tell him. "This bar is a front."

Bob gets me in a headlock. "Listen to Elliot Ness over here..."

I suck some booze through the slender straw and squirt it into an empty ashtray in front of the beer taps.

Bob sees my empty glass, "I thought Jews couldn't drink…"

The bartender gives me a second look to see who's drinking this rotgut and slides me another. The slightest sip makes my eyes tear. "Takin' a piss," I say. I thread my way through the swaying bodies at the bar. Hiding the glass behind me I spill the rest of my drink on the floor in front of the bathroom.

Jimmy G. is telling how he picks up stewardesses. "Go to the Traveler's Inn, on the Southern State, right outside Idlewild. It's where they stay on their layovers…"

"Hey Skip…" A guy is waving a soggy cigar butt. "Why don't you wipe the ashtrays around here?"

The bartender wipes the ashtray where I squirted my drink.. I take another sip for show. The room spins and I have to hold onto the bar until it slows down.

"Them stewardesses play around all the time," Bob says.

"They all do," says Jimmy with surprising bitterness. "They're all hooers if they can get away with it…"

I'm back at the jukebox behind a cop's broad back. Uniform pants, flannel shirt, suspenders. Gun in a holster poking out of his belt. I could grab it right now. Hold it to his head. "See stupid, I coulda killed you…"

There's a commotion in back. A woman is shrieking and waving a broken heel. "I'm not drunk. Somebody spilt a drink…"

"Get over here, it's your round." Bob calls. "Fuckin' Jew, disappears when it's his turn, think I didn't see?"

I dump the rest of my drink behind the jukebox and walk back to the bar.

"You mad I said that?" Bob says.

He tries for another headlock, but I twist away. "I don't give a fuck what you say."

"Call me a shanty Irish mick."

"I don't wanna."

"C'mon do it, then we'll be even…"

"Shanty Irish mick," Jimmy says.

Bob turns on him. "Not, you faggot..."

Jimmy lurches off his stool. "What'd you call me?"

A sputter... A shower of sparks... The jukebox goes dark.

"Hey Skip, the box just shorted out... Plug's all wet..."

On the street trying to get Jimmy into the wagon. I can still feel the imprint of the bartender's thick fingers on my chest. "I don't ever wanna see you in here again..." I lunge for Jimmy, but he slithers away—"Get offa me..."—and staggers out on Coney Island Avenue, cars swerving and honking. I go after him. "Jimmy..." I grab him from behind and pin his arms in a bear hug. He tries to kick me in the shins, but I put my knee between his legs. Lock my thumbs and squeeze his ribs. He's frail and boneless. A few jerks and he sags in defeat. "You're too strong." I feel queasy. This wasn't a fight, I just wanted to get him into the wagon.

He's in the back seat, dead white pupils under half-open eyes. Bob shakes him. "You okay, Jimmy?"

"Okay..." His head droops like a ventriloquist's dummy.

"His car's in the lot," Bob T. says.

It's a blue two-seater Thunderbird.

"How'd he get a fancy car like that?"

"He says an old lady gave it to him," I say.

"Old lady my ass. He hustles those old faggots outside the Botanical Gardens..."

"How do you know?"

"Let him sleep it off here," Bob says." He runs into the garage and comes back up pushing a dolly. "Put him on this." He pushes him into the morgue. The white embalming tables glow in the dark. "Gimme a hand," Bob says.

We lift Jimmy off the dolly onto a table. Bob takes a pillow out of a casket and slides it under his head. Then bends and whispers in his ear. "Nice and cool, huh?"

"Mmm," Jimmy says.

That queasy feeling again. The stories Jimmy tells about women, which never quite ring true. The way he sagged in my arms and said "you're too strong…"

November 4, 1962.

REDS BACK DOWN, says the *Daily News*. The *Times* is more measured. U.S. AND SOVIETS REACH ACCORD ON CUBA.

Khrushchev has agreed to "dismantle and remove" the Russian missiles from Cuba and Kennedy promised to remove our missiles from Turkey. Not a concession, Bobby Kennedy tells John Scali, an ABC reporter with a comb-over that starts above his right ear. "We were going to take them out anyway."

It's portrayed as a victory. *Time Magazine* puts a portrait of Khrushchev on the cover, looking bald, puffy and confused with the banner: AFTER KHRUSHCHEV'S RETREAT.

In the morgue I see somebody took bites out of my veal and peppers hero, leaving mostly bread. There's a magazine under the wax paper. Cover photo of two muscle guys in tiny bathing suits. "A Biscuit, A Basket" in bright yellow letters. Inside, it's a typical dirty magazine, only this one is two guys. They arm wrestle on a blanket, beach scene with palm trees painted behind them. One guy forces the other to his knees. Takes out a huge dick with balls like pink balloons and makes him suck it.

Veal and peppers forgotten, I'm turning the pages. Broad shoulders, muscular, thickly tendoned arms, narrow waists. This is what I tried to look like as a kid, doing pushups and chins until my chest ached, sending away for Charles Atlas books on "Dynamic Tension."

Big, pink dicks. How much bigger than me? Shit! I've got a boner. Am I turned on by this? I don't feel horny, but I'm hard as a rock, dick pushing through my pants.

Whoever left this knew I ate at this spot every night. It's the kind of prank Bob T. would play. He talked about getting blowjobs in the cab. Jimmy was all squishy when I grabbed him. Maybe the two of them are queer and I'm the odd man out. They're trying to recruit me like the queer in the Village who followed me one night, "Don't knock it 'til you try it, honey..."

That night. Feeling weird in the Figaro. Not blip-fishing the girls. Just watching the guys. Wondering what their asses look like, their balls, how big their dicks are. Have I lost interest in women? Was I queer all along and I didn't know it? Tormented, I can't stop thinking about it.

Friday night I go to Dr. S's psychologist. The office is on the ground floor of a Deco building on Riverside Drive. Smudgy, white brick, glass door, marble floor, murals of satyrs and nymphs. An old, bent doorman in worn livery points to a warren of small suites. "The shrinks are down there."

Dr. F. is at a glass-topped desk filling a pipe. "Mr. Gould?" Doesn't get up or offer his hand. Short, in a brown suit, a few strands of hair carefully arranged across his bald head. Lights his pipe and takes out a legal pad. "Heywood... Unusual name..."

I was named after Heywood Broun, the famous writer..."

"I know who Heywood Broun was. Did Dr. S. tell you I would give you a note for your draft board?"

"Yes."

"No student deferment?"

"I dropped out of school."

"Why?"

"To be a writer."

"Was your father in the Army?"

"He was a Lieutenant in the Engineers. Won a Bronze Star."

"And you don't want to follow in his footsteps..."

"Guess not."

He flicks an ash off his pants. "So what's your objection to military service?"

"I've heard you have to sew your patches on," I say. "In the sixth grade we had to sew our own shop aprons and I had to get one of the girls to help me with a basting stitch..."

He's taking it all down.

"Also, they say you have to make your bed so tight that they can bounce a quarter off the blanket."

"And you couldn't do that?"

"Also, I heard you get in trouble if you don't fold your clothes..."

"Couldn't do that either..."

"My mom always did it for me..."

"Your mom... Never went to sleep away camp?"

"No."

"Never been in a dorm or a cabin with other boys?"

"Locker rooms with guys on the basketball team..."

"And how was that?"

"I never took a shower..."

"Why not?"

"I don't know. I guess I didn't want the guys to see me naked."

"Has anybody ever seen you naked?"

"A few girls..."

"How many?"

He's filling his pipe out of a leather pouch. "That many that you have to think about it." "Not that many..."

"But you were uncomfortable at the thought of being naked in front of your friends on the basketball team..."

I tell him the story of the magazine. My sudden fear that I might be queer. Astonished that I'm doing this, but it seems to be what he wants to hear.

He stops writing. "Do you think every muscular man is really a homosexual?"

"I just never thought queers looked like that. I thought they were, you know…"

Raises his hand for me to stop. "And after looking at this magazine you feel you might have homosexual tendencies…"

"I don't know…"

"And that if you go into the Army you won't be able to suppress them…"

"I don't know. I've been feeling weird…"

"Okay, that's good enough, Mr. Gould. You've been trying to convince me that you are psychologically unfit for military service. You've succeeded. I think you have serious issues that need to be explored. Come back next week and we'll start from the beginning."

Come back?

"Are you going to give me a note?" I ask.

"After a month or two."

"My physicals in a few weeks…"

"If they reclassify you there are still months before they induct you. I can always send a note to the Draft Board or have you bring it with you. The fact that you've been in treatment with me for months will add credibility, but you'll have to stay with me for a year. And if you renege I'll report you to your Draft Board and they'll induct you on the spot."

So that's the deal. I come every week, pay him off, nice and legal, and he gives me a note. If I stop coming he snitches to the Draft Board.

"How much do you charge for this fancy shakedown?" I ask.

"I'll give you the student rate. Thirty-five dollars…" Checks his calendar. "Next week, same time. You can pay Mrs. Rubin on your way out. Good night, Mr. Gould…"

Mrs. Rubin is whispering urgently into the phone. I glide by without paying. She calls, "Excuse me…" I keep going.

There has to be a better way.

"A YID FROM YIDSVILLE"

April 1961

My scholarship check has arrived. I buy eight hundred dollars in American Express Traveler's Cheques and put the leather folder in the bottom of my valise. Along with my savings account money and the eleven hundred I've saved from work I should have enough for a year in Paris. By then I'll have a novel published and my mother will forgive me for lying.

Winter is dying hard, attacking with sleet, stinging flurries, slippery slush on the subway steps, patches of black ice lying in wait for the careless walker. But on some nights it is disarmed by the softness of Spring, drawing people anxious for the park life to begin. One night I wander the streets looking in the coffee houses for someone I know. The fountain is bare. No wine drinkers, folk singers or bongo drummers. I follow the murmur of voices along Waverly Place to the southwest corner of the park. The chess players have gathered in the stippled shadows of the bare trees, drizzle glittering on their jackets, clustering around twenty stone tables, chessboards etched into their tops. Kibitzers razz the players "Terrible move…" The players retort. "Think you can beat me, patzer? Put your money down."

I haven't played chess since I got a game board for my ninth birthday and quit after three weeks when I couldn't beat my friends. I watch the games, trying to predict the moves and getting them wrong every time.

The players try to lure suckers. "Wanna play, I'm just learnin', need to practice." But one has a different approach.

"Wanna lose two dollars fast, fish?"

It's a slobby kid with greasy hair, greenish face under the lights, sitting alone at a corner table. A gold Jewish star around his neck.

"Whadda you, a waiter with that crummy black suit?" He holds out his closed fists. "Pick one." I pick his right and he opens it on a white piece. Makes a few opening moves. I recognize the Fool's Mate, a trap that was described in the instructions with my game board, and don't fall for it. "Okay, so you're not a total imbecile," he says and checkmates me in ten moves. "You should pay me double for giving you a lesson. This time I'll play black, I'll spot you a knight and we play for a fin."

I take the dare and lose in ten moves again. Two hours later I'm broke. I have to jump the turnstile as the train pulls in.

Next night I go straight to the tables, determined to beat him. When I sit down he crows, "Here's my dinner." He's oily and smelly, and eats gooey baloney sandwiches, grabbing my pieces with mayo-slicked fingers.

In an hour I'm out ten bucks and he won't play owsies—"Cash on the barrelhead, patzer"—so I drag home at four in the morning. Stare at the squares on the bathroom tiles, replaying every game of the night, reliving the slob's sneers until my jaw aches from grinding my teeth.

I become a familiar face, part of the school of "fish," perpetual losers, obsessed with the game. Every night I return for my ritual humiliation at the slob's hands. When I'm broke I join the crowds watching the "strong" players. There is Duval, an elderly Haitian, brown suit, shiny brown pate, who sets up ornate ivory pieces and a chess clock and dispatches all comers at a dollar a twenty-minute game. "Patzer!" he cries, slapping down the pieces. "You lose!" Next to him is Jimmy, hunched and intense with prematurely gray Toscanini hair. Five dollars for unlimited time, but when the loser makes a bad move he mutters "blunder," and forces him to resign. Joe the Russian, shaved head, walrus mustache—the Gurdjieff look —puffs furiously on Parliament cigarettes as he bullies his opponents. "Stupid move, patzer.

Don't insult my intelligence..." And Franz, a massive Black guy with a white beard, who analyzes every move. "You think I'm gonna do this so you can do that, but I'm gonna do this. It's a forced move, you can't do nothin' but resign."

The weaker players are consigned to tables in semi-darkness under the trees. I try them all. "Atrocious would be a promotion for you," a bald DA named Jack says, slamming down the winning move. An intern named Serge who comes from St. Vincent's Hospital in his surgical blues screams in mock pain: "You are torturing me with your ignorance," and traps my Queen. Even Stanley, the retired postman, who everyone says is senile, wags an arthritic finger. "Don't you see the train speeding down on you, patzer?"

One night the slob plays the Queen's Gambit, an opening which confounds weak players. As I touch my Knight someone sneezes. A lanky guy with greasy shoulder length hair is standing behind the fat kid. He covers his mouth and shakes his head slightly.

Is it a signal? I touch another piece. He lights a cigarette and purses his lips, which I take for a "no." There are a few more possible moves. I touch the pieces until he lowers his head, which I read as "yes." I make the move.

The slob twitches. He makes a move. I touch a piece. My benefactor shrugs and brushes his hair away from his face, which I take for a "what else?" The move initiates a furious exchange of pieces which results in an even position.

"Okay, you got lucky," the slob says. "I can't take the time to beat you so we'll call it a draw..."

"You said you'd pay up if you didn't win," I say. "A draw isn't a win."

"Whadda you, a fuckin' lawyer?" The slob digs into his pocket and comes out with a torn bill which he throws at me. "Here's a buck. That's all you get."

I rise, victorious. The longhaired guy turns away quickly, which I take for a "don't talk to me."

At dawn he is sitting on a rail as I leave the park. Tall and bony, blue veins running up his wrists to his shoulders. Sniffing. Clawing at the pimples on his forehead. I've seen him at the hustler tables, leaning back to blow smoke rings while his opponent agonizes over a move. Passed him once, looking away with a distracted air as an astonishing blonde with a perfect tan, clutched his arm, whispering urgently. He points to the book I'm carrying. "Myth of Sisyphus," he says. "Is that for reading or picking up girls?"

"Both," I say.

"How come you wear black?"

"I work in a funeral parlor in Brooklyn."

"And major in Accounting during the day. The American Dream…" He has a slight accent. English? Snotty Manhattan?

"What's your story?" I ask.

He imitates me. "My stawrry?" He turns quickly down the block. "Let's go, I don't want anyone to see us." As we walk he explains: "Look, maybe you can make B player someday, but you'll never get better…"

"Why not?"

"Chess players are born," he says. "You can study all your life and a seven-year-old kid who's never read a book can mate you blindfolded. By the time I was five I was beating grown ups. From twenty to death there are no big jumps in skill. You just try to conserve."

"Okay, so I stink. What do you care?"

"Ronald's a psychopathic hustler. Feeds on weak players." He gives me a sly look. "You want to crush him don't you?"

Ronald… So that's his name. "You promoting lessons?"

"Something quicker. Look, you've seen me around, I know you have. I'm blackballed in the park. Nobody will play me."

"Because you beat them?"

"Because I didn't learn how to play in Sing Sing or a Bessarabian Yeshiva. Or a Haitian banana boat. Or the City College Chess and Pastrami Club. Because I come into their little bailiwick and remind them what second raters they all are. They're all on the brink of starvation. Living with their parents or some pathetic woman. Surviving on welfare or unemployment and the few dollars they make hustling fish like you. I love to crush them."

He's building up to a proposition. "But you need my help to do it," I say.

"You're perfect for my plan," he says. "Good enough to show sudden improvement without causing suspicion. Also, you're a born grifter. You picked up on my signals immediately. I'll give you the moves like I did tonight. You'll beat everybody in the park. I'll give you half your winnings. As a bonus you'll acquire a reputation for brilliance."

"I'd rather get that without cheating."

"Forget that, you're not good enough," he says. "Hypothetically, if an invisible spirit whispered winning moves to you would you call it cheating?"

"No…"

Another sniff. "So… Think of me as your invisible spirit."

Next night. I meet my partner on the uptown side of the West 4th Street station. He won't shake hands. Won't tell me his name.

"The only thing you have to know about me is that I'm going to make you rich and famous. I have a simple system of signals you can learn in five minutes. We can't lose."

"As long as you always have the winning move."

"I always will. I'm a Master, 2200 rating… I played for Harvard."

"What'd you major in?"

"Majored?" he asks with a sniff, as if that question betrays my humble origins. "I guess I *majored* in chess and amphetamine. After I destroyed Yale they had no further use for me. Or I for them."

He looks around. "Walk ahead of me like we don't know each other…" I take a few steps and he falls in behind me… "I use the standard system of notation, dividing the board into numbers. I flash the numbers by touching my nose with my fingers."

"What about numbers over five?"

"If you shut up and listen, I'll cover everything. When I pinch my nose it means the number is over five. First signal indicates the piece to be moved. Second signal the designated square. As the game develops and most of the pieces are deployed I'll signal the square. By then you'll know which piece I'm indicating. You can play the first few moves of any opening so I'll walk around watching other games. When you need me light a cigarette. I'll come over, take in the board and give you a signal."

"You can do that?"

Another sniff. "There is not now nor will there ever be any position in this park that I cannot analyze in ten seconds. That's the beauty—or in your case, the tragedy—of chess. I'll hang long enough to maneuver your opponent into a hopeless position. You'll get all the credit for the win."

"Can I beat Ronald?"

"Destroy him. All the big fish, too. Use their vanity against them. They'll be shocked when you beat them. They'll double and triple up. When you're done leave the park. Don't look for me. Stash the winnings in the change cup in the phone booth outside the West 4th Street station. I'll divide it and put back your share."

We split up and I walk into the park alone. Ronald welcomes my arrival. "Lamb to the slaughter…"

I sit down. "For five dollars?"

"Uh oh, the fish read a book last night. Make it ten if you're so confident."

I take out another five. "Okay, ten…"

He gives me a quizzical look. "Ten then…" He plays a simple Ruy Lopez opening and I keep up with him for five moves before I need help. I light the cigarette. My partner strolls over as if he's making a tour of the tables. He flashes me a signal. Four moves and he has Ronald backed into a forced position where only one move is possible. Ronald stares at me in astonishment and knocks over his king.

"Again," he says.

"Fifteen bucks," I say.

He blinks. It's over his limit, but he can't back out. "Okay, fifteen," he says. "Lightning never strikes twice…"

I play the Giuoco Piano, a simple opening used by most beginners. My partner stands across the park, smoking and talking and flashing me the signals. Ronald flicks bloody boogers and stares at the board, head in hands. After two more games I've beaten him for sixty dollars. He crumples the bills and throws them in my face. "You hustled me, you scumbag."

At dawn I put three twenties in an empty Gauloise pack and leave it in the phone booth. I cross the street to a newsstand and see my partner crossing the other way to the phone booth. He waits until I cross back to make sure nobody comes into the booth between us. There's a twenty and a ten in a Marlboro box under the phone. It's neat, like a spy movie. I ride home feeling very cool.

Next night I meet him outside the station.

"Ronald will spread the word that you hustled him, which will make the strong players want to beat you." he says. "We'll save Joe the Russian and go to Franz. He's a jailhouse player. A lot of natural ability, but no theory. He'll try to trick you with the King's Bishop, but it's the kind of opening where the attacker loses his advantage if the defender plays correctly. His friends will be watching so I'll give you the first eight moves now. Be careful, hustlers can get violent."

Heads turn as I enter the park. They've heard about my move on Ronald. Word spreads fast in this tiny world.

I see my partner talking to Franz's entourage of tough Black guys. Is he making side bets? When a loser gets up I slide in.

"Five dollars," Franz says. My partner wanders away as the game begins. Sure enough Franz plays the King's Bishop opening.

"You're gonna do this," he says after making what he thinks is a kill move.

Armed with a sure thing I can't resist a little kibitz. "No, I'm gonna do this," I say and make the move that blunts his attack. A few moves later he resigns. "Beginner's luck," he says. He pays the five and sets up the pieces. "Make it ten," he says.

This time I take white and play the King's Bishop. "You can't beat me at my own game, boy," Franz says.

I can't, but my partner can. Sixteen moves later Franz resigns. He triples to fifteen. I beat him again. He stares long and hard at me. I offer a rematch, but his backers confer behind him and he waves me off. "People are waitin'…"

By the end of the night I've taken Stanley, the senile postman for thirty and Jimmy, the resident hustler, for twenty-five. With Franz's money it adds up to an eighty-five dollar night. Leaving the park one of my fellow "fish" slaps me five. "My man! You hustled the hustlers." I put four twenties and a five in the Marlboro box and watch my partner cross the street. Coming back to the phone booth I find two twenties and two singles. He owes me fifty cents. I see him going into the Twin Brothers diner with his classy blonde girlfriend. She is wearing a short black dress like she just came from a party.

They're in a corner booth. He's stirring heaping spoonfuls of sugar into his coffee. I tap on the window. The blonde looks scared. I'm hoping he'll invite me in, but he gets up, lighting a Gauloise and comes out.

"You owe me fifty cents," I say.

"Can't trust me for the piddling sum until tomorrow?"

"Just to keep everything straight."

He beckons to the blonde. Watches me watching her. He sniffs… "This whole charade is about meeting her, isn't it?"

The blonde comes out. Tall in her high heels, but not taller than me. Little brown mole on her neck

"Do you have fifty cents for my funereal friend?" he says.

"I'll get my purse" she says. And goes back inside.

"I saw you talking to Franz's boys," I say. "Making side bets?"

"Side bets aren't part of the deal," he says.

"Then there's no deal," I say.

"I don't need you. I can always get somebody else."

"And I can always tell everybody what you're doing," I say.

"And I can say it was your idea."

"Either way you can't hustle in the park anymore."

He's trapped. "I made forty dollars," he says.

"How do I know?"

Now he's nervous. "Take twenty, okay. We'll figure something out for tomorrow night. Don't tell her…"

The blonde comes back, searching in her purse. "Been to a party?" I ask. She ignores me. I see myself in the diner window, hunched and haggard, sleeves flapping in that stupid suit. I must look like a crazed speed freak to her. She finds two quarters. "What's this for, Getty?" she says.

So that's his name.

"Not what you think so don't worry," Getty says. "I'm giving him chess lessons."

"Oh chess, of course," she says. She smiles at me to make up for her rudeness. "Is he a good teacher?" she asks.

"Very good," I say.

"And he's a good pupil," Getty says." He drops the two quarters into my hand. "He's already forced a draw."

Next night as I walk into the park I am greeted, "Hey undertaker, how's business?"

"Dead," I answer. The players nod, the equivalent of a standing ovation.

Joe the Russian is holding court at the main table. "The undertaker arrives in time for his funeral," he announces.

I look around for Getty. "Just going for a coffee," I say.

I make a frantic tour of the park, all the way to the fountain.

"The dummy in search of the ventriloquist."

Getty and his girlfriend come out from behind a tree. His pupils are pinned and he smells like a wet ashtray. She's slouched and hollow-

92

eyed in jeans and a Harvard sweatshirt. Like she's been up all night with him.

"Joe the Russian wants to play me," I say.

"Perfect. I'll enjoy cooking that *poisson du jour*. Take off before somebody sees us…"

Joe the Russian rises and gestures like he's reeling me in. "Look how the fish takes the bait. For twenty?"

"How about thirty?" I say.

"Be my guest," Joe booms.

In the crowd, Getty is in intense conversation, waving cash, making side bets. Joe opens with the Queen's Pawn. I make the standard responses, but before I complete the opening, Getty starts flashing signals. He exchanges pieces, clearing the board, building to an endgame. Taking Joe out of his comfort zone.

But Joe is not discomfited. "You can't play scorched earth with a Russian. Remember what we did to Napoleon, not to mention Hitler."

Soon, only kings and rooks and pawns are left on the board. The game becomes a race: first pawn to reach the last rank gets a queen and the win. "Your pawns are lost in the space-time curve, undertaker," Joe says. "You cannot stretch the time or compress the space."

I stare at the board to see if I can figure the next move by myself. I can't and when I look up Getty is gone. Does he think I can win without him? Is he afraid he'll be spotted? I miscalculate an exchange. Now Joe is two pawns up on me.

"My foot is on your throat, patzer," he says. "Accept your fate."

No hope. I knock over my king.

Joe is generous in victory. "Good idea to force endgame with a superior player. But after inspiration must come execution…"

I see Getty in the shadows under the trees, counting money. He must have bet against me. Had it planned all along. Built up my rep with a few big wins. Worked the crowd for the bets. Made the game look close by clearing the board. Walked away and left me to lose.

I fish out a twenty, a five, four singles and four quarters. "Did you break open your piggy bank, patzer?" Joe says.

Is everybody smirking at me? I can't see through the hot blur. Are they laughing at the scarecrow in the black suit with the flapping sleeves?

I search the Village. The coffee houses are crowded and festive. At dawn I give up. Broke... I'll have to jump the turnstile again. I turn onto Sixth Avenue. Getty and the blonde are walking into the West 4th. Street station.

"Hey!"

Getty cowers as I run up. The blonde steps in front of him.

"Why'd you take off?" I say.

"You had a clear advantage."

"I was a pawn down."

"But your rook controlled the rank. It was a sure winner."

"Then, why didn't you stick around for your cut?"

His eyes widen. The liar's reflex, I know it well. "I knew I'd see you tomorrow..."

"Are you so stoned you think you're invisible? I saw you counting money."

The blonde mutters over her shoulder. "Just give him his thirty dollars back."

"Why should I?" Getty says. "He lost a winning position."

I take a step toward him. "Gimme my thirty, plus half of what you made tonight..."

He tries to stand his ground, but his leg wobbles and his voice breaks. "Better not mess with me, buster. I know people..."

The blonde slides between us. "Wait, wait..." She puts her hands on my chest. "Let's work this out..."

I'm locked into her sky blue eyes. Her light pressure becomes a caress. "Just take your money, no harm done," she says.

Getty sneers from behind her. "He doesn't care about the money, he wants the glory. Right patzer? Think I've never dealt with guys like you? You would have played for nothing. You would have paid *me* to make you the big frog in this little puddle."

Larceny is pure, but my desire to steal honor shames me. I reach around the blonde and poke him. It's like pushing a screen door. He goes down on his ass with his leg twisted under him.

"Please leave him alone," the blonde pleads. "He's pathetic, can't you see?"

We're drawing a crowd. People standing in a circle... "Get your bread, man..." "Don't let the bitch talk you out of it..."

"Take this." The blonde thrusts some crumpled bills into my hand. "Please, before somebody from the park sees us."

Too late. I see Ronald smirking in the crowd as they run across the street to the subway. Now I'll be exposed as a crook. Word will spread. I'll be blackballed in the park.

"What'd he take you for, beat grass?" Ronald asks.

I'm saved! Ronald thinks I was the victim of dope hustle.

"He's a real scumbag," Ronald says. "Ripped off some really bad people. Lucky he didn't get his ass kicked."

"I wanted to kick his ass for saying bad stuff about Jews," I say.

Ronald laughs. "Schmuck! whaddya think he is? His family owns Pastrami World on 59th. They got one on Queens Boulevard, too. Don't be fooled by that Ivy League act. He's a yid from yidsville."

"IT'S A PROTEST"

They played on the hard, jagged concrete of the schoolyard. Ruts made the ball bounce off at crazy angles. After a winter rain the yard was slick with slush. A fall would mean an ugly scrape or a banged knee that would stiffen quickly. The backboards were half moons. The rims were rusty and bent, making it harder to sink a shot. He couldn't move his arms in a heavy coat so he played in shirtsleeves in the freezing cold. Couldn't feel the ball through gloves so they came off. His face burned with cold and there was a stabbing pain in his ears. At dusk the street lamps splashed enough light on the edge of the court to keep the game going until somebody said "I have to go…"

He came home with itchy blisters on his arms and cheek. Mom put smelly lotion on them. "Don't scratch them or they'll get infected." She felt his forehead. "You're cold as ice…"

His bedroom ceiling was nine feet high. In the beginning he could barely touch it with his fingertips. But after a month of deep knee bends he could hit it with his palm, even from a standing jump. He practiced spin moves, left and right. Jumped and jumped until Mom came in. "What's going on in here? Mrs. Dorsey downstairs says it sounds like a herd of elephants…"

He read the Red Auerbach book How to Play Basketball so often the pages came loose from the bindings. Dribble with your fingertips. Shoot at the top of your jump. Bounce the hook shot off the backboard. Practice layups with both hands. Crouch on defense like you're sitting in a chair and jab at the ball. Aim for the front rim. Shoot free throws underhanded. Box out the man behind you. Protect the ball after a rebound. Pump fakes, jab steps, get your shoulder past the defender. Watch the opponent's eyes to steal his pass.

He got better. The big kids chose him when they needed a player. "How'd you get so good all of a sudden?" his friend John asked. "I don't know," he said. He didn't tell him about the book.

On Sunday, in Hebrew school, he sped through his Torah portion so he could go to the gym. Mr. Rossman stared at him in mock amazement. "Am I hearing things? You made one little mistake so don't get a swollen head." Saw his glance at the clock and pushed the door open. "Go..."

He ran down the hall toward the sound of balls bouncing, whistles blowing. The temple had a real gym. A wooden floor, baskets with nets. A square on the glass backboard where you could aim your lay ups. New balls rolling around where anybody could pick them up. There was a game going on so he could only shoot when the players ran down the court to the other basket.

Dribbling was easy on this floor. The ball bounced straight back into his hand so he didn't have to look. His shot went through the net with a pleasant swish.

He turned and saw Dad glaring in the doorway, "I've been waiting outside for fifteen minutes."

"I finished early."

"Didn't I tell you we were going to Gorelick's?"

"I forgot..."

Dad had already gone to the appetizing store on Flatbush Avenue. There were fish stained white bags of lox and smoked sable on the back seat. He got the corned beef and pastrami at Skilowitz's on Church Avenue. It was Mom's favorite, bright, crowded, music playing, the waiters wearing mustard yellow jackets. Dad liked Gorelick's on Utica Avenue. "They smoke their own pastrami," he said.

"So does Skilowitz," Mom said.

"That's what they say," he said, "but they get it from a distributor. The truck parks in the back alley so nobody will see."

"I don't like places that cook in the basement," Mom said. "If they find a dead rat in the soup they serve it anyway."

"They make the soup with dead chickens, what's the difference?" Dad

said.

Dad sped down Church Avenue, past blocks of rusting signs over vacant stores. Shoe stores, stationery, butcher, with "kosher" written in Hebrew. Children's clothing. Empty storefronts with bags of garbage in the doorways. Past a church. Black people all dressed up. Men in dark suits, women in long dresses with fancy hats.

"Why are all these stores closed?" he asked.

"All the Jews ran away when the Negroes started moving in after the war," Dad said.

He parked in front of a pile of black garbage bags. They walked under a scaffold. "A neon sign blinked weakly in a store window. "Gorelick's Delicatessen... Glatt Kosher..." It was dark and narrow. He could hardly see the people at the tables. An old man sitting behind the counter watched them walk in like he didn't really want them there. "How's the corn beef today, Harvey?" Dad asked.

The man got up slowly. "A day older," he said.

"Give me one corn beef lean. A frank with mustard for my son..."

"You taking my job?" The waiter came out of the dining room, his sallow face glowing in the gloom. A few black hairs plastered across his head. A bow tie dangling untied from his collar. "No scabs, this is a union shop," he said. "Sit by the counter so I don't have to walk so far."

"I know Felix for thirty years," Dad said, as the waiter walked into the kitchen. "Used to come here with Grandpa when we went to Ebbets Field. Look, there's your teacher."

Mr. Rossman was standing on tiptoes over the display case. "How's the pastrami today, Harvey?"

The man behind the counter got up again. "Wait, I'll go ask it..."

Dad whispered: "For thirty years everybody asks the same question—how's the pastrami, Harvey—and he gives the same two answers. It's a ritual like a Seder."

"Don't slice off the end, Harvey, start me a new piece," Mr. Rossman said. "Gimme a half sandwich on a plate, I'll eat it here. A half in a bag, I'll take home for my wife. Gimme a half order of potato salad for here, half cole *slaw to take home. How many pickles to an order, three? So give me one-and-a-half here and another in the bag…"*

"A half of this, a half, of that. What am I, Einstein?"

Dad nudged him. "They should make a movie about this place before it disappears and nobody knows it ever existed…"

"Hey Mister, I 'm next…"

· *There was a Black man standing in the shadows by the door. A painter's cap and paint blotched overalls.*

Mr. Rossman stepped aside. "Harvey, take care of this gentleman."

"It's two ninety-five for a sandwich," Harvey said.

The man leaned over the display case, waving some bills. "I got money. I'm working across the street."

"Congratulations. Whaddya want?"

"Gimme a corn beef on rye bread and slice it lean…"

"Sorry sir, I didn't see you," Mr. Rossman said.

"Yeah, you saw me," the man said and turned away from him. "How much meat you put on the sandwich?" he asked Harvey

"Quarter pound," Harvey said.

"Junior's puts a half."

"You want a half pound, it'll be six fifty…"

"Make it a half and weigh it out…" He watched as Harvey dropped meat on the scale. "Smear a little chopped liver on the bread," he said

"No shmears," Harvey said. "You want a corn beef, chopped liver combo? Seven-fifty…"

"Junior's puts a smear on the bread for me…"

"So go to Junior's. I'll call and tell them you're coming…"

The man shook a finger. "Better not get smart with me, old man…"

"You think you can threaten me?" Harvey said. "Get out of my store, I don't want your business."

The man started around the counter. "I'm takin' my sandwich…"

"Felix call the precinct," Harvey yelled. He ducked and came up, waving a policeman's billy club. The man grabbed it in mid air. Harvey tried to pull the stick away with two hands, his voice cracking.

"Get outta my restaurant, you sonofabitch!"

Mr. Rossman tried to step between them. "Please sir…"

The man froze for a moment, big fist on the stick. Mr. Rossman put a hand on his chest. "Why make trouble for yourself?" he said. The man looked down at him as if he didn't understand. He raised the stick and threw it crashing into the mirror. Turned and walked out, slamming the door so hard dust drizzled from the ceiling

"My God, how did this happen so fast?" Mr. Rossman said.

Harvey came around the counter, a little old man, hardly taller than Mr. Rossman. Gasping, his eyes bulging. He pulled a splinter off the door frame. "Sonofabitch, look what he did."

"It's my fault," Mr. Rossman said. "If I had seen him when I came in I would have let him go ahead of me…"

"They come in looking for a fight. They say they want to be treated equally, but then they want something for nothing."

"Excuse me Harvey, but a little chopped liver wouldn't have killed you," Mr. Rossman said.

"You give in to them it never stops," Harvey said.

Dad jumped up. "Look out!"

The man was outside with a black garbage bag. He ran up and threw it against the window. Trails of grease trickled down the glass

Harvey ran to the door, "Sonofabitch!" he shouted "Dirty bastard! Wait'll the cops get hold of you." He turned and yelled at Mr. Rossman. "You see what I mean? They hate us."

"He could have thrown a rock, or made a fire, God forbid," Mr. Rossman said. "So he throws a little garbage. This isn't hatred. It's a protest."

"THEY MADE HER WELCOME"

June 4, 1961

Tension in Washington Square. Mounted cops gallop through the park several times a night. Radio cars patrol the periphery. A huge, muscular Black man known as Big Brown is attacked by four wiry white plainclothes guys. He's a park regular. Walks around shirtless, poses with tourists and shows up every once in a while with a different blonde.

We watch the cops force Big Brown to the ground. They try to cuff him, but can't get his hands behind his back. He's not fighting, just trying to get free. Laughing, throwing his head back, but I feel his fear in my gut. Two radio cars shriek up. Four more uniformed cops roll out and club him down, two of them sitting on his legs as two more twist his wrists back to cuff him. A busty, dark-haired girl, one of the many who drift through the park, walks by. Sleeveless blouse and tight jeans shorts—"Bronx Bagel Babies," we call them.

What did he do?" the girl asks.

Donald turns and snarls at her. "He's black, that's what he did." She retreats in tears.

Our wary harmony is fractured. The park divides between black and white. Blacks coming together in angry groups. Whites standing apart, vaguely ashamed. The jazz group has broken up.

A young man in a black suit and bow tie is preaching under a banner reading "Nation of Islam." Donald is in the crowd, cheering and responding.

"White man's always tellin' us how to think. Started with FDR.

He had a New Deal for America... Turned out to be the Same Old Deal for the Black man. Now, JFK is the new White Hope-o-crat. Tellin' us to thank God he beat that crook Richard Nixon. He got his own cracker Lyndon B. Johnson in personal charge of keeping the Black man down for another eight years. Just in time for Nixon to come back for eight years of oppression so the Democrats can say put us back in office and we'll give you your rights and then when all you Black people go like sheep to the so-called liberal fold the White Power Structure can keep you in chains for another eight years..."

"And you're playing right into its hands..."

It's an old white haired Black man in a threadbare blue suit with a satchel full of books that he spreads on a blanket under the arch every night. He's bent and his hands shake, but his voice is confident. "The ruling class divides you by race, class, age and gender..."

The crowd turns on the old man. "How many brothers in your ruling class?"

"By endorsing ethnic and gender splitting through its bourgeois cultural constructs the ruling class divides and conquers..."

They surround him. "Answer the brother's question."

He continues doggedly. "The American Negro is conservative and individualist, owing to his roots in agriculture and small business, his indoctrination by the Christian church. But he finds his only real power in the collective action of a union like the United Auto Workers or the Brotherhood of Sleeping Car Porters... One Negro, A. Phillip Randolph, with the collective power of the union behind him forced the integration of the defense plants and the US military. He overcame the most powerful man in the world, the President of the United States"

Jeering... "He shall overcome..."

The old man puts his hand on my shoulder. "Until you unite with boys like this..."

They shout him down. "We don't need him."

Donald glares like we never met. "We don't want him."

Stung by his sudden rejection I follow him out of the park. "My parents fought for equality and civil rights in the thirties…"

He speeds up. "All you white liberals want congratulations. Especially the Jews. We're in the same shit and you keep saying"—he goes whiny and nasal—"why don't you appreciate what we did for you?"

A movement called the Freedom Riders tries to integrate the southern bus stations. On Mother's Day Bull Connor, Chief of the Birmingham, Alabama Police, pulls them off their bus. His cops beat college kids, clergy and old ladies, and turn the dogs on them. The news footage goes around the world.

The demigods of the Democratic Party come out against the Freedom Riders. Say they're tarnishing the image of the US. Harry Truman says they should "go home and mind their own business." Attorney General Robert Kennedy accuses them of being "unpatriotic" because they are showing America in a bad light at a critical moment in US-Soviet relations.

In the park people are handing out leaflets, organizing demonstrations and protest marches all over the city. A tall light-skinned Black woman is seeking volunteers to go on the Freedom Rides. Plain brown dress and flats, hair cropped African style. Hoop earrings glitter as she talks. "We're going to send hundreds of buses down south," she says. Seems to be looking right at me. "Understand people, you WILL be beaten, you WILL be arrested, they WILL put their dogs on you and shock you with electric cattle prods."

"You can't fight cops," I say. "They beat you up and say you were resisting arrest."

"So do we just give up, and give in to oppression?" she says

"NO!" the people shout.

I slip away to an empty bench. A circle has formed around some folk singers singing Weavers tunes. Desperadoes, black and white, wander from group to group, detaching an occasional wayward female or ragged druggie.

The light-skinned Black girl walks by with her friends. They move on, but she sits next to me.

"How do you know so much about cops?"

"I know, okay," I say with a mysterious air.

"Down south they won't even say you were resisting arrest. They'll just beat you and throw you in jail on a phony charge. Send your picture to the FBI so they can open up a special file on you and start watching everything you do."

"Then why go down there?" I say.

"It's the only way. We fill the buses, the stations, the restaurants, the jails. Clog up the machine of repression, passive resistance, just like Gandhi did in India."

"They would have lynched Gandhi in Alabama," I say.

"That wouldn't have stopped the movement," she says. Her bare arm touches mine. "What's your name?"

"Heywood."

"Really... I didn't know they named white boys Heywood. Remember what Gandhi said, Heywood. First they ignore you, then they laugh at you, then they fight you, then you win. The sacrifice of the first wave becomes the moral example that inspires the people."

"Then I'll wait for the second wave. Actually, make that the third..."

She laughs, glints of lamplight in her brown eyes, her hand warm on my arm. "You think I'm not scared? I just hope I've found some courage by the time I get down there." She gets up. "Harlem CORE (Congress of Racial Equality) is organizing a ride for the end of the month. Just ask for Gladys..."

"I'm going to Paris," I say.

"Oh... Junior year abroad?"

"No, I'll still be a man..."

No laugh this time. "Are you ever serious?" she asks.

"Try not to be."

"Because we can laugh but we need serious people. So you have a good time in Paris now..." She gets up and walks away without looking back.

I wait until the night of the 17th to tell my mother. "I'm leaving in two days."

"I thought it was the 26th."

"I got the dates mixed up. We arrive the 26th."

"You'll miss the last week of school. Do your teachers know?"

"Yeah, I told them."

"Your friends at Riverside?"

"I thought you hated them."

"When you're leaving you say good bye." She opens my suitcase. "Did you pack your suit?"

"I'm not gonna move any bodies in Paris..."

"You never know, you might be invited somewhere formal..."

"Okay, okay, I'll pack the suit."

"And a couple of nice shirts with a tie."

I have to check in by ten-thirty. My grandfather decides at the last minute he wants to see me off. In the car he pokes me. "What's the big deal about Europe, I was born there."

We drive through the glare of the Battery Tunnel into the blackness of the West Side Highway. Dark shapes of docked ships against the sky. The Bremen is glittering under floodlights at both ends of the pier. Trunks and suitcases piled high on the dock. Passengers walking up the gangplank, saluted by pursers in blue uniforms with gold braid. Everybody's speaking German, even the high schools girls in green and yellow jackets that say *Milwaukee Lutheran*. The pursers switch smoothly to English for the Americans. But my grandfather insists on speaking German to them. *"Das ist mein Enkel, gut zu im sein."* The pursers smile politely. *"Natürlich..."*

"What did you tell them, Grandpa?" I ask

"I said you're my grandson and they should be nice to you," he says.

"I didn't know you spoke German."

105

"I studied in the Gymnasium…"

My cabin is on C-deck, six flights down. They've made me a going-away party. My Aunt Rae and Uncle Bernie, my brother , my twelve-year-old cousin Chet, my grandparents, and my Uncle Sam in from Chicago. He's a traveling salesman—"name a city, buddy, I got drunk and laid there"—with the style and the patter of one of those old-time movie stars. Wearing two-tone brown and white shoes, camel's hair sports jacket, a soft yellow shirt. He helps my eighty-year-old grandmother down the stairs on her swollen ankles, takes somebody's stuff off a chair so she can sit and stare coldly as my aunt whispers in her ear.

My new roommates look in, murmuring apologies. A small neat man in a brown suit, his cheeks twitching as if he's trying to hold a smile, bows slightly. "Bauer… Which berth, upper or lower?"

Behind him, my uncle points up. "Upper," I say. Bauer nods—" very good"—and puts his pajamas, toiletries and folded pajamas on the lower—"excuse me"—and steps out. "Always take the top, buddy," my uncle says. "This way they gotta smell your farts instead of the other way around…" He opens a bottle of champagne. "Let's start the trip off right…" And pours into paper cups.

Another roommate, white-haired, fleshy, thick-lipped. "Thank you, very nice…" Offers a puffy hand. "Tollner, how do you do?"

A dark guy, short and trim like an acrobat, black brows over black eyes, black shirt buttoned to the top, grabs my hand in a wincing grip. "Stefan," he says. "Croatian… From Staten Island…"

My grandfather is speaking German to Mr. Tollner, who replies in English. "I'm here thirty years. I'm a waiter in Luchows…" My father takes my grandfather's arm and says something in Yiddish that sounds like "red knish…"

"What did he say?" I ask my mother.

"He told him not to talk German," she says. "They'll guess by his accent that we're Jewish and they might give you a hard time."

My Uncle Bernie is tall and bald, brush mustache, always in a suit and tie. As an Army lawyer he prosecuted German soldiers for war crimes against American POWs. He tells me his trial stories, always ending with: "We went home too soon and a lot of those bastards got away."

My Aunt Rae, tall in a tailored blue suit and a velvet hat. She tried for a modeling career in the '30s, but didn't make it and ended up the fastest typist in the east coast office of Metro Goldwyn Mayer, which earned her a photo with Clark Gable. She's full of worries and warnings and wet kisses that leave a lipstick print.

"Of all the boats, he had to pick a German one?" she says.

My mother sags in annoyance. "You think there were a hundred boats, Rae?"

My uncle refills my cup. "Why'd you pick this kraut boat, buddy?" he asks.

"It was the cheapest one," I say.

"Better keep it in your pants or it'll be Jew overboard."

I stay on deck until the lights of the city disappear. Stars twinkle through a hole in the clouds. Lights and music on the top deck. The metal steps are slick with mist. A purser in a white uniform with epaulets and military style ribbons stands at attention behind a chain. Behind him, people in tuxedos and gowns whirl on a round dance floor.

"First Class only," he says. "Your bar is the Taverna on C-deck..."

C deck... Corny dance music. Red lamps over the tables. On a bandstand above the bar a combo of violin, accordion, bass and snare drum. Thick, jovial couples crowd the dance floor.

"Hey Brooklyn..."

It's Stefan waving at the end of the bar. He has shaved and put on a dark suit and tie. His black hair is gleaming, his eyebrows look like he wet them down. "Have a cognac with me..."

The band strikes up a clunky version of *Fascinatin' Rhythm*. "Look at these cows, they think they're Fred Astaire," Stefan says. "So are you a student?"

"Writer."

"You could write my story. I'm running away from a shotgun marriage. Six years making pizza for her father, Croatians make the best Sicilian on Staten Island. Ugly bitch, but it's the boss's daughter so I had to screw her. Had my nights off. Came into Manhattan and met women at Drake Hotel bar. Some widows, some married. Sophisticated, Jewish women who know what they want. Beautiful clothes, even the lingerie. Take good care of themselves, not like this smelly bitch, a few seven and sevens and she's anybody's pussy. Now all of a sudden she is knocked up and putting pressure to get married. Father is offering a ten per cent partnership to work eighty hours a week. I save for a ticket, make my escape without telling nobody. I'll go back to my uncle's cafe in Dubrovnik and they can fuck themselves on Hylan Boulevard..." Leans in and whispers, "Look, we have a spy..." Mr. Bauer, a few stools, down is watching us. "Herr Roommate, have a drink."

Bauer raises his glass. "Thank you, I have a wine." He offers me a Camel. "I was visiting with my daughter and new grandson," he says. "In Washington Heights, you know it? Very beautiful, by the Cloisters... Where is your destination?"

"Paris."

"He's a writer," Stefan says. "Going to write the story of my life."

"So," Bauer says, "you have an interesting story?"

"My experiences in the war."

"A hundred million people had experiences..."

"I was taken when your army came into Croatia."

"My army? I didn't own it."

"Fourteen years old, my brother seventeen, to be slaves for the Waffen SS. You know what was the Waffen SS? Bigger killers than the Gestapo, right Herr Roommate? They took us to shine their boots and make their coffee and steal food for them so that the fat old men in the supply units could have a rifle in their hands. My mother was crying in the road. Good story, no?" He snaps his fingers, a cardinal sin in New York, but the bartender doesn't seem to mind and walks over with the bottle.

Bauer puts his hand over my glass and tugs my sleeve. "Too much cognac and you can't sleep and you are sick in the morning..." He pulls harder. "Please. Your grandfather made me promise to take care of you."

Stefan jumps up. "I'm going to find a fat *fraulein* to keep me company."

"Good luck to you," Bauer says. Pushes me through the crowd. "Don't believe this story he tells," he says. "Everybody lies about the war..."

Silver starlight streams through the windows of our cabin.

Bauer switches on his lamp. There are some photos between the bunk and the wall. "My grandson." Kinky hair, thick lips. Bauer takes a snapshot out of his wallet. A blonde lady is holding the baby on her lap. A Black guy is smiling behind her.

He wants me to say something. "Cute baby," is all I can think of.

"They met at the base in Wurzberg. She was working in the PX, he was a sergeant. They came back to Brooklyn, but there was trouble with his family. In the Red Hook houses with his own people. The Black women wouldn't talk to my daughter. They had to move..."

"There's still a lot of prejudice in this country," I say.

"*Mischlung,*" he whispers. "Mixed race children. This was a crime in Germany to pollute the Aryan race. Not a crime in America, but not accepted..."

Another snapshot of Bauer holding the baby on a couch. "Joseph, he was named for me," Bauer says. A few smiling old people standing around a birthday cake. "My daughter has good friends in Washington Heights now," he says. "Jewish people. Many came here after the war. "They are good people..." His pale blue eyes search my face. "They made her welcome..."

"SIX BUCKS, VINNIE," HE SAID.

Mom hated Vinnie T. "He's a gangster, I don't want him in my house."

"He's a good friend to have," Dad said.

"For you maybe. To go to bars and pick up women..."

"Oh c'mon Stella..."

"Thinks he's a real charmer. The big smile, brings flowers, but he can't look me in the eye. And his wife sits there like a little mouse with her hands folded in her lap, dripping with diamonds. The girls at work used to say the Italian husband gives jewelry to make up for cheating."

"And what does the Jewish husband do?"

"Breaks up his home because some woman he met in a bar tells him what a great lover he is..."

"He's expecting an invitation to the Bar Mitzvah," Dad said. "He'll give a big present."

"He's not invited," Mom said. "We don't need his dirty money."

But on Bar Mitzvah day Vinnie was in the last row of the temple, tan and smiling in a silver suit with a blue tie, his wife in a fancy purple dress and a big necklace with glittery earrings. "This is what she wears to a daytime affair?" Aunt Rae whispered. When the service was over he pushed through the crush of well-wishers, a gold ring with a big green stone sparkling on his pinky. Green stones in his cufflinks, a big gold watch. Wrapped him in a heavy, cologned embrace. "I've been to a lot of Bar Mitzvahs, never saw a kid memorize the whole service like that? Kid's a genius, Bernie..." Slid an envelope into his jacket pocket. "Here y'are genius, don't say I never gave you nothin'."

Then he showed up to the party, bursting into the living room, waving a big cone of red roses, his wife trailing in a fur wrap with little fox heads on the ends. "Thank you so much for allowing me to share this memorable occasion," he said to Mom.

"Beautiful roses, thank you," Mom said.

But when he went for a drink she turned on Dad. "I told you I didn't want him here."

"He gave us five hundred dollars, Stella... Look at the flowers. He really respects you."

"If he respected me he wouldn't come to a party he wasn't invited to."

When summer came they drove out to Vinnie's beach club. Aaron got carsick and had to stick his head out of the window. Mom sat stiffly in the front. "What kind of shady deal are you two cooking up?" she asked Dad.

Driving home, Dad said to him, "Vinnie wants you to come out bluefishing with us next Saturday."

"He just started working at Mrs. Black's," Mom said.

"He can call in sick."

Dad woke him in the darkness Saturday morning and gave him a little pill to take for sea sickness. They drove all the way down Ocean Avenue to Sheepshead Bay. The lights of a diner blazed on the dark street. There was a line around the block to get in. The place was packed, men with army jackets and fishing rods and tackle boxes jostling at the counter. Vinnie was alone at a round table in the back. "Better get a good breakfast, it's gonna be choppy. Hey Stevie, got any donuts?"

A man in a white apron came out from behind the counter. "Just made fresh for you, Vinnie..."

"Jelly donuts for the kid?"

"Comin' up, Vinnie."

The donuts were hot and crunchy, not stale and crumbly like the ones in the package. There was jelly in the whole donut, not just the top. Stevie came back with a white bag. "Made up a nice assortment for the boat, Vinnie."

The fisherman moved out of their way as they walked out. "Good luck, Vinnie," Stevie called. They crossed the street to a big white boat. The motor was rumbling, water steaming under the hull. "Susie Q" was painted in red on the both sides..." One of your daughters?" Dad asked. "The former owner's wife," Vinnie said. "Haven't had time to change it."

A man in a sailor's cap greeted Vinnie as they came aboard. "Morning sir..."

Two men came up from the cabin. "My brother-in-law, Sal," Vinnie said to Dad. "Arnie, you know..."

A sunburned man in a US Navy cap came off the bridge and saluted. "Morning Mr. T." He shook hands and said "welcome aboard, sir" to everybody one at a time, even to him.

Boats were speeding away from the dock. Fishermen waved. Foghorns blew... "Fifty-four feet, bow to stern," Vinnie was telling Dad. "Fastest boat in the Marina. New engine, new radar. We could outrun the Coast Guard..."

The motor roared and the boat thrust forward, its bow rising. He slipped on the deck, banging his wrist against the rail. Everybody laughed. "Watch it, kid," Vinnie said. "Your mother will never forgive us if you go overboard, will she Bernie?"

"I'll have to sleep on the couch," Dad said.

They sped past the other boats, bouncing over foam-flecked waves, cold sheets of spray splatting the deck. On the horizon the night sky was turning blue. Gray dawn rose over the dark waters. Dad and Vinnie went down to the cabin to play poker with Sal and Arnie. The sailor gave out rolls of quarters for chips. He opened a cooler full of fried chicken and sandwiches and the men jumped on the food even though they had just finished breakfast.

Up on the bridge the captain pointed to a dark spot on the radar screen. "That's the sand bar like a mountain under the water. Blues like to hang around it taking pot luck. Swim in schools, twenty, thirty or more... They'll eat anything smaller than them." He got on the phone with the other boats. "Any runs?" Cracked a pack of Chesterfield, staring into the screen. "Vinnie likes action. Sometimes the fish just aren't biting, but he doesn't want to hear it."

Down in the cabin everybody was smoking cigars. Dad had three neatly stacked piles of quarters in front of him. Vinnie poured whiskey into coffee mugs. "Cent' anni," he said and everybody drank.

The sailor called down. "We're here, gentlemen." The boat slowed, the motor subsided and died. There was a splash as the anchor dropped. On deck the sailor was placing rods along the rail. There were other boats in the distance. The jubilant cries of the fishermen.

"Sounds like they're having a good day," the Captain said.

The boat began rocking back and forth, waves lapping against the sides, the bow rising out of the water like a seesaw then dropping so quickly he could feel the food moving up and down in his stomach. A burning lump of donut rose in his throat. He gagged and gulped it back. Arnie ran to the rail retching yellow puke.

Dad pulled him away. "Don't look..."

The sailor tapped his forehead. "It's all up here. Don't think about it." He brought a bucket of garbage to the rail "Take a big whiff of this and you'll never get seasick again," he said. "This is chum. Chopped up pieces of stale bread and rotten fish. It'll attract the blues and start a feeding frenzy."

"The fish eat that?" he asked, turning away.

"They're in the barracuda family, they'll eat anything, even each other. Even Arnie's puke..."

He dropped the bucket over the side.

"Current's taking it, go round to the starboard side, "the Captain said.

The sailor dropped another bucket. Went to the bow and dropped another. They watched as it spread in the water. "It's gotta stay in a clump," the sailor said, "or the blues won't spot it."

They watched the chum float away. "So this is your is a secret location," Vinnie said to the Captain. "So secret the fish don't even know about it."

"They usually come around when it's cloudy like this," the Captain said.

"Why don't you go closer to the other boats?"

"They're out in the sun. The fish see the shadow of the boat and don't bite..."

"Fuckin' fish are that smart all of a sudden?" Vinnie said.

"I'll check the radar," the Captain said and went up on the bridge. The sailor emptied another bucket of chum. It was quiet. Even the waves stopped. It was like the whole world was holding its breath.

There was a dark mass moving toward the boat. "What's that?" he asked.

The sailor came to the rail. "Dinner, thank God," he said.

In a second fish were slithering under the surface. Swimming in circles, bumping each other, crashing into the boat, rising to snap at the chum. The water started churning like it was going to boil. "The captain shouted from the bridge. "We hit a school!" The sailor put a chunk of the chum on his hook. "Try to drop it right on top of one of 'em..." There was a tug, then a pull like something was trying to yank the rod out of his hands. "Kid got the first one," Vinnie shouted. The captain moved over behind him. "Pull him in nice and steady, son. Don't horse him, just keep reeling." The reel started slipping, he couldn't turn it. "Walk it back," the Captain said. The fish was bucking and twisting as it came out of the water, frantic to get off the hook. The sailor grabbed the line and dropped it on the deck. Silvery blue. Tiny sharp teeth like a rat's. "Watch out he don't bite you," the sailor said. He banged it on the head with a club and yanked the hook out, tearing its mouth.

Fish were swirling around the boat. The men were laughing, shouting, "I got one... Got another one... I got a fuckin' whale here." The sailor ran from one man to the other, grabbing the lines and dropping the fish, writhing and jumping, on the deck. Clubbing them. Tearing hooks out of their mouths and rebaiting them.

"The fish look mad," he said.

"You'd be mad, too, if you had a hook in your mouth," the sailor said.

"But I thought fish didn't have any feeling," he said.

"They fight to stay alive even if they don't know why they're doin' it. Plus, they're mad they got caught. They hate us. We been killin' them forever. Think they don't know?" He pointed to a few fish swimming away. "There's the smart ones. They let the kids do the bitin' first to make sure it's not a trap..."

Behind him, Dad shook his head like that wasn't true. "Great day, Vinnie," he said.

"Best fishing we've had, all summer," Vinnie said. "Let's go home, Skip."

The sailor pulled up the anchor. The motor roared. The boat turned, and sailed into the sun, the sea sparkling all around them.

They stepped over fish, on deck, twitching and flopping, eyes bulging, mouths bloody. The sailor knew how many each man had caught. "You got five," he said to Dad. "Your son got seven. And this six pounder. That's like a twelve pound flounder, the way the blues fight." Sal had caught a seven pounder. "I win the pool, Vinnie," he said. "Uh uh, the kid wins it," Vinnie said. "He gets a three pound handicap." Vinnie gave him a twenty-dollar bill. "Don't spend it all in one place..." Everybody took a swig from the bottle of whiskey. Vinnie offered it to him. "Okay, Bernie?"

"Don't tell Mommy," Dad said. The whiskey burned his throat and made him dizzy.

Vinnie turned the bottle upside down—"kid killed it..." He put a dollar in it and threw it overboard. "This is for the fish gods to thank them for a good day..."

On the way home the sailor opened the cooler. He ate a tuna sandwich dripping with mayo. Then some cold fried chicken. "Everything tastes better on the water," the sailor said. He took his cap off and rubbed his gray crew cut. He had seemed like a young guy in the morning, but now he looked old. "Long day," he said.

They put their fish in a black mesh bag. Some of them kept flopping all the way back to shore. People were waiting at the dock. Mostly Black people or Puerto Ricans with their little kids. The fishermen from all the boats lay their catch out on the boardwalk. "Everybody eats tonight," Vinnie yelled. The people walked up and down, haggling over the price. Sal yelled at a woman "whaddya complainin', for four dollars you'll feed your whole family..." And Arnie kept saying, "This would be ten bucks in a fish store..."

An old Black man stood over his six pounder for a long time. "I'll give you three dollars," he said to Dad.

"Take it, on the house," Dad said.

The man put the fish in a garbage bag and walked away without saying a word.

"He didn't even say thank you," he said.

"I didn't do it for thanks," Dad said. "He needs that three dollars more than I do."

Sal waved a fist full of bills. "We're cleanin' up, Vinnie…"

"Hey Bernie," Vinnie called. "What'd you get for that big one?"

Dad winked at him. "Six bucks, Vinnie," he said.

WAIT'LL I TELL LENNY AND BENNY

My Uncle Sammy is right. Brooklyn boys *are* better at everything.

The ship's shuffleboard course is made of smooth green wood. I'm used to the crumbly cement outside Cousin Abe's bungalow at Rockaway Beach with its pebbly ruts and faded numbers, weeds sprouting between the squares. I'm unbeatable on this surface. The coaster slides right onto the middle of the number. Old guys applaud.

Some of the kids from Milwaukee Lutheran are throwing a football around the narrow lower deck. I grab the ball. "Go long," I say. "Don't throw it overboard," a blonde girl teases. "You kiddin'?" I say and hit a kid in full stride with a perfect spiral.

The pool is small but deep with a platform lower than the sixteen footer at Ravenhall Pool in Coney Island—an easy dive. I climb it and feel the blonde's eyes on me. I do a "chair," raise my knees and try to land in a sitting position, but come down flat on my back. It feels like I've fallen through a plate glass window. The pain forces my mouth open in a scream and I take a few gulps of chlorine at the bottom of the pool. As I surface I see the girls coming to the edge. I come up laughing like I do this every day. The blonde offers her hand. "Oh God, your back is all red."

Stefan is strutting around the pool in a tiny black bathing suit with a bulge. Did he stuff a sock in his crotch? He's really short with his shoes off, wiry like an acrobat, knotty back muscles and tendoned arms. Black hair on his arms and legs, but his back and chest are shaven smooth. "Don't waste your time with these girls," he says. "All you'll get is stupid American necking."

"That's how it starts," I say.

"And where it ends. In Europe if you touch a girl's boob you will definitely fuck her. But the American girls want you to fold your tongue up and kiss until your mouth is paralyzed. And then hug like your old grandmother..."

He points to two older women on beach chairs. "There's our bon voyage..." Glasses, sundresses, heavy legs. "The chaperones, who are here to protect precious American virginity, but not their own. While the little cheerleaders are looking at cathedrals they'll be in the hotel fucking the bellboys. This is their vacation, to fuck everybody they can and nobody will know in the hometown."

There is bingo and ping pong in the rec room, but chess is the big game. After my months at Washington Square I recognize the "patzer" strategies and easily beat a few of the high school kids. Second day out I've drawn a crowd of admiring kibitzers. By the third no one will play me.

One day to go before landing at Cherbourg, Bauer watches me stuff clothes in my valise. "Ach, not like that... "Tollner smiles from his bunk as he folds my clothes and repacks them. "I don't want your Grandfather to be mad with me."

At dinner Bauer drinks Riesling with his fish and winces at my Cokes. "Please have a glass of beer for our last night," he says. He won't let me pay. "I'm inviting you..." The beer comes strong and bitter in a frosted mug. I have another one. Then a blackforest cake and a double demitasse...

I'm whirling through the crowded taverna. The jukebox is playing German rock songs with heavy backbeats and sado-masochistic lyrics—*"I knock you to the floor I kick you out the door"*—sung in English with thick German accents. Stefan is at a corner table with the two chaperones. Names get lost in the noise. He yells in my ear, "they're roommates. Pick one, either one." Shots of Steinhager with beer chasers. We all clink glasses. I turn and there's the blonde from the pool. I bow—"may I have this dance?"—and offer my arm. *Don't be*

Cruel in German. I try to mimic the lyrics and she laughs, "that almost sounds like German." She knows how to Lindy, turns one way and then another. "It's like we've been dancing together forever," I say. She smiles and slides her hand along my shoulder. I feel her suppleness under the silk of her blouse. Other dancers give us room. Now a ballad. *I want you/I need you/I love you...*" I draw her close in a "grind." Feel the soft skin of her cheek. Breathe the lyrics in her ear. *"With all my heart..."* She laughs and eases gracefully away. "I think we'd better sit down." Takes my hand and leads me off the floor.

"I need a name, any name," I say. I'm saying all this suave stuff and she's playing along like in a movie.

"Will Adelaide do?" she says.

"Will Heywood do?" I say.

"No, I want a better name."

All smiles at her table. Women with beers and cigarettes, a blond German guy in a blue suit with a cognac and a cigar. "You dance very well..." Snaps his fingers *"Herr Ober! Cognac..."* Where do you live? Brooklyn. Brooklyn, the Dodgers? Not anymore. Oh yes, I'm so sorry. But we still have the bridge, I say. Laughter. Yes, the bridge... Adelaide is beaming. I clink with the blond guy... *Proste...* "I'm from Frankfurt, but I am living two years now in Chicago," he says.

"My uncle lives in Chicago," I say. Lakeshore Drive right by Lake Michigan... Eyebrows up. I know it, yes... He turns and says something in German to the woman on his right. *Ja ja.* She turns to the woman next to her. *Ah...* The woman next to her leans in to hear what they're saying and looks at me. The air freezes. Adelaide looks distressed. Is it about Lakeshore Drive? *My uncle at his picture window, Scotch in his hand, laughing. There's so many rich Jews in this building we'll have to change the name to Lake Meshugenah...* Rich Jews, is that it? They're ignoring me. Can't catch Adelaide's eye. Not wanted here... I rise... Better get back to my friends... Polite smiles. Yes... Nice meeting you...

Head down, hot with shame I push through the crowd... All

these thick, flushed faces. The clumsy dancers mocking the grace of the Lindy. The clunky backbeat, the English lyrics, sneering parodies of our innocent American love songs—*"I'll tease you 'til your tears drop/ Squeeze you 'til your eyes pop, baby"*—

In the morning a purser is walking through the corridors hitting an electric gong. "Cherbourg..."

There's a booth at the purser station for changing dollars into francs. I take out all my traveler's checks, but Bauer stops me. "The French will cheat you. Always get cash at American Express..." Tollner gives me a bag of soaps and sundries that he took off the housekeeping cart in the corridor. "Tell your grandfather we took good care of you," he says.

Stefan meets me on deck, bleary but triumphant. "What did I tell you? We fucked all night in the lifeboat. That ugly bitch almost killed me... I'll see you in New York..." He leans over the rail, waving as I go down the gangplank. "We'll pick up broads in the Village..."

An old guy in a dirty blue smock with a purple nose grabs my valise "Votre baggage, monsieur..." I yank it back. The conductor runs down the platform. "It is the porter, monsieur..."

Passengers shove onto the train. The compartments are full so I stand in the corridor. The countryside melts into vacant lots and abandoned sheds. Meager suburbs thicken into towns. Junkyards, wrecks, telephone poles like any American landscape. Highways pinch the tracks, cars race the train. We go into a dark tunnel and come out in... Paris!

Gare St. Lazare. Men in dark suits, starched shirts and ties, carrying leather portfolios, hipsters in leather jackets and tinted glasses, more purple noses in blue smocks. French soldiers in oversized berets and floppy khakis, looking like kids in their father's uniforms.

Lovers holding hands, stop to embrace while people walk around them. Don't see that at home. *Gendarmes* looking like toy soldiers raise their white batons to their caps to salute people who come to talk to them. Not like New York cops who gather in tight groups, staring down anyone who dares approach.

Cafe Tabac. Waiters in white coats, carrying bottles and water carafes on trays. Men peering over their newspapers at passing women. Women alone, legs crossed, stirring their coffees, scanning the crowd as if they're waiting for someone. At the bar a guy ahead of me orders "u*n crème.*" I repeat "*Un crème,*" not knowing what I'll get. The bartender brings two silver pots, one with coffee, the other steaming milk, and pours them into a huge cup. Someone runs up—"*Gitanes*"—and gets a box of cigarettes. I lean over the bar. "*Gitanes...*"

The coffee is thick and sweet. The Gitanes are harsh and loosely packed—almost like reefers—and burn unevenly. A girl at a table—blond ringlets, red lips, white dress like a painting—looks at me then back at her book—then sneaks another look. A woman brushes by. Slim, brunette, shoulder bag. She meets my eyes then lowers her gaze down my pants to my shoes and moves on. I've gotten more blips, dick checks and secret smiles in ten minutes than in my whole life. Take that you bitches in Dubrow's!

The Metro doors open and I walk into a cloud of stench. In the New York subway you'll get a fart, some cheap perfume, a blast of booze, or an occasional shot of herring and onions from the Orthodox Jews who get on at Delancey Street, but almost everybody else will pop a stick of gum or a candy or a spray of Binaca. Here I'm getting cigarettes, coffee, garlic, BO, rotten teeth. A respectable man in a blue suit has teeth like a Bowery bum. A redhead in a see-through blouse, tight skirt and heels, opens her mouth to reveal gold fillings.

At the next station young soldiers open the door and jump off while the train is still moving. At Raspail I try it, but misjudge the speed of the car and trip over my valise. I lurch and stagger, people jumping out of my way, and go down on my ass.

Boulevard Raspail. I walk through another miasma of funk and tobacco and see a public toilet, men hurrying in and out. It never occurred to me that so many people you pass on the street are dying to take a piss.

People in sidewalk cafes are watching the passing parade. Lovers arm in arm, kissing, embracing. Guys chasing girls, yelling, "Jacqueline, Susanne, Madeleine," hoping they hit on the right name." In Brooklyn the girls would call a cop. Here they keep walking, pushing the guys away when they come too close or smiling and stopping to talk before moving on.

I turn onto a broad avenue, *Boulevard Saint Germain*. Guys with long scarves, even though it's a warm night. Shrimpy, pimply, long hair, tinted glasses, tight pants.

A cafe, *Snack Bar Cujas*. In the window a kid in a chef's hat is cooking steaks on a grill. He's making a sauce, squeezing lemon juice over a lump of butter, mixing in some mustard and a shot of booze.

Yellow light like an old painting. An old waiter in a white jacket hands me a menu. The only words I understand are *"soupe"* and steak. "Steak," I say. The waiter points to the menu. *"Prix fixe. Un h'ors doeuvre et un fromage..."* I'm stumped so I just say *"oui."*

He comes back with a basket of hot bread. No butter, a little pot of brown mustard. The bread is crisp outside, soft inside. The mustard burns a trail up my nose. He brings a plate with a few slices of radish and a pat of butter, a hardboiled egg with a dollop of mayonnaise, a few sardines, a chunk of salami with more butter. Makes a drinking motion. "Coca Cola?" Wiseass, huh? *"Vin ordinaire,"* I say, remembering that from some Hemingway book. He shakes his head in rebuke, "Vin *de maison."* Comes back with a carafe of red wine. It's sour, unlike the Manischewitz at Passover and the Italian Swiss Colony in the Village.

A young couple leans across a table, hands clasped, looking into each other's eyes. She has short hair like Jean Seberg in *Breathless*. Short black skirt, black tights, slim, long white arms, graceful fingers stroking her boyfriend's wrist. I get the chills watching it.

Diners are smearing butter on sardines, radishes, salami, mustard on the bread. The waiter brings a plate with a sizzling steak covered with a yellowish sauce studded with black peppercorns, and thin, golden fries, crusted with salt and still bubbling. The sauce flows into the juice of the meat. I sop up every drop. When I run out of bread another basket appears. Then there's a plate of lettuce with a tangy dressing. He must have forgotten to bring the salad earlier. Okay, I'll eat it, don't want to get the old guy in trouble. He offers a plate of cheeses. I pick one with holes that looks the most like swiss. A pear on a plate. I'm about to take a bite when I see someone slicing it with a knife. "*Cafe, monsieur?*" the waiter inquires. Okay, I've got that down. "*Un creme,*" I say. Shakes his head, I'm wrong again. Comes back with a demitasse. "*Cafe noir, monsieur...*"

I light a *Gitane* with a feeling of utter contentment. It's a cheerful place. Everybody seems to know each other. People enter and greet the cashier. The waiter is laughing at the bar with three men who are drinking huge glasses of red wine. I feel funny calling him "*Garcon.*" It's French for waiter, but also means boy. I wave. "Check," I say. "*Non Francais,*" he answers and his friends laugh. Twenty-eight francs for all this food? That's $5.75. The old guy must have made a mistake. I'll leave him forty francs in case he has to make it up.

The lady at the register is reading a newspaper called "*L' Humanite.*" She looks up and says "*au revoir monsieur*" like she's singing it. I walk toward a neon sign up the block, "*Hotel Cujas.*"

"*Monsieur...*" The waiter comes huffing after me. He hands me ten francs and shows me the menu. "*Service compris.*" Oh yeah, I remember that from the brochure: "Most French restaurants add a gratuity of 15 to 18 percent to the check." He's giving me my money back. Mr. Bauer wouldn't believe it.

Hotel Cujas. A dark, narrow lobby. Woman at the desk, her face haggard in the harsh light of a single bulb over her head. I remember a phrase: "*Est-ce que vous avez une chambre.*" She squints at me and calls into the darkness. "*Est-ce que nous avons une chambre?*" A large, bald man, sinister behind smoky glasses limps out from behind the mailboxes on a thick wooden cane. "*Pourquoi pas?*" he says. "*Cinq nouveau par nuit,*" she says. At five francs to a dollar, it's a buck a night.

I can live here for months. She hands me a large metal key like the ones that open the prison cells in the old movies. *"Trois-quinze,"* she says. Three-fifteen.

The steps are so dark I have to hold onto the bannister. A man brushes by me, head down, shrugging into a suit jacket. A toilet flushes and a girl comes out of the bathroom at the top of the stairs. Blonde, chubby legs in a short skirt, pink woolen sweater. *"Ca va, cheri?"*

Trois-qinze is at the end of the hall. I have to jiggle the key to turn the lock. Grope around the wall, but there is no light switch. Find a lamp in the corner. A table, a large bed with an iron bedstead, coarse sheets and a faded flowered spread. A sink and a mirror, rusty around the edges. A little bathtub on the floor, looks like toilet without a lid. Okay, this must be the *bidet* I read about in *Tropic of Cancer*. I look it up: "Bidet: Primarily used to wash and clean the genitalia, perineum, inner buttocks, and anus. Also used to clean any other part of the body such as feet." Miller talks about women "douching." *Douche* means shower. In Brooklyn it's an insult—"you fuckin' douchebag!" B*idet* is derived from the old French for "pony" because of the way it is straddled when used. Pretty cool actually, a special tub to wash your balls and pussy and asshole. Miller is obsessed with bidets. Has several scenes with women squatting over them, carrying on casual conversations. One where a Hindu student mistakes a bidet for toilet and drops two huge turds causing the women to shriek in horror. Okay, I've some done some dumb things, but at least I won't shit in the bidet.

A chair by the window overlooks the street. I see the chubby blonde run out to a car parked at the curb. She leans over and talks for a while, then gets in. Holy shit! I'm living in a cathouse. Wait'll I tell Lenny and Benny.

"I WANNA KILL COMMIES"

Paris is a horny city. Parisians look in the eyes of every passerby, searching for romance. There are blips, dick checks and inviting smiles. But not for me. Those aren't blips, but alarms going off as some gawky teenager, which is me, startles a young girl with a gape and a sudden lunge. Her inviting smile isn't for me, but for a pimply shrimp with greasy hair and a long scarf who is walking *behind* me. The chic lady in the cafe isn't checking me out, she's looking down to avoid eye contact. The closest I'll ever get to her is watching from an adjoining table, as the inevitable old, bald guy in a suit shows up and whisks her off in a taxi.

Madame has a rule about guests on the third floor patronizing the girls on the fourth and fifth. I try to talk to a girl on the steps. Madame shoots her the ray and she walks away without a word. Customers come from the outside. I hear them clomping up the steps and walking by on the squeaky floor outside my room. *"Mes clients,"* I hear a girl calling them. A line of cars outside in the morning. The girls rush out and get in with the old guy in the suit. Nice life. Have your *crème*, kiss your wife goodbye and drive off to screw a teenaged hooker. At night the girls talk to their pimps. Dark guys in wide-shouldered suits, Algerians or Moroccans. They never come into the hotel, but stay across the street in the shadows. One of them smacks a girl in the face so hard she goes down. Her high heel comes off and her bag goes flying, everything falling out. She crawls over, picks up her stuff, puts on her shoe and grabs a garbage can, arm trembling, to pull herself up.

Early morning. Trucks and shouts in the street. The blue smocks call "*Bonjour les gars*" as they enter *le Snack* and the old waiter pours red wine right up to the brim of a *ballon* or huge glass. A basket of croissants, a large bowl of coffee, half milk. Dunk the croissants, flakes float away in the coffee. I eat the whole basket and the old waiter charges me three francs, which is sixty cents and starting to seem like a lot of money.

My khakis are a dead giveaway that I'm American. Luckily, my mother made me pack my suit. Got a pair of tinted sunglasses, let the beard grow a couple of days like a gangster in a French movie.

Le Jardin du Luxembourg is a short walk from the hotel. Flowers and winding paths. Mostly tourists and old people taking pictures of the gardens. The Germans are boisterous and hog the paths, making people walk around them. Don't they know they lost the war? An American tour leader, a plump, frazzled lady with a bunch of bored kids, stops and asks me something in high school French. I shrug in the Parisian way. "*Je ne sais pas.*" She says "*merci*" and moves on. Had her fooled.

Down the steps to the Seine. Old guys sitting in beat up armchairs in front of their bookstalls. At lunch they eat on upturned crates. Plates of food, bottles of wine. People passing wish them "*bon appetit.*" I try a "*bon appetit.*" The guy raises his glass, "*merci, Monsieur.*" I think I've fooled him but then he says: "Monsieur, I have a good collection of books in English..."

Walking the city like I did so many nights in New York when I couldn't find anybody I knew at the fountain. Pass a restaurant that looks good, but it's small and crowded and I'm too shy to enter. Cross the street so nobody will see me pass again and know I'm just a lonely kid walking aimlessly. Turn down a narrow, crooked lane off the boulevard and I'm in Quasimodo's Paris. Stunted tenements, you can almost reach across the street from one house to the next. A movie theater, *Cinematheque*. Posters advertise "The Maltese Falcon" and "The Big Sleep." A restaurant a few doors down called "Cous Cous..."

African students in black suits and starched shirts, calling "Cous Cous Mouton, Madame." They get a mound of something that looks like barley and a bowl of lamb and vegetables with a little pitcher of brown sauce. The students are pouring the meat over the rice and splashing on the sauce. I do the same and have to stifle a cough as the sauce flames up in my chest. A huge carafe, twice the size they give me at the Snack. Did the waitress ask me, "*Grande?*" And did I nod because I wanted to be cool? Drink it all so they won't think I made a mistake. Dizzy, stumbling down that twisty street trying to find my way back to Saint Germain to pass out in my room.

"Heywood!"

It's Donald! Running across Boulevard Raspail like I'm his long lost brother. Last time it was me going, "Hey Donald," and him snubbing me in front of all his Black Muslim friends. I should snub him back. Instead, I run to meet him—"Hey Donald!"—overjoyed to see a friendly face. We shake hands and slap five. He's wearing the American uniform, khakis, workshirt, white bucks. Clocks the suit, the beard, he's impressed.

"I'm on a college trip," he says.

"Which college?"

His light skin seems to darken. Is he blushing? "Columbia."

Now I've got him. "I thought you were living on the street, you're an Ivy Leaguer."

He is definitely abashed. "I'm just staying in school to keep my 2S. How about you, what are you gonna do about the Army?"

"I'm gonna live here," I say.

"Where you staying?"

"In a whorehouse. I'll show ya..."

I've been practicing the Metro jump. I open the door and hit the ground running. Donald waits until the train stops.

I take him to the hotel. A few of the younger girls walk by. "They look like cheerleaders," Donald says. Up in my room, he sees the bidet. "You use this?"

"Yeah, you know, the chicks wash themselves off."

"The hookers?"

"No, you know, students. You can pick chicks up on the street here. Just walk up to them and say '*Je vous admire mademoiselle, prenez-vous un verre avec moi?*' Means I like you. Wanna have a drink with me?"

"You speak enough French to have a conversation?" he asks.

I give him the Parisian shrug. "You don't need much if they like you."

At night we walk down Saint Germain to the *Cous Cous*. Africans, Arabs in their wide shouldered suits, sitting in blue clouds of *Gauloise*. I get a *"bon soir"* from the waitress. Donald is knocked out. "They know you here?" *Cous cous mouton, grande carafe of vin rouge, yaourt* with sugar for dessert, c*afe filtre*—"man, this coffee's strong," Donald says. I give him a *Gitane*. One puff and he coughs his guts out. I inhale easily, swallowing to make the acrid smoke stream through my nose.

Back on the street he shows me a piece of rolling paper with a scrawled address. "An old hipster at the fountain gave me this. It's a club owned by a guy from New York…" We follow the numbers down Saint Germain to a small bar called *Les Nuages*. "Wasn't that a Django tune?" Donald says. Two chic ladies get out of a taxi, jewelry glittering, perfume wafting. I wait at the curb while Donald opens the door and looks inside. Comes back, shaking his head. "A little too fancy…"

We start down the street, but a guy comes out, "Where you boys goin'?" Sharp beige suit with a brown shirt, yellow tie, gold watch. Looks and talks like Benny from the Bronx. "New York boys, right? I can always tell New York boys." He opens the door. "I'll buy you a drink."

Inside it's moody. Red banquettes against the wall. Like one of those literary photos of famous writers around a table. Glasses, ashtrays, bottles, cigarettes, some staring into space, others leaning in to whisper important secrets in cocked ears. The guy stops at a table full of older women. Thin brunette in a black dress. Bony chest.

"Found a coupla New York boys," he says. She says something that ends in "New York" to her friends. And they cheer. "*Bravo...*" "*Formidable, Johnny...*"

A bartender in a white jacket with a boxer's battered face puts two cocktail napkins down in front of us. "George, give these guys whatever they want," the guy they call Johnny says.

"Cognac," I say.

Donald looks at me and says, "Cognac."

"Where you boys from in the city?" he asks.

"Manhattan Avenue," says Donald.

Suddenly, I can't remember my neighborhood. I stammer "Prospect Park..."

"What are you a bum, man, you sleep in the park? So how do you know each other, school?"

"Washington Square," I say.

"All detours lead to the Village," he says. George slides a glass of yellowish liquid across the bar. Adds water and it turns cloudy like a chemistry experiment. The guy raises his glass. "Welcome to Paris." Donald chugs his cognac and coughs, eyes watering. "That's for sippin', brother," he says and waves to the bartender. "George..." The bartender slides two more cognacs in front of us. "I'm Johnny Romero," he says.

Donald shakes hands. "Donald B..." I shake his hand too hard and blurt "Heywood..."

"What are you into, Heywood'?" he asks.

"I'm a writer," I say.

He points at a table of women. "Francoise Sagan. Know her?" (Actually, I do. My mother is reading her best seller *Bonjour Tristesse* and I've seen her photo on the jacket cover.) "James Jones comes here. Know him?"

Is he's testing me? "*From Here to Eternity*," I say.

"Jimmy Baldwin is a good friend... What are you into, Donald?"

"I'm studying Political Science," Donald says.

"Good time for that. Kennedy's gonna make big changes."

Donald starts the Black Muslim line. "It's just old wine in new bottles. The liberal lull before the hammer comes down..."

Romero walks to a table in the back. "Got some New York boys, here..." Three big Black guys in sports jackets. "Kid's a writer like you, Bill," Romero says. No handshake. No intro to the females, two skinny French girls, heavy rouge, plucked eyebrows, zero blips. Donald is hanging back. "Donald B... from Manhattan Avenue," Romero says. Smiles. "Harlem boy?" They slap him five. A waiter brings a chair for Donald. No chair for me. I sit on a banquette. Bill turns his broad back, excluding me.

"Say hello to a friend of mine," Romero says. A lady at the next table. Dracula's Daughter. Black hair, sleeveless dress, long black gloves on white arms... Dead pale face, black eyes bulging, large silver crucifix, tiny diamonds glittering. "Sandrine, this is Heywood," Romero says. *"Un ecrivain, de New York..."*

She slides down the banquette to make room for me. Slips off a glove and offers a warm hand with a smooth blue stone on the third finger... "Enchantée, Aywoud," she says.

A little guy pops out of the darkness, startling me. "Christian. No English, pah doo too." Leather jacket, peering through tinted glasses on the bridge of his nose, sleek brown hair to his shoulder. Looks into a Leica. A flash blinds me.

Sandrine slides closer. Black skirt creeping over her knees. Warm thigh against my leg. "So, you have just arrived," she says.

Donald's voice rises shrilly out of the hum... "Frantz Fanon says it's a universal struggle to free all colonial peoples,"

"Frantz Fanon was never in Mississippi," somebody says.

Donald writhes like his chair is hot. "You're all behind the times..."

The guy next to Bill K says: "Africa will be free one day, brother, but they'll still be kickin' old ladies off buses in Alabama..."

Sandrine lights my cigarette. Holds the flame up to my face. Flicks her tongue at me.

"Every place has gotta have its niggers," Bill K says. "Arabs are the niggers here."

Donald jumps up. "Oppression is the same in any language and can be overcome in the same way for all people..." His chair goes out from under him. "Cynics will be punished for their opportunism..." He trips over the chair, stumbling out.

They laugh. "Come back, brother..."

Romero nudges me. "Go take care of your boy, he's loaded."

I catch up to Donald rubber legging down the street. "C'mon back man, they were only kidding." I use the clincher. "A lotta chicks in there..."

He pulls away so violently that he almost goes down. "You can't co-opt me with white pussy."

I slip on a wet spot chasing him. People laughing... "C'mon, this is a cool place. James Baldwin goes there. Richard Wright..."

"Richard Wright would never set foot in that scumhole," Donald says.

"Those guys were just putting you on," I say.

"They're obsolete. They're in the dustbin of history with white phonies like you..."

That word upsets me, too drunk to know why. "Don't say that, man." I give him the schoolyard shove, high on the chest under the shoulders. He stumbles back and almost goes down. Then comes at me, swinging "Dustbin, motherfucker!" I duck under a wild punch and try to get him in a jumping headlock.

There are people between us. *"Calmay-voo..."* I'm pulled away by the back of my shirt. Someone pats my shoulder. "Ca va? Okay, my friend?"

A car rolls up, headlights blinding. "Hey man, where you think you are, MacDougal Street?" Johnny Romero behind the wheel. A Jaguar sedan. Floor shift with a mahogany knob. "Sandrine saw you on the curb. Sent me out to take care of you."

"Where'd she go?"

He laughs. "She'll be around. Let's eat."

We drive across a bridge into a market. Narrow street, stalls on both sides. Little motor scooters with big baskets on the back. Blue smock guys pushing barrows. "*Les Halles*," Romero says. "Like the fruit market on Washington Street..."

A restaurant, lights blazing. White tablecloths. Waiters in tuxes, Blue smocks at the zinc counter with their *ballons*. Well-dressed Parisians finishing off the evening. They hold their knives like pencils and don't switch hands to eat. Push the food into forkable piles with their knives instead of using their thumbs like my father does. They hold their wine glasses by the stems. Eat with precise movements like it's almost a ritual.

"Ever have pigs feet?" Romero asks "I don't mean the sickass pink pickled knuckles in them Irish bars..." He squeezes my shoulders, squinting. "You kosher? I spent a lotta time on Eldridge Street, know where that is, *bubbeleh*? Ever go to Ratners on Delancey under the bridge? Blintzes there, *chicharrones* next door, pork fried rice a few doors down. Hang on the Lower East Side you got the world covered."

The pig's feet arrive. Two long bones, lined with fat with a knob of meat at the end. A silver pitcher of white sauce, a pile of sizzling fries. "Best after hours food in the world," Romero says. "I admit sometimes I get a taste for fried eggs over hard, black around the edges, burnt bacon and greasy home fries flipped across the counter by some guy in a filthy apron..."

A bowl of bubbling cheese lapping over the rim. Hunk of soggy bread in the soup. Pale strips of translucent onions...

"Ever hear of Minetta Tavern on MacDougal?" Romero asks. "Nah, that would be before your time. My joint. Only Puerto Rican who ever owned anything in the Village. White women came from all over the city—all over the world—to mingle with the dark brothers. Purple lighting so you couldn't tell who was what. We had all the ballplayers, fighters and musicians. Socialites, singers, movie stars, you wouldn't believe me if I told you. It was takin' a big risk for some of these women. This gets out, big scandal. Career's over, lotta money down the drain. The guys too, if they got caught. Brother bangin' a white woman? Hang up your spikes, nigger, pick up a broom. But they kept comin'. You could feel the excitement every night. Like cheatin'. It's more fun when you've got something to lose..."

"The place took off. I was more surprised than anybody. I knew what white women liked, but I didn't know what they would risk to get it. Word was gettin' out who was comin' down. I had to stand at the door to keep the riff raff out. People tryin' to get next to me. I ate it up, who wouldn't?"

"I paid protection, but couldn't protect against success. Old time Villagers were warning me. Cops too. Slow down, you're gettin' too big for a Rican from Division Street. Okay, but how do you slow down when the place is packed every night? Tony Bender, know who he is?"

I do. There's a strip club on Third Street called Tony Bender's. Benny and I would stand outside and watch the show through the window until they chased us.

"He sent guys to raise the weekly rate on me. Finally, he came in himself. Mousey little prick, but he ran the neighborhood. Told me I had a partner... Him. Fifty percent, then ninety. You think they'd throw me somethin' for makin' so much for them, but they only give up what they have to. I had to pay sales tax outta my end, re-ring the tapes so it wouldn't look like we were making too much and kiss their asses for the crumbs they threw me. Then, somebody dropped a blind item in Winchell's column. 'What blue-eyed apple-cheeked warbler is making secret trips to a shady bar in the Village to meet her dusky Romeo?' Number One Box Office, "*que sera, sera*," guess who that was. The word came down from the top: Shut this motherfucker down. I had Building Inspectors, Liquor Authority, cops finding marijuana in the Men's Room. I fought back, shot my mouth off. Thought I had political friends. Turn around nobody's there and I'm a day away from goin' for a swim in the lime pit in the Third Street Garage."

I knew that garage. Always, a few guys sitting on bridge chairs. Waving cars away—"garage is full…"

"I cashed out and came here," Romero says. "Built up my old lady's bar. My writer friends commute between Paris and the Village like it's the D train. Always somebody droppin' in. Musicians, tired of being fucked over in the States. Don Byas, Kenny Clarke, Sidney Bechet. Bud Powell's here, too. French are happy to have 'em. They love our music our cars, our movies, even our cheeseburgers, but hate us. They bent over for the Krauts, some of them will admit it. We showed up and chased the motherfuckers, you think they'd be grateful…"

Some girls are hanging in the doorway of a little hotel down the street. Young blondes, short skirts, high heels…

"Girls this beautiful don't have to be hookers," I say.

"They make more in a night than in a month workin' in factories or waitin' tables," Romero says. "Some of 'em stay in the game long enough to open a store or a cafe. Get fat and married and hang with the priests. Always find hookers around the markets. Back home, too. Fulton Fish market, Washington Market has 'em. Only they're mostly skanky junkies or dumb hicks. A lotta drag queens. Follow one into a doorway and wait'll the light hits her… Adam's apple. Big hands like a bricklayer. When you're back home take a walk down there."

"I'm not going back," I say.

"What's the matter, you knock somebody up? Cops after you?"

"No… just the Army…"

"You can beat that," he says. "At your physical go up to the guy with the most stripes and medals and tell him gimme a gun, man. I wanna kill white people. Wait a minute, that won't work for you…" Snaps his finger. "Commies, that's it! Tell him gimme a big gun, man, I wanna kill Commies."

134

"IT'LL KILL MY MOTHER"

Hemingway worked in a cafe with a handful of sharpened pencils and a *café au lait,* the story "rushing along faster than I could write it." In the summer he switched to white wine, in the winter a rum St. James, which "warmed" him as he wrote.

I start the day with a *crème* at le Snack, but the story doesn't come. Another *crème* and another. Saucers piled on the table to keep track. I go through a pack of *Gitanes.* Crack another. Sharp pain in my chest. The waiter looks concerned. *"Monsieur, veut manger quelque chose?"* (Do I want to eat something?)

In my room. Exhausted but can't sleep. Coffee is worse than being drunk. Can't just puke and pass out. Footsteps on the stairs, whispers. No drunken jokes from the clients or giggles from the girls. In Brooklyn sex is kind of a joke. Here they take it seriously. Always looking for a few spare minutes. On their lunch hour or after work. Mornings when the nice cars pull up, doors open as the young girls cross the street. Do these girls douche themselves before and after? Do they worry about the clap or getting pregnant? Can they give it up, move away, marry some guy, have kids and never tell anybody like Romero said? How many women have done it? And their husbands never know.

My father was overseas for three years. I heard him talking about the Philippine women. "Great legs, great asses." My mother was alone for three years. Never think about what she did, but men like her. Andy, the school janitor, stared when she walked by. Mr. Warren in our building, always takes his hat off when he sees her in the elevator.

135

Steps back to let her go out first so he can sneak a look at her ass. Once she was laughing in the kitchen with my grandmother and Aunt Rae. "Oh God, my Bernie takes forever," my aunt was saying. "I tell him, Bernie get it over with already…"

Coffee not working, I try white wine for inspiration. No disturbing memories, but it twists my guts into a pretzel. Maybe a rum St. James. The waiter brings a shot in a cordial glass on a saucer. A tentative sip burns going down. Soon I'm inspired, optimistic, but I don't know where to begin. It's like I'm posing as a writer, but Hemingway was posing, too. Sitting there with his white wine and his oysters, fuckin' flannel shirt, sleeves rolled up to show his brawny forearms, mustache neatly trimmed, rolling papers. That story about how the owner let him sit all day because the French love writers. Crap. He had to keep eating and drinking or the guy would have kicked him out. Explains his style. He was so busy pouring wine and opening oysters, rolling cigarettes, sharpening his pencils and saying "*bon jour*" to all these adoring tradesmen that he didn't have time to do anything but scribble a couple of simple sentences and go somewhere to sleep it off. He came on like a big expert on bullfighting and boxing to Gertrude Stein. I'd like to see him walk into the schoolyard, bragging about all the guys he beat up. Tommy DeBendedetto would knock him on his ass. He's snotty about that Jewish guy in *The Sun Also Rises* being a collegiate boxing champion, but the hero, Jake Barnes, never fights that guy. And Jake Barnes can't even get it up.

My head won't fit under the sink faucet so I let the water pool in the bidet and get a cold dunk. Little Mennen Speed Stick. Down the stairs, ravenous. Snack Cujas is closing, old waiter stacking the chairs on the tables.

A line of taxis in front of *Les Nuages*. I loiter by the window. Am I welcome without Donald? Packed with the same crowd as the night before. Romero waves for me to come in. "Your boy still mad?"

"Don't know."

"You guys don't hang out?"

"He's on a college trip. I'm living here."

"Where at?"

"Rue Cujas."

He laughs. "In one of them cathouses?" And translates for his old lady and her friends who raise their eyebrows. *"Incroyable..."* *(Unbelievable.)*

Sandrine's banquette. Bottles in ice buckets, ashtrays overflowing. She offers her hand. "Sit here next to Angela, also *Americain.*" Blonde pompadour, shaved sides like a kid's haircut. White suit, black silk shirt with some kind of red brooch at the collar. In animated conversation with two French guys at the next banquette. "Angela, here is Aywoud, un American *journaliste,*" Sandrine says. Angela turns, blue eyes glittering in the shadows. "Where ya from?" Southern accent. "New York," I say. She laughs and imitates, "Noo Yawk... Love it..."

Sandrine's offers me a candy. "Majoum, very especiale..." It's sweet with nuts and honey like the halvah my grandfather brings. I wash it down with a bubbly pinkish wine. Sandrine offers another majoum, but Angela reaches behind me and pushes her hand away. *"Ca y'est salope... Faut pas le tuer..."* "Salope" means cunt or bitch, I hear it on the streets all the time. Sandrine is giving me the French equivalent of pot brownies. Angela is calling her a bitch and telling her she shouldn't kill me. That's funny, protecting me, who'll smoke or swallow anything. "Come to striptease," Sandrine says.

Place Pigalle. Little clubs and bars, barkers outside trying to entice the soldiers. I'm in the back seat of a cab between Sandrine and Angela. Christian is in front, leaning out of the window shooting with his Leica. We stop at a club, neon blinking, *"Chez Michou."*

Short steep flight down to the entrance. Another old guy in a suit at the door, looks like a morning "client" at the hotel. Cheek kisses all around. "Aywoud, a *journaliste* from New York," Sandrine says. Trembly grip, old man trying to show strength...

We walk down another winding flight to a door, the old man

whispering, "This was a false wall during the war to hide our sabotage cell from the Germans..." Behind me Angela giggles. "He was a heero of zee REESISTONCE..." Shadows on the dance floor, smoke floating. A flute trills and colored lights strobe the room, catching couples at the tables. A small stage, palm trees under a smoky green light. The old man pushes me—"Vite, vite..."—up to a reedy person in a red silk smoking jacket, pleated turquoise shirt, a red cummerbund, short black crew cut, downy mustache, cigarillo... "Michou's the queen bee," Angela whispers, and says *Mon ami, un journaliste de New York, Mich..*" A slim damp hand. "You will write about Chez Michou?" Waitresses with crew cuts, white shirts, high-waisted pants and red suspenders. I jam into a black banquette next to Sandrine. Angela slides in next to me. Sandrine orders a "Rose brut." I order Cognac. The waitress leans over Angela. "Pour vous, Madame?" Angela slides her hand up the waitress's leg. "Bourbon, rocks, cherie... "And puts her arm around me, pushing me closer. "Who do you write for Noo Yawk?"

The lie flies trippingly off my tongue. "I'm doing a series of articles for Esquire on Americans in Paris."

She gives me her card, *Angela Wallace, Model.* "You should do a piece on me. From the backwoods of Louisiana to the showrooms of gay Paree..."

The green light on stage turns pale yellow. Tree shadows, jungle sounds. Conga pulsing. Black guy upstage, in a loincloth, drumming. The flute flutters. A girl in a green bikini, slim and dark with long flowing black hair comes on stage, looking around like she's lost. Like a jungle movie. Sandrine moves closer. Perfume, wine breath. I'm pretty high, but that Majoum keeps coming on. Sandrine puts her hand in my lap. "Do you go to striptease in New York?" she breathes in my ear. She slides her finger up my crotch looking for my zipper. Is this really happening? On stage, the girl bends and finds a recorder. Turns it over, doesn't know what to do with it.

Angela whispers in my other ear. "They take their burlesque very seriously here. Like bein' in sex church…" Does she know what's going on under the table? Sandrine gets my zipper down. Glad I wore my dad's boxers. I pop out like the cuckoo in the clock. Sandrine puts a napkin over me.

The girl on stage is stroking the flute. Sandrine is stroking me. Angela won't shut up. "I miss the Garment Center. Joke of the day. You hear it in the showroom, then at lunch with the salesmen in Lou Segal's, then at night with *machers* in La Grenouille. Dubrow's on Seventh Avenue, do you know it?" I try to answer in a normal tone. "No…" "I had my first modeling job in that building," Angela says. "Monsieur Francois, he was really…"—tries a Brooklyn accent—"Sid Brody from BENSONHOIST. Sold every small store in every hick town. Hired me on the spot, dropped his pants a minute later. Nothing hornier than a Garmento Jew…"

On stage the girl puts the recorder between her legs, then in her mouth.

"Sid did separates, three outfits for the price of one," Angela says. "For Work or play/Night or day. Good slogan, huh? Cheap clothes for cheap girls, he used to say…"

I try to hold back. Think of baseball, Lenny says. Or the Bible…

"They called me the *shikse*," Angela says.

Duke Snider, Pee Wee Reese…

"When they showed to the out of town buyers Sid would run back and rip the dresses off the other girls Let the *shikse* wear this *shmatte*, make those small town *clutzes* think they can look like her."

Moses… The Burning Bush… Too late, I go off in the napkin… My body is throbbing. Conga is pounding, flute shrieking. Angela pulls my chin toward her and yells in my face. "Sid liked to bend me over his desk. I have a wonderful family, he said while he was humping me next to his daughter's graduation picture. After he'd be all guilty. I never do this, but you're so beautiful. He'd buy me a piece of jewelry to keep my mouth shut. You won't tell anybody, will you Angela, not even the other girls. As if they didn't know and what do you think Mrs. Sidney was doing up in the mountains with all those busboys?"

It's over. The girl steps out of the hollow tree trunk to scattered applause. Sandrine kisses my neck and gives me her card. "Call in the morning," she says and slides down the banquette. Angela drains her bourbon and waggles her glass for another, prattling on like nothing happened. "Tony Lanza, top agent, said I had class. Tells me to go to Paris and break into the French magazines. Gives me a few numbers. I see everybody. Screw a few guys, big mistake 'cause then they pass you around. These Casanovas over here think they're doin' you a favor. Jump outta bed like King Kong. 'I am wonderfool ness pah?' And I'm moaning—'oh cheri, cheri'—to keep from laughing in their faces. Mostly old hags doing the hiring. One tells you to take ballet for your posture, another says come back after your breast reduction. 'Fix your overbite you look like a horse. Develop an attitude for the runway. Throw out that portfolio, try this photographer, that stylist.' The Ford lady told me the truth: 'Face it honey, you're a farmer. Forget covers, try for a catalogue.' Sandrine got me into house modeling for Nina Ricci, the Sid Brody of Paris. Two years goes by like a bad dream in this town, you'll see. First chance I get I'm going back to New York. I swear to God I'll kiss the ground outside Gimbels. Gimme the kikeiest *schnorrer* selling trimmings in the Fur District who fumble-fucks you in the Statler Hilton with his cigar burning in the ashtray, then runs across the street to Penn Station to catch the five-fifteen to Roslyn…"

She has to know what happened? She was right next to me.

"Good story, huh?"

"Great story," I say.

She stops and shakes her head. "Leave out the screwing part. It'll kill my mother."

"A FRENCH GIRL WOULD NEVER DO THAT"

The more fluent I become the more I see how much the French dislike Americans. They call us "Amerdoc," based on the verb "*emmerder*" which means to shit on or irritate. They all speak merchant English, but refuse to respond to anything unless it's said in perfect French. American tourists point to items on the menu, pantomime the act of drinking water or brushing teeth, but they shrug and sneer "*comprend pas...*"

No sour looks for the German tourists, though. Don't even give them a chance to speak French, but start *sprecking* to show off their *Deutsch*. Ask where they're from, which causes embarrassment because any place in Germany is loaded with evil history, concentration camp, army base, Gestapo headquarters...

I pose as a Canadian. Tell the girls at the hotel I'm from Quebec. Tell the old Commies in Le Snack that my father fought in Spain with the Lincoln Brigade. They embrace me. "Comrade!" They were all in the Resistance. Sabotage, ambushes of German troops, plots to poison the beer, assassinate informers. There would never have been a Resistance if not for the Communists, they insist. If not for the Russians we would all be goosestepping today. But what about the Americans? I ask. If Hitler hadn't diverted his troops to fight the Russians—"et tuer les Juifs" (and kill the Jews) the old waiter interjects—the Americans wouldn't have even attempted an invasion, they say.

A letter from my mother. School starts September 22nd. She

checked and there are no boats leaving after September 15. The passenger lines suspend service because of rough winter seas. I'll have to take a freighter, which could be a two-week voyage or even longer.

I can't bring myself to tell her I'm not coming home. In a year I'll have a novel written and sold. Then all will be forgiven.

Two doofy guys latch onto me at American Express, "Hey man, you live here?" Tim and Mitchell. Chunky red cheeks, Michigan Lacrosse sweatshirts. They're loud, jovial, amused by their own ignorance. "How do you say deodorant in French, deodoranto?" They think it's funny to exaggerate their American accents "juh pahle oon poo francay…" They call out to the passing girls—"Hey Mademoiselle, voulez-vous coucher avec moi?"—and laugh at the huffy snubs—"well excusez moi for living."

I take them to Le Snack. Get them a *steak au poivre*, couple of Alsatian beers, *coupe aux marrons* (ice cream with chestnuts). Walk them over to the hotel. They flip just like Donald.

"You got it made in the shade," Tim says. "They gonna let you keep your 2S?"

"As long as I can show I'm taking courses at the Sorbonne."

They laugh. "You think they're gonna let you drink wine and plug French chicks?"

"We're doin' ROTC," Mitchell says. "Drills and calisthenics, lectures about the Cold War, Commie spies in America. Two weeks of camp every summer, you get to shoot guns. They make you a Second Lieutenant. Six months pullin' your pud at some base in the boonies and you're done.

A brunette, black skirt clinging to long legs, walks by. It's my muse, the violet-eyed mystery woman of my fantasies. Our eyes meet for a moment. Before I can shut him up Tim yells the voulez-vous coucher line. She stops—"*non merci*"—and comes to the table. "But may I practice my English with you for a brief time?"

Her name is Colette. She's studying architecture and English at the Sorbonne and is going to spend a year as an exchange student in

California. Her light tap on my leg is like an electric current running to the top of my head. "Are you a student as well?"

"Journalist. I work for the *New York Times*…" Tim and Mitchell give me the secret smile. "Doing an article on what people did during the war."

"You should talk to my father," Colette says. "He escaped two times from the Germans."

She gives me a card Colette K… address and phone. "And yours?"

No card. I write my name and address on the back of a Bière d'Alsace coaster.

"Aywoud," she says. "Can you come Friday night, Aywoud?"

Is she asking *me* out?

"Are we invited?" Tim asks.

She just smiles. Slings her pocketbook over her shoulder in that very French way. "Until Friday," she says to me, and walks away.

"You're in like Flynn," Tim says.

"I love the way they swing their asses when they know you're looking at them," Mitchell says. "They zero in on a guy. Open the door for him, light his cigarette…"

"My girlfriend is always pissed at me, for somethin' I did or said," says Tim. "Holds out on the pussy. A French girl would never do that."

"THAT'S ANOTHER THING THEY CAN THANK US FOR

He liked the lilt of the Christmas songs, "Deck the halls with boughs of holly/Tis the season to be jolly..." Liked the bustle of the holiday. Everybody bundled up, flushed and happy. Stores with special decorations. Red and green lights on the houses. Trees roped to the roofs of cars swooshing through the slushy streets. Dad got cards from his Army buddies and put them on the mantle, "They were the best friends I ever had..." Neighbors wished them "Merry Christmas." Dad answered.... "and a Happy New Year," and Mom said, "Happy Holidays." They never said the word "Christmas." Dad put a twenty-dollar bill in an envelope and slipped it under Leo the super's door. "This'll keep the heat on for another year," he said.

That night they lit the Hanukkah candles. Mom made latkes, and Grandpa Dave brought special jelly donuts from Ebinger's bakery. He and Aaron sang the blessing. Mom drank a glass of wine and her eyes got bright. They spinned the dreidel and sang "I have a little dreidel/I made it out of clay." Bubbe gave them Hanukkah gelt, chocolate mints wrapped in gold paper.

In Hebrew school Mrs. Friedman talked about the "real meaning" of Hanukkah. "We know the Maccabees fought the evil King Antiochus, who tried to desecrate the Temple with pigs and garbage. We know the miracle of the lamp that burned eight nights with only a little oil..." She was a big woman in a saggy black dress with black brows and an angry voice. "But this is not an ancient story," she said. "It's happening today. The Christians resent us for not celebrating their holiday. Life would be easier if we gave in and became like them. But we must follow the Maccabees and defend our traditions, with our lives if necessary, as our fellow Jews have done for centuries and as they are doing right now in Eretz Yisrael."

In school he helped trim the tree for the Christmas Assembly, standing on the top step of the ladder as girls passed him tinsel to drape over the branches. They took a school bus to Rockefeller Center to see the tree rising high, lights twinkling, "White Christmas" playing, people clustering in the cold to snap photos. Mrs. Bradley snapped a class picture and put it in front of their little plastic tree in her classroom. At Christmas Assembly they sang the Carols with Mrs. Walde playing the piano. The words were happy— "God rest ye Merry Gentlemen/Let nothing ye dismay/Remember Christ our Savior was born on Christmas Day." On the day school closed they sang "Silent Night/Holy Night" and the girls' voices rose on "All is Calm/ All is Bright." Walking home Dorothy Hansen asked "Do you have a tree?" Goofy John Macdonald snorted "how can he have a tree, he's a Jew, right?" Dorothy pushed him away, "who asked you?" and turned to him. "But you're allowed to celebrate Christmas, aren't you? Have a tree, give presents?"

"Yeah sure," he said, not to disappoint her.

She waited until John Macdonald turned down his street and gave him a little box with a ribbon around it. It was a Paper Mate ballpoint pen. "So you won't have ink all over your hands," she said. "Merry Christmas."

At home he showed Mom the present. "Is Dorothy Hansen that cute little blonde girl?" she asked. "Now you have to give her something…"

They went to the A&P on Prospect Avenue. There was a Christmas section at the back of the store. Mom went through bins of scarves and gloves and sweaters. "Junk," she said. "Wait, here's something." She pulled out a book, "Reader's Digest Book of Great Christmas Stories." "Does she like to read, I'm sure she does…" She bought a roll of red and green wrapping paper with stars and floating angels playing harps—"we'll never use this again— "and a plain little card that said Happy Holidays. "Write something nice," she said. He wrote: "I'm using my new pen to thank you and hope you enjoy these stories." Mom read it with her little smile. "Now drop it off at her house," she said.

Dorothy lived around the corner on Vanderbilt Street in a house with a green metal awning over the front porch. Red and green lights twinkled around the windows, and a green wreath with pine cones hung on the door. Through the window he saw Dorothy and her sister clipping colored ornaments onto a big tree in the living room. He ducked so she wouldn't see him and tried to slide the book through the mail slot, but it didn't fit and he had to ring the bell. Dorothy came to the window and waved. In a second the door opened and she was standing there, breathless like she had run. "Hi..."

He gave her the book. "This is for you. It's a book of stories..."

"Don't tell me," she said, "I wanna be surprised..."

"Oh okay, sorry."

She hugged the book to her chest, "Wanna come in for cocoa?"

"No, I gotta go." He jumped down the steps, anxious to get away. "Happy Holiday," he said.

They didn't sing Easter songs in school. Mrs. Bradley didn't decorate the classroom. Some of the kids came in with smudges on their foreheads. The girls were asking, "What did you give up for Lent?" He asked Dorothy, but she said, "I can't tell because it'll sound like I'm bragging."

On Good Friday he saw Mrs. Dorsey wishing people "Happy Easter," but she looked away when he passed and he thought maybe she was mad because he practiced jumping in his room. On TV there were pictures of the Pope in Rome blessing the crowds of people. "On the most solemn day in Christianity," the announcer said. But then they showed kids on the ground pushing colored Easter eggs with their noses across the White House lawn and President Eisenhower giving the winner a huge box of candy.

Passover came first this year. It wasn't a holiday, not even an excused absence. They didn't talk about it in school and it always felt like a secret they didn't want anybody to know. Bubbe came the day before with a big black fish wrapped in newspaper. She put a kerchief around her head like the photos in her bookcase and chopped it up with a special knife for Gefilte fish. They said the blessings and Aaron said the Four Questions. Mom watched them eating her Matzah Balls. "I used seltzer this year. Are they any

146

lighter?"

"Lightest hockey pucks I ever ate," Uncle Sammy said.

In Hebrew school Mrs. Friedman closed the door and switched off the lights. "I want to show you something you should know." She turned on the slide projector. "Easter Sunday was the worst day of the year for the Jews in the Old Country," she said. Photos of dead people and soldiers with fur hats standing over them were projected on the blackboard. "The peasants used the death of Christ as an excuse to murder the Jews and steal their property..." The projector was whirring and changing slides every few seconds. "The Governments encouraged the pogroms to use the Jews as scapegoats and distract the people from their oppression. This is why we sing 'If I Forget Thee O' Jerusalem let my right hand lose its cunning because only in our own homeland will we be truly safe...'"

Mrs. Friedman moved into the light so it looked like she was in the phots. "More massacred Jews, not given a chance to defend themselves... Tel Aviv, 1921..." She pointed to a few men with turbans. "Arabs our new enemies... Sons of Ishmael... The Torah says every man's hand shall be turned against them."

The door opened and Mr. Rossman looked in. "Mrs. Friedman, may I speak with you?"

The projector kept clicking, dead bodies, burnt houses, soldiers. In the doorway Mr. Rossman was arguing in a soft voice. "It is not historically accurate. Arabs are not Cossacks..."

Every neighborhood had its own Easter Parade. His friends put on their Confirmation suits and the girls wore their new dresses with "bonnets" trimmed with flowers. After Easter dinner they met and walked along the park in a big group, but soon split into pairs, everybody choosing a special person to walk with. He put on his Assembly outfit, white shirt and blue tie and corduroy pants. Mom made him wear his woolen sweater. "You can't go out in shirtsleeves, it's not a complete outfit," she said. He wondered if Dorothy Hansen would be there and if she would want to hold hands.

Uncle Sam came in from playing golf. "Got a civilized tee time. Easter Sunday. All the goyim are in church..." He took a shiny flask out of his golf bag.

"It's three o'clock in the afternoon, Sam," Mom said.

"Sun's over the flagstaff," Uncle Sam said and took a quick drink.

They were watching a special Easter program from St. Patrick's Cathedral. "Look at that fairy Cardinal Spellman," Uncle Sammy said. "They say he spends thousands on his outfits."

Mom brought out coffee. "Who's they? How would you hear this stuff in your circles?"

"They call him Franny. They got a Monsignor whose only job is to keep him away from the altar boys..." He took another drink. "What are you all dressed up for, Buddy?"

"He's going to walk around with his friends," Mom said.

"Got a cute little shikse girlfriend? Better not tell your grandmother or you'll get all the stories about how the drunken Polacks rampaged through the shtetl on Easter Sunday. How she and Aunt Annie hid in the potato cellar while they were upstairs wrecking the house. Guys her father knew, did business with. Spitting on him, slapping him around. We heard that every year, didn't we Stella?"

"Every Jew's got a story like that," Dad said.

"I don't know what they're so pissed off about. If we didn't kill the bastard they wouldn't have a religion..."

"Shut up, Sam," Mom said and put a dollar in his pocket. "Go, have fun..."

"They sing White Christmas 'til it's coming out of our ears," Sammy said. "We wrote that..."

"We?" Dad said. "Since when did you collaborate with Irving Berlin?"

On TV Perry Como was singing: "In your Easter bonnet/With all the frills upon it" to a row of old ladies holding corsages.

"Irving Berlin wrote that, too," Dad said. "That's another thing they can thank us for."

"I'M STAYING HERE"

I dream a subject. Innocent Young American discovers Decadent Old World. I'll call him Danny Miller to make the Daisy Miller reference obvious for the critics. I've got the first chapter, Sandrine and Angela. I can see the reviews: *"A recently unearthed work from Gould's Paris period. Bawdy and life affirming... In the great tradition of Tristam Shandy and Tom Jones..."*

I find a few crumbs of Sandrine's majoum in my pocket and eat them on the Metro. Colette lives on Rue de la Victoire on the Right Bank. Cooking smells in the hallway remind me of my grandmother's building. Colette answers, thick dark hair tied in a bun, tight black skirt, white blouse buttoned to the top. She reaches for my hand. "Be brave." There is a long dark foyer, like in my grandmother's apartment. Mourning candle flickering on the kitchen sill. Couches and overstuffed chairs. Heavy, dark furniture, books behind glass doors. Tables with candy dishes and figurines. Do all Jews live alike?

Colette's the tallest one in the family. Dapper dad—wavy white hair, thick black brows like Colette, pinstripes, light blue shirt, red tie. I catch his wary look: Is this bum banging my little girl? Little chubby sister, frizzy hair. Old lady, *Tante* Something, in a long black dress with a lace top. That'll be her burial dress. See her in a coffin, can't blink it away. Mom hasn't come out of the kitchen. She dead in the war?

Colette brings out a clear soup with fish, onions and carrots. No wine. Green bottles of Perrier water. She explains that I'm doing a story about what people did to survive during the war. "People on my street," I say. "Rue Cujas…"

Papa objects in a torrent of French and Colette has to translate. "He says if you want to speak about survival you should come to *Le Marais*, the old Jewish quarter…"

Tante lights a cigarette, bored stiff, heard it a thousand times. Baby sister brings out a roast chicken on a bed of potatoes and carrots. There's a plate of *haricot verts*, string beans. Tasteless, look like green worms, don't understand why the French love them.

Papa takes a loose leaf binder out of the sideboard. "*Notre histoire,*" he says. Pages of neat writing in blue ink. Talking quickly. Colette explains. "My parents were born in Lodz in Poland. My grandfather was an *importeur* of cloth. They shipped the silk from Shanghai to Hamburg and then to Lodz. There was much demand to make robes, pajamas and his father was a silk painter *par excellence…*"

Tante offers a plate of *rugelach* she could have gotten at any bakery in Flatbush. Baby sister brings out a teapot with Chinese figures. My grandmother has one just like it.

"Silk was very much the mode," Colette says, "and they were prosper. They came to Paris, to the Marais, Jewish quarter, center of the clothing industry. They rearranged to send the silk to Vladivostok by ship, then by train across the Polish border. Then, the Germans came…"

Papa leans over and grabs my wrist. "*Vel d'Hiver, vous avez entendu parler?*"

"This is the Velodrome, the large stadium for bicycle races," Colette says. "So first they said the men had to report there and they would be transferred to transit camps."

"*Bousquet,*" Papa prompts. "Say to him, Colette…"

"René Bousquet, Chef of Police. The Jews trusted him, but he lied. He said the women and children wouldn't be taken. My mother was pregnant with me. They brought everybody into the arena. Twenty thousand. No food, no toilets, just to sleep on the ground. My mother was very afraid and they thought she would lose me, but there was a doctor there and he helped... And a guard took them to a door and let them escape..."

Papa pokes me. "*Miracle!*"

"They went to the north. The farmers there in the Resistance hided them. My father went back to the apartment to get some jewelry. But the concierge had stolen it and informed on him to the Germans. They came and took him to the transit camp at Drancy where they put the prisoners before deportations. He and some men jumped off a train going to Auschwitz. The Germans shot with *mitrailleuse* but he got away."

"What happened to your mother?" I ask.

"She got sick after my sister was born. She was in bed and I didn't like the smell..."

Papa pushes the notebook across the table. "*L'histoire complete.*" He presses it into my chest. "Take, take. Write in the *New York Times*..."

Colette walks me back to the Metro. I try to return her father's book. "Look, I lied, I don't work for the *Times.*"

She doesn't seem upset. "Why fabricate a story?"

"To impress you."

"And you don't want to impress me now?"

"Sure, but I don't want to lie to a girl who was born in a concentration camp."

"Now you have a *crise* of conscience. Don't worry, I don't suffer. No one can remember when they were born."

She comes down into the station with me. She has taken her shoulder bag, I hadn't noticed. Does that mean she's coming back to my room?

"Isn't your father going to miss you?" I ask

"They think I'm going home to the student residence."

We cuddle on the Metro like young lovers. I'm feeling very Parisian. Walk arm-in arm into the hotel past Madame at the desk. "*Bon soir, Madame...*"

The girls clatter down the stairs. "Ca va, Canadien?"

"You're not Canadian," Colette says.

"It's a better story," I say.

She slaps me playfully. "If one of those girls was born in a concentration camp would you have a *crise* of conscience for her, as well?"

The room is gloomy even with all the lights on. It's better in the dark with a few splashes from the streetlights like in an old movie. "*La vie Bohème*," Colette says and sits on the bed.

I'm a bumbling boy, embarrassed by my eagerness. Afterwards, she slips on her skirt and leaves and I think I've lost her. But she's back from the bathroom in a few minutes. "I thought you had gone home," I say. She undresses and gets back into bed. "I'm coming to live here, didn't I tell you?"

I awaken to her, standing nude at the window of my sun-drenched room, curtains fluttering. Every artist has tried to paint this and now I know why. Later, she is douching in my bidet. I'm moved by her delicacy.

"You see," she says, wiping herself, "just an ordinary Parisian girl with ordinary Parisian ideas…"

She's slipping into her underwear. Like watching a ballet.

"What are the ordinary Parisian ideas?" I ask.

"Oh you know, complete my *diplome*. Get a job… Then get married because I will want to have children one day, although now the idea is *unsupportable*. Then, like a good Parisian girl, take a lover…"

I stretch in the dappled sunlight. "And that lover will be me."

"No, no, cheri… You're the husband."

Colette is taking an English course at the Sorbonne and comes to me after class to "practice."

"I'm practicing, too," I say to her one blissful afternoon.

"But you are not improving," she says with that playful slap.

In August all of Paris goes on vacation. We are in our own parallel universe, moving unseen among hordes of tourists. Colette gets a singing "*Bon jour*" from Madame every time she comes and an "*au 'voir*" when she leaves. She disdains Le Snack, "It is like a station cafe."—the old waiter watches as we pass. She takes me to a long, narrow restaurant with red banquettes where the owner, impeccable in a sleek suit with *boutonnière* in his lapel kisses her hand and hands me a menu in ornate script. The food is better than Le Snack—amazing how much better—and doesn't cost that much more. The owner always gives us a bottle of wine "*moins cher*" (inexpensive), free coffee and one dessert to share.

She watches the door like she's looking for someone. "Do you come here with your lover?" I ask her.

"Is this what you imagine for a story?"

"Yes. You bring me here so he can see us together."

"But like a good bourgeois he is on vacation with his wife and children."

"Will he leave his wife for you?"

"Never... France is a Catholic country. We don't have divorce..."

"So you will only see him when he can get away..."

"Until we are bored..."

"And then you will find another... And another..."

"Until I am old and no one wants me anymore. Or if I marry a rich man and can buy gifts for young lovers..." She laughs at my expression. "Oh look, romantic boy..." Her brown eyes are brimming. "Will you marry one woman and stay faithful for your life?"

"That's the idea."

"But it never happens so why believe?"

We go to all the tourist spots. Eiffel Tower, Sacré-Coeur, the museums, boat ride on the Seine. Walk in the Bois de Boulogne. One Sunday she shows up with her father's Peugeot. She speeds through the narrow streets, laughing at my fear. "This is how we drive..." Onto the *autoroute* to a quiet country inn where we drink Rose at a picnic table and feel the first autumn breeze scattering the leaves. Again, she seems to be looking for someone.

"Hoping to see your lover here?" I say.

"Ah my imaginary lover..."

"Comes in for lunch with his wife... Sees you... No, wait a minute, you don't care about his wife, you stole him from her. He comes with his new girlfriend. You've never seen her, have you? You've been wondering what she's like. It's driving you crazy..."

She laughs. "You imagine a good story, but I am not as devious as you imagine..."

Did the laugh last a moment too long?

On the Monday after Labor Day, I'm walking with Colette in *Jardin du Luxembourg*. The night before we had been shivery in bed as the rain rattled the windows. Colette had reached out to me in her sleep. I put my arm around her. She nestled under my shoulder.

"I am leaving for my year in California tomorrow," she says.

Of course, I had forgotten.

"I leave in the morning."

The ground is still damp, last night's raindrops glittering on the grass.

"You should have told me," I say. "I would have you brought you a going away present."

"I didn't want to spoil our last night..."

I pick a pink flower from the borders along the walk and offer it with a courtly bow. *"Bon voyage..."*

"And this is for you." It's a brown box wrapped in pale paper, tied with blue ribbon. A Mont Blanc fountain pen on a plush lining. "This will help you paint every word as you say the great writers always do."

How did she know I love fountain pens? "I'll have to find a store that sells ink," I say.

"Call my sister, she'll help you. I'll be at Berkeley University of California"

"Big school, you'll have a good time... You'll..."

She puts her finger to my lips. "Please don't tell me all the handsome lovers I will have. Give me your address in New York."

"I won't be in New York," I say. "I'm staying here."

"I CAN OFFER YOU FOUR THOUSAND"

I wake up in the middle of the night. Colette is standing by the window, silhouetted in the moonlight. I call to her...

My chest aches so badly I think I'm getting sick. The whole world seems to share my desolation. Madame at the desk nods gravely, the waiter at Le Snack whispers to Madame at the counter when I come in. Even the girls in the hotel stop the happy chatter when I pass them on the stairs.

In mid-September the Parisians return and the tourists go home. All the landmarks that seemed so special with the cameras clicking now recede into the workaday world. The only Americans are the professional expats. The business guys in the suits, their Donna Reed wives determined to be as un-French as possible. Expats at the jazz clubs, Blue Note, *Chat Qui Peche*. The Black guys in a tight circle at their tables, white guys in leather jackets with their French friends. I sit at the bar, drinking cognac at ten francs a shot—five times what I pay at le Snack.

Running out of money. Maybe I can peddle the *Tribune* on the street. I take the Metro to the office. Copies of the paper are pasted on the window. Thick, ruddy guys in white shirts and suspenders slouch at desks pounding Underwoods, cigarettes dangling, like in the movies. A woman at the switchboard shakes her head. "Pretty girls get preference, or didn't you notice."

Next day, the American Embassy. The Marine guards block the door and make me show my passport. The lobby is bustling. Khakis and madras shorts, simple, open faces, cheerful voices. I feel out of place among my own people. In the "Information" booth, a kid trying to act older in a heavy gray suit, face scraped raw from shaving. "We don't get jobs for people here." I must look suicidal because he softens his tone. "If you know French really well you can get a job translating at *Agence France Presse*. They have Americans working in the English section..."

Next day, *Agence France Presse*. Two crowded floors on the Right Bank, wire machines rattling out reams of copy, which coils unread on the floor. A kid rushing by with a tray of demi-tasses points to a cubicle in the corner. Four guys who look like aging Village beatniks are putting up pieces of French wire copy on easels and translating them into English. Marty H., a dark-haired guy with the biggest, blackest eye bags I've ever seen. "Where ya from, Brooklyn? I thought so..." His accent is so thick I think he's making fun of me. Foddah name ya after Heywood Broun? Everybody read Heywood Broun in dose days... Can't hire ya, but I'll buy ya a drink..."

He takes me to a cafe next door. Waiter pours two shots of yellow liqueur, Johnny Romero's drink, and we fill the glasses with water from a carafe. The cloudy liquid tastes like licorice.

"Line forms at the rear for this gig," Marty says. "GI's who never went home. Guys who came here after the war to get laid and write the Great American War Novel. This is the only job we can get, nobody leaves. Done with the army?"

"I have a 2S. I can keep it if I stay here and keep taking courses..."

"They won't let you get away with that. Better get it over with before the next war starts."

"Next war?"

"Yeah, we're overdue. Every fifteen, twenty years like clockwork. Kennedy got a bloody nose in Cuba, he's gotta show how tough he is. This time Berlin will be the excuse, which is funny because we'll be defending the same scumbags we just beat... See where they're doublin' the draft. Calling up the Reserves. Boost the economy, kill a lotta young guys who might make trouble for the ruling class. I was thinkin'

I wanted to be back in the States when it starts, but the Russians'll probably bomb New York... 'Lotta Commies in Paris so they'll leave us alone... Do you have an idea for a novel?"

"I haven't really had time to make up a story."

"You don't make up a story, it happens to you. A lotta guys go trout fishing, Nick Adams happens to Hemingway. Decadent expats on the Riviera, Fitzgerald gets *Tender Is The Night*. Guys are drunk and stupid in the Army, James Jones has *From Here To Eternity*. I was a supply sergeant, quartermaster, titless WACS they called us. I got a commendation for capturing a wine cellar..."

"That's a good story," I say.

"I know," he says. "I've been trying to write it for ten years... You're a Jew, right? Me, too... Great American Jew Story. My grandfather fixed zippers in a shithole on Rivington Street. My old man got into trimmings, making buttons and belts for Brooks Brothers trench coats. Got rich making uniform epaulets and patches during the war. He's got congestive heart disease, but refuses to sell out and retire to Miami like any other self-respecting Yid. My mother says he'll die if he loses the business so I'm supposed to come back and run it for him... Just another boring bubbe meise, every Jew has one. See, but Bellow and Roth made a best seller out of it. 'Cause they know a story when they see one... But what they really know is how to create an act that goes with it. Become an art phony. That's your real creation, the stories are just journalism... So while you're figuring what kind of phony you can be..." Takes a book out of his shoulder bag. *Lust Weekend*. "Think you can write one of these?"

"Pornography?"

"You can make it art with the right act. Girodias, Olympia Press, same crook who published *Lolita*. Dirty book about a guy who fucks a little girl, but Nabokov strikes an esthete pose, waves his butterfly net around and it's a literary event. That's better than Beckett, who writes boring shit that nobody understands in bad French and everybody thinks he's a fuckin' genius. Women throw themselves at him...

Girodias will want you to write the first one for free and if he don't like it he won't hire you again.

"Two thousands new francs is four hundred bucks," I say. "That would keep me going while I wrote a novel."

"Only trouble is you won't," Marty says. "You are what you write. You can't grind out crap all day long and then come home and turn out a few pages of gorgeous, polished prose. But Paris is a good place to bum around. Cheap rent, food's good, always a woman around..." Gives me a card, *Editions Mauve, Place Pigalle*... "Try this guy, Bela, old fairy, he'll give you a chance..."

Next day. Place Pigalle. Day shift hookers on the stroll. A client approaches. A blue smock, or an old guy with an umbrella. A business suit comes out of a taxi checking his watch. Even a kid, who looks like a student. A little conversation and into the hotel.

Down some steps to *Editions Mauve*. A bookstore in front. Paperbacks, bondage magazines. A skinny kid with shiny black hair and traces of pinkish eye shadow sends me down a narrow hallway past an old man with a visor at a drawing table, a woman typing labels. I come to an office overlooking a weedy garden. A jowly guy in a blue velvet jacket watches me from behind a huge cigar.

"Bela?"

"And you are?"

"Heywood. Marty H. recommended me..."

"Ah yes Marty, unhappy boy... I support half the young writers in Paris. Maybe a future Nobel Prize. I should get a dedication, don't you think. I pay two thousand francs per book... Four hundred dollars. Twenty chapters, ten pages a chapter... Have you done pornography?"

"Yes, in America," I lie.

"American porn is like burlesque. We are like serious strip tease in Europe. Ambiance is important. Do you have a story?"

I think of Sandrine. "Young American becomes the sex slave of aristocratic decadent French woman and her lesbian friend. They take him on their yacht..."

"And then you can do the homosexual version."

All of a sudden I want to get out of there. "I've never done it…"

"You can steal from other books. Readers are fetishists, they're happy with the same thing over and over again. It's a simple formula. An innocent boy with a giant penis is at the center of the story and you add masochistic embellishment…" He takes a few books off a pile on his desk—Muscular young guys and older men, *The Protege*, *Berlin Bathhouse*. "Maybe these will give you inspiration…"

"Yes okay," I say, backing out.

He takes a long sucking puff on his cigar. "I can offer you four thousand."

"NOTHIN'," HE SAID

June 1954

Every night he put his catcher's mitt under the mattress wrapped it tight around a ball with rubber bands to deepen the pocket. He kept the mask, shin guards and chest protector in Dad's overseas bag. Catching was the best way to get on a team if you weren't a fast runner or a power hitter. But it was also the best position. He wasn't just standing out in the field, waiting for a ball to come to him. He was calling pitches, chasing pop ups and bunts, yelling instructions to the fielders. He was admired for his ability to catch a pitch when the batter swung and missed. To throw on a fly to second base and nail a runner stealing. He loved when foul tips banged into his mask or wild pitches bounced off his chest protector. When he blocked the plate from a runner trying to score and got bowled over, but came up waving the ball as the ump yelled "You're out!" and the kids cheered. He was proud of his scrapes, bruises and bent fingers. They showed how tough he was without having to fight.

He awoke, elated. The sun was leaking through the blinds, burning lattice patterns on the floor, which meant it was nice out and there would be a game. And later the Dodger-Giant game would be on TV.

But the skies were already starting to gray when he got to breakfast. "Looks like it's going to rain," Mom said.

The spreading gloom seemed to chase him as he ran down the park side to the Parade Grounds. His teammates were playing catch on the field. Coach Urban squinted up at the sooty clouds drifting overhead. "Maybe we'll get a few innings in," he said.

Big drops started coming down as they went on the field to warm up. "We can still play in this," Coach said. Then cold sprays of drizzle blew across the field. The coaches were talking. "We can play if it stays like this..."

They took the field for the first inning, but then it was like somebody was pouring a pail of cold water on them. In no time his woolen uniform was drenched. "Get off the field guys," Coach called. They stood under the trees watching the driving rain kick up clots in the grass and dredge mud puddles in the infield. "We'll try again tomorrow," Coach said.

He walked home under the trees in his shin guards and chest protector, his spikes clacking on the sidewalk. The rain slowed and turned into steaming vapor. His sodden uniform sagged.

Junior and Frank were hanging outside Arrnie's candy store across from the park. "You get rained out?"

A flatbed truck loaded with cinder blocks turned down Vanderbilt. In a second there was a traffic jam. People honking and cursing. A car couldn't get around the truck on the narrow street. The truck driver got out and tried to guide it—"you got plenty of room—" but the driver leaned out of his window. "You gonna pay my body work if I don't?"

A police car rolled up. Big red-faced cop, sweat blotches on his shirt. "Back outta there..." He held up oncoming traffic as the truck backed onto Prospect Park Southwest.

"I gotta dump this load," the driver said. "I'll give you twenty minutes," the cop said. "If you're still here I'll impound the rig as an unsafe vehicle." The truckers started arguing as the cops drove away. "All they wanted was a fin," one said. "I'll give' em ungotz," his partner said. "I'm sick of these pricks shakin' me down... Rather give it to these kids. Whaddya say, fellas, you wanna make five bucks?"

They jumped up. "Yeah."

The driver wiped a trail of grime through his dusty forehead. "Gotta unload a coupla hundred blocks. Bring 'em down to the site. Can you help us do that?"

"Yeah."

The blocks were stacked in piles of eight on the flat bed. A guy with *huge arms jumped up and grabbed one in each hand. "These weigh forty-five pounds apiece so two hands for beginners. I'll give 'em to you, you load 'em on the hand trucks and take 'em down to the masons."*

He grabbed one in each hand to see if he could do it. It was easy, no strain. He loaded eight on the hand truck, feeling strong. "One of you stay here to load," the big guy said. "The other two take the loads to the masons..." He pushed the hand truck to the construction site halfway down the street. There was a slight grade. He pushed harder to maintain speed. The masons watched as he took blocks off the hand truck. A mason's helper put his arms through the holes, slid the blocks up to his shoulders, a hundred eighty pounds on each arm, and walked stiffly like Frankenstein down a hill to a foundation where the masons slid them off his arms, slapped cement on them and lay them on a wall they were building, scraping the excess back onto their palettes and yelling up to them: "what are you lookin' at, let's go."

He passed Frank pushing a hand truck on the way back. Junior wasn't working fast enough and the driver had joined him, stacking the blocks, one hand over the other. He had already made four piles of eight. "C'mon fellas load those hand trucks."

After the third trip the load seemed heavier, the slight grade a lot steeper. He had to back up for a running start to go over a rut in the sidewalk. The masons were shouting up to him. "Hurry up, we gotta get to another job."

The driver passed him. "Need another man on the truck." A mason's helper ran by, pushing an empty wheelbarrow. By the time he got to the truck the helper had thrown ten blocks into the wheelbarrow and was running back to the site. The driver took the hand truck. "Get up on the bed and pass 'em down." He was in a maze of blocks. "Take 'em off the back end and work your way up," the driver called. As he got further from the edge he had to walk longer and the blocks seemed heavier. He couldn't go any faster. Couldn't hold the blocks with one hand anymore, had to hug them like grocery bags. Junior had disappeared, his place taken by a mason, yelling, "C'mon pass it down." There had to be at least fifty blocks left. He picked one off the top of the pile. A sharp pain shot up his back. He dropped the block on his foot, but kept going, trying not to limp.

The driver waved him off the truck. "Okay, kid, we can take it from here." His arms were shaking, forearms burning. Couldn't turn his head, calves throbbing. Frank had torn his pants. Junior had a bloody scrape on his arm. "Those guys throw them things around like nothin'..." They watched the last block come off the bed. The truck roared. Black smoke shot out of its tailpipe.

The driver came over snapping a five. "Here y'are fellas..."

His partner called from the truck. "How they gonna split five dollars three ways?"

"Yeah, okay." The driver peeled six singles off a roll of bills. "That cop's gonna be pissed he didn't catch us..."

They watched the truck rumble away. Whacked up the six singles, two dollars apiece.

"I'm gonna get a frappe," Junior said.

"Me too..."

A frappe was a quarter. He could also get a grilled cheese for a quarter and an egg cream for a dime and he'd still have a dollar forty left.

Arnie kept the papers in a pile outside, didn't even cut the twine around them. Everybody took a paper and left the change on top of the pile. He never came out to collect it, but would send one of the kids, "hey, go out and get my paper money," would give him a dime and put the coins in the register without even counting them. It was so dark you couldn't see anything when you walked in. There was hardly any space between the magazine rack and the counter and you had to be careful not to knock down a whole shelf of candy. Arnie made a frappe with two scoops, chocolate syrup, candied walnuts, a mountain of Reddi Whip and a cherry on top. He had a grill where he made eggs in the morning and burgers and grilled cheese all day. In the winter you could hardly get in, the store was crowded with cops and guys from the gas station, drinking coffee. Arnie made big egg sandwiches with extra slices of bacon for the cops and never charged them. At night you could see him sitting under the light at the end of the counter smoking a cigarette in the empty store.

The doorbell jingled. Arnie was at the back of the store with Blackie and Jose. Blackie was a few years older, skinny and dark, lived by Greenwood Cemetery. They said he was Syrian. Junior's brother Sonny said, "Watch he don't pull a knife on you." Nobody knew where Jose lived, but he was always with Blackie, a big kid, glaring behind him. In the third grade Blackie and Jose would show up sometimes outside the movie theater and take their fifty cents ticket money. Once he put the two quarters in his socks when he saw them up the block. "I don't have nothin'" Blackie smacked him on the side of the head. "You always got money you little fuckin' hebe..." They backed him into the shadows under the trees on the park side. Stood over him and made him turn his pockets out and take off his shoes, cars driving by.

Then Blackie was gone. Sent to Juvenile Detention, they said. Now he was back. He had been coming around the schoolyard, hanging with the older guys. Cigarette butt between his fingers. Skinny and hunched over like he was cold. He came out of the gloom, sniffling, red-eyed wearing a black silk shirt, black pegged pants with white saddle stitching and pointy "french toes," Jose glaring behind him.

"You got big all of a sudden, but I can still take ya, right?" Blackie said.

"Right," he said and felt ashamed that he had answered so quickly.

"Your brother Sonny around, Junior?"

"He's workin'," Junior said.

"Seen yiz humpin' them blocks out there, too. How much that cheap prick give ya, buck a piece?"

"Two bucks," Junior said.

"Two bucks, shoulda been ten. What are you gonna do with it?"

"I don't know, get a frappe," Junior said.

"A frappe, you kiddin'? How would ya like the best blow job in Brooklyn? Two bucks. Beautiful broad. Chorus girl at the Elegante... Whaddya say?"

Junior shrugged. "Yeah okay..."

"How about you?" he asked Frank.

"Yeah, yeah," Frank said.

*"You go first Mickey Mantle," Blackie said. "She's parked in back...
Name's Agnes..." He shoved him. "Go ahead, whaddya a faggot or
somethin'?"*

*He walked through the narrow passage past boxes of empty soda bottles
into the alley. There was a blonde head in the back seat of Arnie's baby blue
Chrysler Imperial. He walked around and opened the door. "Hey, a ball
player. Didja win today? "We were rained out," he said. She looked pretty
young, make up covering her pimples. Red lipstick like Aunt Rae's. Tight
black sweater and a short red skirt. "Blackie's friends get special treatment,"
she said. She pulled up her sweater and her breasts flopped out. They were
big like an old lady's and had powder on them. "You can feel 'em, but don't
touch my perm..." He felt around the top, avoiding the nipples. She bent
over, feeling around his pants and he could see the dark roots at the back of
her neck. "Don'tcha have a zipper?" She pushed him back against the seat.
"Cmon, get 'em off, while I'm still in the mood..." He leaned back and pulled
down his uniform pants. "Okay, baby relax, I'm not gonna bite ya..." He
felt her cold fingers, pulling him up. Her lips wet and cold..." Mmmm, I like
you, baby... I really do..." He closed his eyes and tried to think of all the girls
he lusted for, Lucy, the super's daughter, Jane Russell in the movies...*

She let him go. "Dead as a doornail, honey," she said.

"I'm sorry," he said.

*"Happens, don't worry about it." She sat up. "Gimme the two bucks, I
won't tell your friends..."*

Junior was waiting outside, eyes wide. "How was it?"

"Best blow job I ever had," he said.

Blackie was at the counter. "Didn't I tell ya? She's the best, right?"

"Best I ever had," he said.

"That's high praise coming from you," Arnie said.

They were laughing at him. Like they knew what had really happened.

Junior came back. "She said I almost choked her to death..."

"We'll hafta charge you double next time."

They were laughing at him, too.

Frank was taking a long time. "They're probably trying to find it," Blackie said.

"You want an egg cream?" Arnie asked. "You can owe me…"

"I gotta go," he said.

"Next time you wanna see Agnes just ask Arnie," Blackie called as he walked out.

Outside, the sun was breaking through. It was always brighter after the rain. They might even be playing the afternoon games. The ball would be muddy and heavy and would splash through the puddles and stop dead in the grass.

He smelled Mom's meat loaf in the hall. "Take your spikes off," she called from the kitchen. "Throw your wet socks in the hamper."

Aunt Rae was drinking coffee at the kitchen table. "Did you play in this rain?"

"Game was called."

"So what did you do all day?"

"Nothin'," he said.

"DADDY KNOWS SOMEBODY IN THE UNION"

November 1961

Without Colette to talk to I haven't said an English word in days. I pick up a copy of the *International Tribune* and automatically translate the English to French.

I'm in a panic. My grand plan didn't work. I came here to become a great writer and haven't written a word in months. And now I'm losing my language. I've been a flop at everything I ever tried. Now I can add this time in Paris to all my other failures.

I cash my return ticket at Nord Deutscher Lloyd, the shipping line, and buy a cheaper one for a freighter leaving Bremerhaven, Germany for New York in two days. The night before I pack in the dark and sit at the window until morning. I rush down the stairs past the desk. Madame doesn't even look up. On the train I buy a *saucisse* sandwich and sleep most of the way.

Bremerhaven is still bombed out from the war. New buildings next to piles of rubble. American troops rollick by in a jeep. Pretty soon I'll be one of them.

On the dock, the longshoremen push dollies loaded with crates and sacks up the gangplank and down a slide into the hold where others stack it methodically, leaving just enough room to clamber out. Trim guys, not wide and close to the ground like the Brooklyn longshoremen. Cloth caps, cigarettes. Disappearing under burlap bags of cocoa beans so huge all you can see is their feet, like ants carrying crumbs. They stop for lunch, spread drop cloths on the dock, huge white loafs, plates of meat, bottles of beer. They smoke and snooze after lunch. These guys have it easier than the guys on the Red Hook piers, tossing crates into a net as a foreman screams into the hold, "Fuckin' greaseballs, better move your asses if you wanna work on my dock..." They don't have to be great. Why do I?

I thought art was pure, but it's just a con like Marty was trying to tell me. Find a urinal and call it sculpture. Write a porno about screwing a little girl and call it allegory. Go to the bullfights with your drinking buddies and call it literature. Invent a character—tough guy, beatnik, dadaist, Russian exile...

Everybody's an art phony. The so-called poets in Washington Square, who keep the talented people out of their clique. The guys who know two chords on the guitar and everybody sits at their feet. The revolutionaries, who act like everybody else is a bourgeois asshole, while some of them take money from their parents and others are spies or informers. Everybody's got an act but me.

Liquor isn't allowed on board, but there's a washtub full of Rignes, Norwegian beer, in a bed of cracked ice in the dining room for the passengers only. The crew is mostly Arabs and Greeks with a couple of yellow-eyed Africans thrown in. The captain is a wind-burned German who stays on the bridge and eats in his cabin. The officers walk the ship in full uniform, giving brusque orders in English, which the crew jump to obey.

We're housed in a low-slung prefab with a tin roof on A deck. Narrow allway, six cabins on each side. People snoring, farting, moaning in their sleep, no sex sounds. My cabin has a bunk, a porthole and a filthy sink. Bathrooms at each end, busy all the time. After the first day one of them is out of order. "How much you wanna bet there's Kotex cloggin' the toilet?" says Warren, a junior high geography teacher from Sarasota. "Happens in my school all the time." Warren says he and a buddy couldn't stand the latrines on the troop ship going to Korea so they shit in the lifeboats. Another American, a longhair named Bill from Portland, Oregon, says he was constipated for three weeks in boarding school and had to go to the hospital for an enema. I tell about the time I tried to squat over a hole in Le Snack and ended up shitting down the back of my pants. They laugh. "Jeeze, that'll spoil your night."

Passengers and crew crowd together in a small dining room next to the galley below deck. No smiles, or "good mornings." Breakfast is canned juice, two fried eggs, all the black bread you can eat and a bitter Italian instant coffee that sends you right to the crapper. Lunch is a slice of cheese or salami between thick slices of the same black bread, dinner a stew or macaroni with canned fruit for dessert, more bread. The crew has their own table. The officers watch sternly, making sure they don't talk to the passengers.

Two of the passengers speak a guttural language I can't identify. Three ladies in headscarves and long skirts dragging on the ground take their plates back to their cabins. Two chain-smoking young women, bleach blondes, cracked nail polish, leather jackets over their short skirts, look at us like, "do you really expect me to talk to you?"

There's a game room with a chess table, checkers set, old magazines. Warren cracks a pack of Winstons, first American cigarette I've had in months. He draws a flag on the table—"American territory"—and nobody comes in.

Three days out the wind starts blowing. The ship pitches and rolls. Waves break over the deck. Cold spray shoots through my porthole, drenching my mattress. Crewmen with mops and buckets. The officers, in black ponchos, vomit over the side.

Warren taps on my door. "I puked on my floor. Can I come in?" I make him eat a hunk of black bread and drink a couple of beers. "You gotta get something in your stomach." He's reluctant—"you sure this works?" He crams the bread in his mouth and runs out gagging. Next morning he's in the dining room with a smile. "I'm better, thanks…"

I reread *In Our Time* and *Tropic of Cancer*. Bill's *On the Road* is creased and dog-eared, Warren has a bagful of Western paperbacks, lurid covers, swooning blondes with cowboys and snorting stallions.

We sit around the game room, smoking and beering and trying to top each other with tales of defeat and lost illusions.

"I was in my Kerouac bag," Bill says. "I was gonna bum around the world. Got a job pulling nets on a fishing boat up in Alaska…"

"That was the dream of the guys in Washington Square," I say. "I knew a kid who made a fortune on a tuna boat up there."

"Pretty hard to do, 'cause there's no tuna," Bill says. "You can get salmon, or groundfish they call it like halibut or pollock. They'll even take you on a drift boat to pull salmon in on a drop line. They need another pair of hands, you don't have to know what you're doin'. The nice guys'll give you a quarter share, but most of them pay a day rate. Everything's so expensive, fuckin' buck a beer…"

"I was gonna make a fortune, too," Warren begins…

Bill isn't ready to relinquish the floor. "I wanted to find my own path, like Siddhartha," he says. "Got a student rate to Katmandu with a Buddhist group. All Dutch, German, Aussies, American kids, too. They hung out on a place they called Freak Street, kids walkin' around like zombies, everybody strung out on heroin. This American guy, Matthew, said 'wanna make some easy money? All you gotta do is carry a valise on the next flight to Sydney. One stop in Bangkok, but Thai Customs won't bother white people. Take the valise to this address in Sydney, they'll give you five hundred US plus enough Aussie pounds for a hot weekend and a flight home…' Me and this girl from Denver said we'd do it. I got a shave and a haircut, khakis and loafers. She tied up her tits and looked like a twelve-year-old. Like they said Thai Customs waved us through. They told me to leave smelly socks and underwear in a sloppy mess on top of the valise. It worked. The Customs guy in Sydney said, 'why don't you learn how to pack?' and shoved my valise back at me. I took a cab at the airport. The girl went off in the opposite direction. Little cafe at the end of a dock. Walk in out of the sun and it was so dark I could hardly see. They took the valise and gave me fifty pounds. 'Good job, mate…' I'm supposed to get five hundred, I said. Heard a chair squeak. Next thing I'm on the street, head poundin', blood pourin' into my eyes, people walkin' around me. Three guys sitting outside the cafe staring at me like if I talked I was dead. I told the cops I got jumped from behind and didn't see who it was. They stitched up my head, see?" He has a scar above his nose between his brows. "Broke my hand, when I fell I guess. They fucked up the cast..." He has a lump of bone under his knuckle. "Aussie cops didn't give a shit, but the people at the Embassy gave me the third degree. Why'd you come here? Surfing? What kinda board do you use? Lucky I was a beach kid so I could give them the right answers..."

"What happened to the girl?" I ask.

"Nothin' good, I'm sure... They held my passport until my mom sent me a ticket to Seattle and two hundred dollars in traveler's checks. Dropped me at the airport. I didn't wanna go home. Some of the kids in Kat had been talking about the freaky scene in Tangiers so I snuck over and exchanged my ticket for a flight..."

"Jeeze," Warren says. "Tangiers is halfway around the world."

"Took thirty hours, I think, with a coupla stops. Fuckin' freaky scene is right. A lotta rich Americans but you have to be a writer or artist. I never heard of any of them, but they act like they're friends with all these famous people and tell you stories, mostly about how everybody's really a queer or a lesbian. I got myself up to Rome, but this time my tight-assed Jew stepfather said no more money and told the Consulate to put me on the first boat home."

"What are you gonna do about the Army?" I ask.

He cracks the bone under his knuckle. "Can't do a lot with this hand so that might be enough. If not, I got two DUI's and a ton of shrink's notes. How about you?"

"I've got a 2S. I took this semester off..."

"They won't let you keep the exemption," Warren says. "You don't get to have fun on their time."

His eyes are always red-rimmed like he's been crying, but it could be the beer. "My buddy, this guy I was in Korea with…"

"The one you shit in the lifeboat with?"

"No, that guy got out on a medical. Walked around barefoot until he got frostbite and they amputated a couple of his toes and sent him home. No, this guy was Company Sergeant. I was Company Clerk and took care of all his paperwork. Made him look good with the Captain. Also, helped him cheat in the poker games. We'd have signals like a code. Dumb hillbillies never cottoned on. He'd send me out in a jeep to bring the mooses back…"

"Mooses?"

"Yeah, gook girls, you know. Gave me the money to bribe the guys on guard duty to let them on post. It was all fixed, but still it's a general court martial bringing on unauthorized personnel. Ten, twenty below and the guys would stand outside the barracks against the wall and these mooses would go down the line, givin' blowjobs, two dollars a head. I don't know what the sergeant paid them…"

Bill makes a face. "Ugly Americans."

"Yeah, yeah, Imperialist Mercenaries, I heard it all in grad school," Warren says. "What kinda mercenaries if we didn't get anything out of it, but frostbite and two dollar blowjobs?"

Bill tries to make amends. "Korean War was years ago."

"It was in '52, yeah. I was discharged, got my teaching license. Fuckin' dumb kids don't wanna learn. I had a small apartment, beat up car, sorry-assed women, you know, divorced or just lookin' for help with the bills. All of a sudden I hear from the sergeant last year. He's back in the Army, got his stripes back, too, and he's stationed in Wurzberg… He's got a racket selling mutual funds to GI's. I should come over there and help him run it, he says. I had nothin' goin' for me so I go. He's got this Kraut partner who knows how to put it all together. He needs somebody who can write proper English to do a prospectus, letters, contracts. Puts me up with the Kraut and his wife… We get all the paperwork done and looking real official. He promotes himself a booth in the PX. Puts me in there 'cause I'm a civilian and he's gotta stay out of it. I sell a few, not a lot. Hard to explain mutual funds to these hicks. But after a month he starts payin' dividends, fifteen, twenty percent. Word spreads. GI's don't have any dough, not even officers. New guys rotatin' in and out with the mobilization."

"What mobilization?"

"All that shit about a standoff in Berlin and how we were gonna go to war with the Russians… They're lining up at the booth. Like an avalanche, the money's rolling in. I'm selling during the day and at night I'm writing out checks, fifteen, twenty percent payouts every month. I was riding a good thing, didn't ask questions. Wads of Deutsch marks. I was goin' out with the Kraut's sister-in-law. Huge knockers. Take her shopping and you get anything you want. Krauts love money."

"So how was your friend making all this money?" Bill asks.

"Ponzi scheme, old as the hills. He was paying off one guy with other guys' money. Like Treasury Bonds, he told me, what's the difference? Crooks are the biggest suckers, I found out. They'll steal from you and then turn around and let someone steal from them in exactly the same way. They were losing the money on bad deals. They opened a GI bar but the MP's made it off limits after a brawl. Then they bought into a dog track, but couldn't get it licensed and the Krauts took all their money.

"They started bouncing checks. Sarge tells me don't write no more but it's too late. I'm a stationary target, standing in that booth in the PX. My name's on all the contracts. Guys comin' up to me, sayin' where's my money, motherfucker? So I ask what's going on and he looks at me like I'm nuts. 'It's all a swindle, didn't you guess?' That night, my girlfriend warns me they're runnin' away and I'll be left holdin' the bag…" I snuck out to Bremerhaven. Hopped this tub. Those guys escaped into the Russian zone…"

Dock at dawn. Customs comes aboard. "Form a line, please." The passengers are questioned and searched. "Hayward Gold?" a Customs officer calls. "Gould," I correct. He waves me up to the front of the line. Stamps my passport. "Welcome home, Hayward."

My parents are waiting on the dock. Awkward hugs.

"You lost weight," my mother says.

"I ate like a pig," I say.

Bill and Warren wave at the rail. I feel guilty I got off so easily. "They didn't ask me any questions or search my stuff," I tell my mother.

She points to my father, talking to a guy in a suit. "Daddy knows somebody in the union."

HE HAD GOTTEN DADDY IN TROUBLE

Aaron came into his room, pressing his blanket to his face. "Mommy and Daddy are fighting again."

He snuck out and slid against the wall outside the kitchen like the guys in the cop movies. Mommy threw the soup spoons in the sink and slammed the refrigerator door. "Morris, the big hero of the Lincoln Brigade," she said.

Daddy lit a cigarette with a shaking hand. "He saw action in Spain," he said. "Shrapnel in his leg kept him out of our Army…"

"That's the story this week. Remember when he was saying it was rheumatic heart fever?"

"That was only when he didn't want people to know he'd been in the Party, Stella. Why do you always bring this up?"

"Because everybody—but you—knows the FBI exempted him so he could spy on the unions during the war."

"Who's everybody?"

"And Dina always acts like I'm a dumb housewife and she's the big Hollywood star. Watch, she'll tell that same story about the night John Garfield propositioned her…"

"It was the big moment of her life…"

"And Ben, the big martyr. The blacklist is the best thing that ever happened to him. Gave him an excuse for failure…"

"Look, it's our turn, we were there last month…"

"And Dina got Chinese…"

"So you can get deli…"

"No I can't because your friend Morris put in an order for stuffed cabbage."

"He said if you felt like making it."

"And while I'm slaving in the kitchen that slut wife of his will be all over you..."

"She was a dancer, it's a more liberated mentality."

Another crash, like a cup falling and spinning on the floor.

"Why do you always defend them?" Mommy said.

"They're my oldest friends, Stella..."

"They wouldn't cross the street for you. What do you think they say about you behind your back?

"What do YOU think they say?" Daddy shouted.

Mommy ran past him down the hall to the bathroom and came back, whipping a towel through the wisps of smoke over Daddy's head.

"How many times do I have to tell you I don't want the boys eating breakfast in polluted air."

Daddy dropped his cigarette with a soft sizzle into his coffee.

"Am I supposed to wash that cup now?" Mommy said.

"You wanted me to put it out, I put it out," Daddy said.

Mrs. Schiller made the kids line up and walk by her globe. "I want you all to see this." She pointed to a pink area. "This is South Korea. A free people like us with a growing Christian community..." Slid her finger to a large blue country above it. "This is North Korea. After World War Two, the traitors in our State Department allowed Russia"—she slapped a large red area so sharply with her pointer that Dorothy Hansen shuddered and grabbed his arm—"and China"—another slap on a yellow country with CHINA written in red—"to take over this country and turn it into a Communist dictatorship. The Russians gave guns and tanks and planes to the North Koreans to invade the south. The Chinese sent millions of troops. Our American boys went into battle, fifty thousand versus millions. They are fighting in sub-zero weather, enduring frostbite and constant attack to protect our way of life. Chinese soldiers would be bayoneting American babies on Coney Island Avenue if it weren't for these brave boys."

She showed them an Army photograph like Daddy's of a smiling man with two bars on his shoulders, Daddy only had one. "This is my nephew, Captain Armand Schiller. He's with the Eighth Army fighting in Korea. Your homework is to write him a short letter, saying how much you appreciate what he's doing for us. Make sure you check your spelling in the dictionary. We'll pick the best one and everyone in the class will sign it."

He wrote the letter at the kitchen table while Mommy was making dinner. There was a speech in a Batman comic—"we must be forever vigilant against the forces of darkness." He had seen a war movie where the general was pinning a medal on a soldier. "For courage under fire," the general said. He remembered a priest on TV talking about "the struggle against Godless communism." He put them all together: "Dear Captain Schiller, I know you are fighting under constant attack in subzero weather and I appreciate your courage under fire. I know that we must be ever vigilant against the forces of darkness. I hope one day to grow up and join the Army so I can join the strugle against Godless communism."

"What are you working so hard at?" Mommy said.

"A letter to a soldier in Korea."

She read it with a little smile. "Struggle has two "g's," she said.

Daddy's friend Ben had a big, bald head like a cartoon character with a fringe of hair over his ears. Dina was wearing a black blouse that looked like one of Mommy's brassieres. She sat with her chubby legs folded under her and he could see right up to her panties. Ben tripped over the coffee table, sitting down. "Ben got a head start," Dina said. "When's the star gonna make his appearance?" Daddy asked Dolores, Morris's wife. "Search me," she said. "It'd be a pleasure," Ben said. "Shut up, Ben," Dina said and everybody laughed, even Mommy. Daddy poured a big glass of whiskey for Ben and a smaller one in a shot glass for himself. They clicked glasses, "Nostrovya."

The door buzzed and Morris came in and took a big smell. "Just like my mother used to make. With raisins and pine nuts, I hope." He gave Mommy a big bouquet of roses. "Sweets to the sweet." Gave Daddy a big bottle. "Try some vintage hootch for a change." Daddy sniffed the bottle. "Vintage means the bathtub was older" and Dolores laughed "Hah!" really loud. Morris's face was as tan as Bubbe's, and she sat outside the building on a bridge chair all day. He was wearing a green shirt with yellow palm trees and blue mermaids on it. Dolores was real tan, too, smooth brown arms, combs and flowers in her black hair, a dress like the Chinese women in the war movies, with a slit so he could see up her leg. Daddy was wearing a white shirt and his suit pants from work. "You look like the foreman of the sweat shop," Morris said. "Smell like him, too." Daddy didn't get mad. "Did you have fun in Miami with the rest of the class enemies?" he asked. "I was downtown at the end of Collins Avenue," Morris said. "Three tenements where all the old Commies live. Shoulda heard the war stories. Everybody was in the Brigade. Everybody stormed the Winter Palace, everybody liberated Madrid..."

Mommy was wearing a white blouse and black slacks. "Look at the tush on this broad," Morris said. Daddy leaned over Dolores. "Freshen your drink?" She smiled and held out her glass.

Other men who visited would try to make conversation with him and Aaron. Ask who they rooted for. Who they thought was the best, Mickey Mantle, Duke Snider or Willie Mays. But Morris just called them stupid nicknames like "Slugger" or "Tough Guy," and Ben drank a lot of whiskey with his head down and stumbled over to the sofa before dessert. Other women would say how cute they were or how they looked like Daddy or Mommy and then talk about their own kids and even show pictures, sometimes. But Dolores looked at them like they shouldn't be there. And Dina had a phony smile like a teacher. "He doesn't like the cabbage, Stella, he's just eating the meat." Mommy gave him a dirty look like he had embarrassed her so he put a big piece of cabbage in his mouth and tried to chew it. Morris poked him. "You don't know how lucky you are, Slugger. If I had ever found a Jewish girl who made stuffed cabbage like your mother I would have married her on the spot..."

"What makes you think a nice Jewish girl would have married you?" Dolores said.

Morris rubbed his fingers together. "Cause I know the way to her heart..."

"You may know the way, but you can't afford the ticket" Daddy said.

Dolores kept laughing until Morris said, "Shut up, it's not that funny."

After dinner they sent him and Aaron to bed. They were talking and laughing so loud he could hear them with the door closed. He waited until Aaron was asleep and crawled down the hall like the soldiers in a battle and peeked around the corner. The bottle of whiskey was on the table. Everybody was talking at once.

Dolores had her arm around Ben. Her dress was pulled all the way up her leg. "He said I looked like Yvonne De Carlo," she said.

"Yvonne De Carlo was the easiest lay in Hollywood," Dina said.

"Easier than John Garfield?" Mommy said.

Daddy and Morris were arguing.

"It was agreed after the war that the Party should give priority to the struggle for civil rights," Daddy said.

"Maybe in Trotsky Wonderland," Morris said. "In the real world the first priority was bringing an alienated class together in collective action…"

"And telling those rednecks not to let the New York Jew bosses exploit them," Mommy said.

"We were up against the Confederate mentality, Stella. It had to be portrayed as a struggle against outsiders."

"There were no Jewish bosses in the South," Daddy said. "Local grandees owned those textile mills. You distorted the analysis and sold out your own people…"

"My own people? Is nationalism back in style?"

"Jews are a separate case," Daddy said.

"Jews are headed for the dustbin of history along with all the other counter-revolutionary element…"

Ben got up and fell back on the sofa. "Where's the head?"

"Same place," Daddy said.

Mommy pulled Ben up by his arm. "I'll take him. Don't want him waking the boys up…"

He crawled fast down the hall and hid in the shadows as they came out.

"Gonna hold it for me, Stella?" Ben said.

"That's your wife's job and she can have it," Mommy said.

Morris was yelling at Daddy. "Theory is fine for the cafeteria revolutionaries, but we're changing the world in the field…"

"You're not changing, you're perpetuating," Daddy yelled back.

Mommy walked back into the living room. "Somebody wanna get Ben off the bathroom floor?"

"Let him lay on the cool tile for a few minutes," Dina said.

"Did you integrate the mills?" Daddy said.

"We needed a victory first," Morris says. "That was next on the list…"

"But it never happened," Daddy said. "The whites got the union, the Negroes got mops and buckets."

He stayed close to the wall, struggling to stay awake. Morris's laugh sounded like the crazy bad guys in the movies. "Murray Lerner hero of the Battle of Aragon. Shot in the back while charging…" He wondered how that could happen unless one of your own soldiers shot you by mistake.

He was jolted awake by a crash. Morris and Daddy were on their knees at the coffee table, arm wrestling. Morris was slowly forcing Daddy's arm down. "Into the dustbin of history you go," he said. Mommy came out of the kitchen. "I could beat you both," she said. Daddy gripped the table, arm shaking, his hand looking tiny in Morris's big red paw. He prayed: "Please God, make my dad stronger." Then, as if God had heard him, Daddy started forcing Morris's hand back. Morris grabbed the table. "That's cheating, Morris," Dolores said. The table went up on one leg and the candy dish flew off "Happy now?" Mommy said. Morris and Daddy sat back rubbing their arms. "I didn't want to embarrass you in front of Stella," Morris said. Dolores laughed, "Hah!" and touched Daddy's arm. "You don't know your own strength, Benny," she said.

All the boys' moms cut the brims off old fedoras and made beanies. The trick was to put more stuff on your beanie than your friends. He had a Jackie Robinson button and a big blue Stevenson for President. Also, a Mickey Mouse and a pin of the Statue of Liberty he'd gotten on a field trip. Mommy gave him one of Aunt Rae's alligator pins and he found some army ribbons in the bottom of Daddy's drawer. He looked in the leather pouch where

Daddy kept silver dollars and old watches and found a little pin of Abraham Lincoln seated at the Lincoln Memorial, above an American flag. At Lincoln's feet, was a caption, "For Our Freedom and Yours." It seemed like a really patriotic medal so he pinned it on the front of the beanie to make sure Mrs. Schiller would see it.

The kids weren't allowed to wear their beanies in the classroom. "You can show them off just before lunch," Mrs. Schiller said. She went from desk to desk. "Let me see your letters." She read his for a long time. "What does vigilant mean?" she asked. "Watching out for trouble," he said. She looked at him so long that he had to turn away. "Does your mother help you with your homework?" she asked. He shook his head. "Copy the letter on a piece of drawing paper and the class will sign it, and we'll send it to Korea." she said. "You're a good writer, I'll say that." Dorothy whispered: "Wow, what a surprise. She never says anything nice to you."

At lunch Mrs. Schiller made everyone line up. "You can show off your little hats now." She walked down the line looking at their stuff. Looked at his for a long time. "Jackie Robinson was just a baseball player, he didn't do anything special... Adlai Stevenson, I might have guessed... What's this?" she asked, turning his Lincoln pin around so she could see the back. "An Army troop," he said. "My father's friend fought in it." He thought she would say something nice like she always did about American soldiers, but her face twisted like a witch's and she hit the pin with her finger so hard it hurt his head. "Did you know they were Communists who took a great president's name to fool people? That your father's friend slaughtered Catholics and burned churches in Spain?" There was a lot of noise like sirens in his head. He squeezed his eyes to stop the surge of tears. "And now your father's Communist friends are murdering our soldiers in Korea, did you know that?" Mrs. Schiller said. She tried to pull the pin off his beanie. "Throw this garbage away right now!" He pulled it away from her. She screamed, "Look what you did!" A trickle of blood was running down her finger. He ran down the hall, head down, so the kids wouldn't see him crying. "You come back here right now," she yelled.

The streets were a boiling blur. Leo, the super was outside the house.

"*You hurt yourself?*" *Aunt Rae was drinking coffee in the kitchen. "Stella, he's here…"*

Mommy came in. "They just called from school…"

"*Did I get Daddy in trouble?*"

"*No, no, of course not. Stop crying for a second and tell me what happened?*"

"*Mrs. Schiller saw the Lincoln pin and said Daddy's friends were killing our soldiers in Korea.*"

Mommy ripped the pin off his beanie. "I thought I had gotten rid of all this crap."

"*Is that true?*" *he asked. "Are daddy's friends killing our soldiers?*"

"*Of course not,*" *Mommy said. "Daddy was a soldier, an officer. He spent four years away from home fighting for his country. You've seen that photo of General MacArthur pinning the medal on him. You can be proud of him… I'm gonna complain to the Board Of Ed,*" *she said to Aunt Rae.*

"*They'll take it out on him,*" *Rae said.*

"*But that bitch shouldn't be teaching.*"

"*They won't fire her, she has tenure. Better hope she doesn't call the FBI…*"

"*Will the FBI arrest Daddy?*" *he asked.*

"*See what you started?*" *Mommy said to Rae. "Absolutely not. Never…*"

"*But I did something bad to him…*"

"*You didn't. Everything's fine. I'll talk to Mrs. Schiller tomorrow. She'll apologize for what she said, you'll see. Everything will be fine.*"

He knew she was lying to make him feel better. He could tell by looking at Aunt Rae. He had gotten Daddy in trouble.

"I WAS AFRAID THEY WOULDN'T TAKE ME"

January 1962

I sleep through my nineteenth birthday. In a semi-stupor I hear my mother outside my room: " I don't know what's wrong with him…"

"Didn't you get any sleep over there?" My father asks.

I thought I had. I was never tired. Walked the city until it shut down and the street sprinklers showed up. Talked and talked all night to Colette. Then, in the morning, watched her sleep, head on my chest, wisps of her hair tickling my nose. Always in a frenzy of expectation, out and about, waiting for something to happen.

I awaken in a sweat as if from a fever sleep and stumble, heavy-limbed into the kitchen. My father has been promoted. He runs fifteen funeral parlors in the city, including Campbells, which buries all the movie stars and celebrities. He's up and out early to get to his office in Manhattan. My brother has left for school. Too tired to eat, I poke at the yolks of my sunnyside ups. Three tablespoons of Maxwell House Instant don't give the buzz of one *crème*. I scorch my mother's saucepan trying to steam milk. She gives me Pillsbury Crescents, the closest thing to the croissants I had raved about in my letters. Pours coffee over her shredded wheat, spoons sugar and mashes a banana into it.

"Daddy comes home drunk every night, you'll see," she says. "They gave him a raise, big office. None of them want to go home. They make up these business meetings so they can pick up women at the bars. Get drunk and complain about their shrewish wives and these

183

women pretend to be so sympathetic just to see what they can get… Miriam treats me like the boring drudge who won't let him have any fun."

"Who's Miriam?" I ask.

"His secretary. He makes her call when he's going to be late. As soon I hear her voice I know he's standing over her and that they'll laugh like they got away with something…"

My father is at the sideboard, hands trembling as he pours a shot. He's changed brands from Haig & Haig to Cutty Sark and from Pall Malls to Kent filters. Sits at the kitchen table with his suit jacket on as if he were getting ready to leave. Licks the white crust of Maalox off his lips.

"What are you going to do about school?" he asks.

"I'll register for the spring semester."

"It's too late," my mother says. "They won't let you back."

"What were you doing over there?" my father asks.

"Working on a case study on a French Jewish family during the war," I say.

"Case study?" my father says with tipsy scorn. That's his rhetorical trick: repeat what you say as a sarcastic question.

Thursday morning there's a letter from Selective Service. *"This is your notice of classification. You are required to carry it with you at all times."* And a new draft card reading 1A…

I've lost my exemption.

"They must have checked to see if you were registered in school," my mother says.

"They'll call you for a physical," my father says. "Then you get a number and wait to be drafted…"

"Remember how long we waited for you, Bennie?" my mother says. "You thought they wouldn't take you because of the Lincoln Brigade."

My father sighs like it's an old argument and they're each going to say the same thing they always say. "They didn't know anything about the Brigade, Stella."

"Your good friend Hermie Summit informed on you to the FBI," my mother says.

"Hermie only knew my *nom de guerre*, not my real name."

My mother turns to me. "Half the party were informers, taking FBI money, it all came out after the war."

"They never would have made me an officer if they knew I was in the Party," my father says.

"You were almost in tears," my mother says.

"I wanted to be in this war," my father says. "I was afraid they wouldn't take me…"

"YOU'LL GET YOURS"

He wanted to get an after school job, but Mom said to wait until the term was over. "Your job for now is to get at least a ninety average," she said. "If you need spending money ask me."

But he hated to ask. Mom's pocketbook was always in another room so she would have to go out and come back, digging in her purse for a dollar or two. Dad would put his hand in his pocket, counting the change, and come up with some coins, lint and tobacco shreds. Once Uncle Sammy was watching and said, "Can you spare it, Benny?" He snapped a five-dollar bill off a gold money clip and stuck it in his shirt pocket. "Here y'are buddy, don't spend it all in the first joint..."

Spring weekends his friends went to Coney Island. You couldn't use your subway pass on the weekends so the kids stood behind the token booth until the train came in and then vaulted the turnstile just before the car doors closed. Some of them had been caught by transit cops and given a Juvenile Delinquent card and he knew if it happened to him he'd be banished to his room for weeks.

To save the carfare he hitched the Coney Island Avenue bus. He and a kid named Harry Cassidy jumped on the back fender and clung by their fingertips to a little niche on the rear window as the bus took off. When the bus stopped they hopped off—hopped back on when it started again. Drivers honked them. People on the street yelled, "Get off whaddya crazy..." Cops rode by, leaning out of their windows, "Get off that bus," and drove on, not waiting to see if they had obeyed. Some bus drivers ran around to chase them. Some stopped short to make them fall off. They hung on, undeterred by stories of kids who had fallen and broken their legs. They let the bus come to a

186

full stop before dismounting, then waited for the whoosh of the closing doors to climb back on. When it crawled in traffic they leaned back and held on with one hand, waving like daredevils to the girls on the street.

They rode all the way down Coney Island Avenue to the boardwalk. The forty cents he saved bought a Nathan's hamburger with fried onions and a frozen custard from the stand next door. They went to Bay 14 where the girls from the neighborhood hung out. Same girls who had played "Spin the Bottle" at the eighth grade graduation party. Rosie Manieri, who had stuck her tongue in his mouth and let him reach under her blouse was lying on a blanket in a one piece bathing suit so tight he could see her nipples and the fresh shaved stubble at her crotch. He called her, but she made believe she didn't hear and turned away as he approached. An older guy with muscles and a Tony Curtis pompadour crunched by him in the sand with franks, fries and sodas and dropped down next to her.

"You playing baseball this summer?" Mom asked next morning.

First day of summer vacation he had always he brought his catcher's mitt to the Parade Grounds in Prospect Park and tried out for a team. In the seventh and eighth grade he'd been one of the big kids. Now he was fourteen in the American Legion league where everybody was seventeen or eighteen and a lot bigger. He knew he'd never get in a game.

"I told you, I wanna get a job instead."

"Not much you can do at fourteen," Dad said.

"Maybe Mrs. Black needs a delivery boy," Mom said. "Go ask her."

Black's grocery was on the corner. Mrs. Black, an old lady in a white apron, sat behind the counter smoking cigarettes and listening to the radio. He walked by the store a few times, looking in the window, but couldn't go in.

Next morning Mom shook him awake. "Get up... I spoke to Mrs. Black. She's got an opening..."

He jammed the pillow over his head. "I can get my own job, Mom."

"When you're thirty, maybe... She says anybody under sixteen needs working papers. It's a New York State rule, probably has something to do

with insurance."

"What do I have to do?"

"Probably pass a physical. We'll go down to the Department of Labor tomorrow."

"I'm not sitting on the subway with my mother," he said.

"A bunch of strangers, who'll know? Sit in another seat. In another car if you want..."

"I'll go alone or I'm not going," he said.

Next morning he bought a Post *at the newsstand. People were gulping coffee, or taking a last drag on a cigarette before going downstairs to the station. He tried to look as bored and pissed off as they did.*

Jammed into a rush hour car. Nose to nose, rubbing against each other. A girl in a tight skirt kept backing against him. Was she doing it on purpose?

The State Department of Labor was in a gray stone office building on Livingston Street. People rushed past him in the swarming lobby. A Post Office cop stood by the elevator twirling his billy club.

"Do I need a physical for my working papers?" he asked.

"Go up to the tenth floor and ask them."

He walked down a dimly lit corridor, past offices with smoked glass doors like in a crime movie. Came to a door with a sign reading State Dept. of Labor. Typewriters were clattering in a large office. A wide-shouldered man in a smudged white shirt looked up from a desk. Cigarette burning in a full ashtray. "What can I do for you?"

"You give the physicals here?" he said.

"The what?"

"Physicals for the working papers," he said. "You give 'em?"

"Who told you that?"

"The cop downstairs..."

"What cop?"

"I don't know, a cop. You give physicals or what?"

The man took a deep drag and squinted at him through the smoke. "Oh yeah sure, we do. Take it easy, kid, haven't had my tenth cup of coffee yet, know what I mean? Rough night..." He got up. "Let's go to the examining room…"

He followed him into a smaller office. Three men looked up from their desks.

"This gentleman is here for his physical," the man said.

"His what?" a man asked.

"His physical for his working papers, Dr. Rothkopf. You wanna extinguish your pipe in a medical facility." He cleared some papers off a desk. "Sit here, sir." Stubbed out his cigarette. "This won't take long. Open your mouth and say Ah…" Pulled his jaw down. "Little wider…" Looked down his throat. "Do you get tonsillitis?"

"I had my tonsils out when I was a little kid," he said

He turned to the men in the office. "It's okay, he had his tonsils out when he was a little kid." The man pried his eyes wider. "Wear glasses? Suffer from pink or wall eye?"

Twisted his head and yanked at his ears. "You've got serious wax deposits, son. Do you use Q-tips? We might need you to come back to check your auditorium canal."

"Auditorium canal?" Dr. Rothkopf said. He rushed out of the office, head down, coughing and sputtering. "You oughta do something about that cold, Dr. Rothkopf," the man said. "Okay, sir, almost done. Face the wall and drop your pants…"

Mom had told him to change his underwear, but he hadn't and now he was scared the stains would show.

"Underwear, too…"

He hesitated. Nobody had ever seen him naked before.

"You want your working papers or what?"

He pulled his jockeys down.

"Hey, Dr. Malin, he's a member of your tribe," the man said.

"Better wrap this up Dr. Mulrain before Dr. Farrell comes in," Dr. Malin said, pointing to the clock.

"Quite right, Dr. Malin. Pull your drawers up son, and go join the work force."

He scribbled a note and folded the paper. "Give this to the nurse across the hall. Tell her Dr. Mulrain said you passed with flying colors and she'll give you the forms."

"You sure that's advisable, Dr. Mulrain?" Dr. Malin asked.

"Sure, sure, she'll approve…"

He walked across to a door marked New York City Board of Health. The office looked more like a doctor's waiting room. A nurse at a desk was putting on lipstick, puckering into a compact mirror.

"Yes?"

"Dr. Mulrain sent me," he said.

"Dr. Mulrain?"

He gave her the note. "He says to tell you I passed and you should give me the forms."

She read it, shaking her head. "Is Dr. Mulrain a big red-faced guy with black hair?"

A chill of suspicion spread through him. "Yeah…"

"Wait here," she said and walked into an inner office, her ass bouncing in the tight, white skirt.

He grabbed the note off her desk. It said: "Lunch, Blarney Castle. Play along. I'll tell you all about it."

The nurse came out with an old man with a droopy gray mustache. Brown spots with little hairs growing out of them on his bald head. He took a gold pocket watch out of his vest pocket. "Nine-fifteen, note it," he said to the nurse. "Did they make believe they were doctors?" he asked.

Make believe?

"Did they touch you?"

That guy who had run out of the office wasn't coughing. He was laughing.

"Well, did they?"

A lump rose in his throat. He was afraid if he talked he would stutter or his voice would crack.

"Do you want to make a complaint against them?" the doctor asked. "You'll have to testify at a hearing…"

And show everybody how stupid he had been? Mom will say it never would have happened if she had come with him.

"We can just tell Mr. Farrell," the nurse said.

"Won't do any good without a complaint. How did you get up here in the first place?" he asked.

"The cop downstairs sent me for a physical," he said.

"You don't need a physical, "the nurse said. "All you need is a parent's consent."

"You're not in mama's kitchen anymore, sonny," the old man said. "You can't depend on others. You have to be responsible for your life."

"Forget it, they're just a bunch of jerks," the nurse said. "Workman's Comp claims, they have nothing to do all day long." She took his arm, a clean, sweet scent rising off her uniform, and walked him to the door. "Go down to the Employment Office on the third floor. They'll give you a form. Fill it out and have your parent or guardian sign it. Then bring it back and you'll be all set..."

The hallway seemed darker now. There were voices and loud laughter behind the office door. They were talking about it. They would tell all their friends, would joke about it for days. Like kids who kept bragging over and over about some crazy thing they had done.

He went to the third floor. The forms were on a table. It was easy, no big deal. That made it worse.

He took the elevator to the lobby, but then turned and got back in. "Tenth floor," he said. The operator gave him a funny look like he knew what had happened.

He went into the tenth floor landing and sat on the steps. He could take one of those ashtrays standing by the elevator and throw it through the glass door. But they were heavy and somebody might see him. There was a stationery store in the lobby. He could buy a bottle of ink and wait until they left for lunch and pour the ink all over the guy's desk. But somebody might catch him.

People brushed by him on the steps laughing like they knew. He could hide here until lunchtime. Jump him from behind, a pull him down by the back of his shirt and kick his legs out, he'd seen kids do that to bigger guys.

Push him down real hard so he cracked his head on the floor. Do it right in front of his friends. And that nurse, too.

More people came running down the stairs. He had to move over out of their way. Must be lunchtime. He opened the landing door for a look. The four guys came out of the office, still laughing about it. He moved back so they wouldn't see him. The big guy went across to the Board of Health while the other three kept walking, laughing. "Maybe she'll like you better now that you're a Doctor..."

He closed the door and waited. Then he heard the nurse: "picking on a kid like that..." And the big guy: "he had it comin', wiseass little Jewboy, you shoulda heard him..."—he made his voice all whiny—"do you do physicals or what?"

He opened the door a crack. The big guy was chasing the nurse down the hall. "C'mon it was just a joke."

"Mean joke... You're a mean guy."

"I wouldn't be mean to you," the big guy said.

"You'll never get the chance."

"Your loss."

She looked over and looked away quickly like she had seen him. "One of these days somebody's gonna get even with you..."

"Never happen," the big guy said.

Her voice got louder like she was talking to him. "Oh yeah, you'll see. That kid doesn't have to worry. You'll get yours."

SHE SEEMS PROUD

February 1963

A newspaper strike is in its third month, none of the seven major papers are printing.

Early morning ice skaters at Prospect Park Lake are horrified to see a decapitated dog, wedged in the ice by the shore. Candle ends are scattered around the head, eyes gouged like in a satanic ritual. Desperate for a gory story the *Brooklyn Eagle* makes it front page news "Brooklynites are terrorized by a maniac haunting the park…"

I've a found a new place to hang out. Cafe Figaro on the corner of Bleecker and MacDougal. Bach fugues in the late afternoon, golden light streaming through the windows. Thunderous Romantic symphonies at night. Village crowd, corduroy jackets, denim work shirts, chess boards, obscure paperbacks on the tables. Boho women, in black with short dark hair, clipped and serious. Poetic blondes, who walk in their own Renoir haze. A cheeseburger and a hot cider with a cinnamon stick buys me a few hours. When the waitress picks up my empty plate I get a coffee and a piece of carrot cake and I can sit there all night.

Been blipless for weeks. Everything will change when I publish my first novel. Those dreamy blondes will make room for me in their soft light.

"You need wheels," Rizzo says "No halfway decent broad'll even look at a guy who don't have a car." We go to a house on Avenue R. Furniture dumped on the street. A pale green '57 Bel Air in the driveway. "Somebody's grandmother died without a will and they're looting the house before the city locks it up," Rizzo says. "Five hundred bucks for this car."

The back seat is ripped, stuffing and springs sticking out. The space for the radio is empty "Take it for a spin," Rizzo says. "Key's on the floor."

The car coughs, rattles and bucks. No heater. Play in the steering wheel. Tires are so worn they drift going around a corner.

"Brakes are squealing," I say.

"They squeal on all Chevys, don't mean nothin'," Rizzo says.

"No radio."

"Go to Mike's Auto, he'll sell ya the one they just stole outta the car... Just kiddin'..."

I try not to show how badly I want the car. "No heater... I'll give you two fifty."

"I can junk it for more than that," he says. "Tellya what 'cause we're friends, four fifty..."

"Three seventy-five," I say.

He wraps me in a headlock and gives me a scalp noogie. "You're a real *hondler.*"

He's too happy. I'm sure I've been taken.

First stop: Earl Scheib's for the twenty-nine-dollar special. I get it painted black. It comes out looking sleek and shiny. Buy a radio from Mike for thirty bucks and I'm set.

No more waiting for a subway, freezing at a bus stop. A new heater burns my feet and nothing else. But the radio works and my life flows to a jazz soundtrack like Belmondo in *Breathless.*

I drive at night, down Ocean Parkway, onto the BQE and across the Brooklyn Bridge. Not a soul on Center Street. Lights are blazing in Criminal Court. Next to it the Tombs, the city prison, windows blacked. Past Chinatown, lanterns glowing in restaurant windows, pagoda phone booths. Left on Canal, right on Sixth to Bleecker. The

Italian funeral home next to the candy store that everybody knows is a numbers drop. A shaggy guy in a pea coat enters the San Remo Tavern and is greeted by every table he passes, girls stepping aside to give him a place at the bar. Must be a famous writer. That'll be me one day. Park on MacDougal in front of the Figaro. In the window I see a tall guy in a black suit cooling out of a black car to a swinging sound track. That's me.

The Figaro becomes my social life. If no one is there I wander the streets of the Village, head down against the icy wind passing it again and again until I see someone I know.

One night Benny slips me a small square of paper with a pink dot in the center. "Pure acid, man, right outta the Columbia lab. Put it under your tongue and keep it there." It sneaks up on me. I'm not giggly, hungry, horny, no brilliant ideas like with marijuana. But the black and white squares on the chessboard are pulsating.

"Chess is about Nature defeating Humanity," I tell Benny. "The pieces are the humans, greedy, petty, slaves to false hierarchies. Condemned to move one way for all eternity, doomed to repeat and die. The empty squares are the universe. In the beginning the pieces invade the pristine emptiness of the square. As the game progresses they are taken off the board. Then, when one pathetic, impotent monarch has surrendered, the battlefield reclaims its emptiness…"

"Sounds like a plan, brother," Benny says.

Dawn on the bridge. A clean, straight road, mist rising over the river. I could squeal to a stop, back up, shift to Neutral, rev the motor, floor it, shift into Drive, lurching, burning rubber and crash through the guard rails. Stay conscious and experience the plunge all the way down into the water. Falling at thirty-two feet a second. I would know what it feels like at the last moment of life. But knowing comes after experience. Knowing is memory, but there is no memory after death. So there is no knowledge. You can't even say "there is" because that implies something. And "nothing" implies absence of "something," but there never was anything… Things deform the beauty of emptiness.

Fucking profound, man…

Driving across the bridge on a winter afternoon. The skyline looms. Tugs and ferries churn furrowed wakes across the river. Traffic snakes down the East River Drive. My heart jumps, I feel the rhythm changing. Exiting onto Chambers Street. Shouts and chants, the occasional low moan of a police car. Daily picket lines around City Hall. Crowds in the hundreds, screaming into impassive cop faces. Civil rights is the issue. Mayor Wagner is the target. They want him to force construction companies with city contracts to hire Negroes and Puerto Ricans or face cancellation. This will force the all-white construction unions to admit minorities.

A coalition of Civil Rights groups calls for a one-day boycott to protest segregation and neglect in the public schools. It seems like just another day in Windsor Terrace, white kids trudging along with their schoolbags. But the schools are closed in Harlem, Brownsville and Bed Stuy, hundreds of kids marching on the Board of Ed in downtown Brooklyn. The boycotters claim they've kept a half million children out of school. Martin Luther King Jr sends an encouraging message.

People handing out leaflets on Bleecker and Sixth. Announcing demonstrations, sit-ins, picketing. "Shut'em down, shut 'em down," they chant, calling for a halt to construction until the unions admit Negroes and Puerto Ricans. Passersby stop for angry confrontations. "Go back to your own neighborhood, you don't live here."

"Heywood Gould!"

A prim little redhead, white blouse, skirt to her ankles…

"Peggy Olson, Mrs. Walde's class?"

Oh yeah, Peggy. Neat and prepared, pencil case and a looseleaf.

"Dorothy Hansen's cousin, remember?"

"Oh yeah, Dorothy. How's she doin'?"

"She just got engaged to Lester Saunders…"

Nineteen and already engaged? Lester, big blonde guy, a few years older, stickball star, hit three sewers. Lived far away on Fourth Avenue.

How would she even know him? My neighborhood, I knew everybody, but I wasn't part of their Christian world.

"Will you join us?" Peggy asks. She's marching with a tall, Black guy who's leading the chants. "Shut 'em down..." Little Italy guys, stocky and square in work shoes with paint crusts or cement dust on their pants. "Fuckin' commie, go back to Russia..." I back off. Don't want to get hit by one of those big calloused fists.

The tall Black guy comes over. "Ray, this is Heywood," Peggy says. Handshake and a hug. "Welcome brother..."

"We're going to picket the Carpenter's Union construction site tomorrow," Peggy says.

"My grandfather is in the Carpenter's Union," I say and feel I have to explain. "He's really a tinsmith, but couldn't get into that union because he was Jewish. The Carpenter's Union was the only one that was integrated. My grandfather had a Puerto Rican guy and a Negro guy on his crew..."

"They were just tokens, man," Ray says.

"My father and two brothers are in the building trades unions that are systematically denying membership to minorities," Peggy says. "I love them, but they represent everything I hate..." She takes me aside. "Can you drive some people to the demonstration on 52nd street tomorrow?" She says it low to spare me from Ray's scorn if I refuse. She's aflame with zeal, but wants to protect me.

Fifty-second Street was the jazz center of the city in the heady days when people were still celebrating the end of the war. Gil Evans had a basement apartment in the neighborhood where everybody came to jam. Music poured out of little clubs between Sixth and Seventh. Errol Garner segueing to Art Tatum to Bud Powell... The clubs are long gone. Now they're demolishing the rest of the neighborhood, the Irish bars, antique stores, drugstore lunch counters; the little retail worlds in the basements a few steps down, which sell old books and records, tell fortunes or alter trousers. Sleek stone and glass office buildings are rising to replace the brownstone rooming houses. The

Time-Life headquarters on 50th was the first, a skyscraper with a famous restaurant on the roof. They're building a block long Hilton Hotel on Sixth from 53rd to 54th. More foundations are being dug all the way down Sixth Avenue to the 30s. Cement mixers and dump trucks. Jackhammers and klaxons. Rusty girders swinging over the street. Workers, thick and surly, going about their work with robotic detachment.

No one will miss a few old bars and junk shops. Or worry about the solitary tenants in the brownstones. Bank tellers, civil servants, school teachers, sales ladies. Pressed suits and starched collars, plain dresses with sturdy shoes for standing long hours. The ones who get to work five minutes early and smoke a last cigarette outside the building so they'll be sure to be on time. Waiting for a seat at the Woolworth's lunch counter, feeding nickels to the machines at the Automat. Hurrying through the dusk with their groceries to make it to their room before nightfall. They're in Gramercy Park, or Chelsea, downtown Brooklyn by the St. George Hotel. The wrecking ball hangs like Damocles' sword over their lives.

I pick up Peggy and her roommates outside her dorm on Fifth Avenue. Flushed, excited, "We were up all night making signs." A dark, sharp-featured girl named Naomi. Thick brown hair parted on the side like a man's, rimless glasses, fierce black eyes. A skinny, cheerful, Black girl named Pam, blinking behind thick glasses. They load stacks of picket signs into the trunk and back and squeeze into the front seat. I'm hoping Naomi will sit next to me, but Peggy pushes in. A cop directing traffic around an accident looks into the car as we drove by. He whistles, and waves. "He wants us to pull over," Peggy says.

I floor it.

"You ran the light," Pam says.

"I'm wanted in thirty-seven states."

Naomi laughs. "I could almost believe that."

They've demolished half a block on 52nd and are digging a deep foundation. Concrete trucks are double parked, buckets turning. A crane is dropping debris into dump trucks, which labor up from the site, gears screeching, wheels spinning. The hard hats are just catching on there's a demonstration forming around them. Kids chanting. "Shut 'em down, shut 'em down."

I park across the street. The girls run out. They're back in a second with Ray, the big Black guy, and a bunch of kids, who grab the pickets. "Okay, form a line, right in front of the driveway," Ray says and walks around the car. "Nice ride my brother. Where'd you steal it?"

I'm flattered that he thinks I'm a thief. "I got it off an old lady who only drove it to church and bingo," I say like it's a cover story.

"See me later. My boy uptown will give you a new plate and paperwork to go with it."

A school bus discharges a bunch of Black and Puerto Rican guys in work clothes carrying signs reading "Bronx Labor Committee..." There are old Commies marching with "Socialist Workers" signs. Kids from Columbia, NYU... A group of ministers, black and white. East RiverCORE, NAACP, Catholic Worker, Jewish Labor Committee. They are milling on the narrowed sidewalk under the scaffolding, chanting "shut'em down, shut 'em down..." The workers are gathering by their trucks, looking at each other like they're waiting for a signal.

"These guys are just trying to protect themselves and their families," I say to Ray. "Maybe we should explain that we're not trying to take their jobs..."

"But we do want their jobs, brother," Ray says. "Revolution is about the transfer of power from the ruling class to the workers."

"But these guys are workers, too."

"White workers are tools of the ruling class, man. Reactionary by inclination. That is why the intelligentsia must wage the revolution..."

A police bus comes down the street, followed by a paddy wagon and a fleet of radio cars. Another bus speeds the wrong way down this one-way street. Cops jump out with billy clubs.

"Every pig in the city is here," Ray says. "We could stick up Chase

Manhattan and get away clean."

A curly-headed kid in a work shirt comes running up. "We've gotten people to lay down on the driveway in front of the trucks," he says. He challenges me. "You comin' with us, man?"

"My car'll get towed if I'm busted," I say.

"That's a cop out..."

"No, no, he's right, we need his car," Ray says. "See if you can find a space under the highway on Eleventh, brother."

I watch from behind the wheel as Peggy and her roommates join hands with some other kids, a few ministers and an old lady from the Jewish Labor Committee. They lie down across the driveway, singing "We Shall Overcome..." A dump truck backs up from the foundation, it's bed full of crushed rock. It stops a few feet from their heads, gears whining. Is he going to drop his load on them? A cop with gold braid on his hat races across the street, followed by a squad of cops, holding their holsters as they run. Ray and the curly-haired kid are egging on the picketers. "Shut 'em down, shut 'em down..." The cops pick up the protesters by their arms and legs and carry them, singing, to the paddy wagon. "We shall overcome one day..." A cop drags a Black kid, his head bumping on the sidewalk.

They have Ray bent over the hood of a police car, cuffing him. The curly-haired kid is walking along the line, shouting himself hoarse. "If we don't work, nobody works..." A hardhat bolts out of the crowd and slams him with a straight right so hard we can hear the thump. Blood spurts out of his nose and he goes down on his ass. Tries to get up but his arms buckle and the back of his head hits the road with a crack.

A cop bangs my windshield with his club. "Move on, nothin' to see."

Another night in the Figaro. A guy at a table, cashmere jacket with an ascot, like the students in Paris. Takes off his gloves to shake hands, European style. Joe M. Works as assistant makeup editor for the *New York Post*, putting the paper together every day. The 114-day newspaper strike just ended and they're looking for copy boys.

"I don't have a degree. I dropped out of college to go to Paris."

"The managing editor's wife is French. Write him a short letter. His name is Al Davis."

I've got one dose of acid left. Should I drop it before I write the letter? Remember what Charley Parker said: *"Any musician who says he is playing better either on tea, the needle or when he's juiced is a plain straight liar."* I go home to my room, close the door and open the Royal Portable. Out comes a torrent of high school pretension about how I was destined to change the world through the noble calling of journalism. Oh shit, just tell the truth. I quit college and escaped to Paris to be a great writer. Ran out of money and came home. I'm a mortician's assistant but I really want to work for the paper I've been reading all my life.

A week later there's a small envelope with the *Post* letterhead. My letter has been jammed into it. There's a scrawled note under my signature: "Interview, Davis," and a card reading: *Leonard Arnold Personnel Manager…"* Tuesday 10:30."

The *New York Post*, 75 West Street, across from the Hudson piers, West Side Highway thundering overhead. Leonard Arnold is a gray-templed, horn-rimmed pipe smoker in a brown suit in a small office in the Classified Department. He glances at my letter.

"Your undertaking services might be needed," he says. "People drop dead in the city room all the time…"

"Glad to be of help," I say.

"You say you've been reading the *Post* all your life?"

"Every day."

"Tell me the names of three sports writers."

I give him the whole department, including Jerry De Nonno who handicaps the horses. He slides me a one-page application. "You start at eight tomorrow morning. You're on probation for thirty days. If you're hired the union will see to it that you make fifty dollars a week for the rest of your life. The rest is up to you."

I go out to Brooklyn and announce, "I got a job as a copy boy on the *Post*."

My father, at the sideboard, repeats: "Copy boy. How'd you get it?"

"Wrote a letter. They wrote back and gave me an interview."

My mother looks worried. "Did you lie about college?"

"What was in this amazing letter?" my father asks.

"Oh just how it would be an honor to work for the paper I'd been reading all my life. And some biographical stuff. It wasn't very long."

"Long enough to show them what a good writer you are," my mother says.

She seems proud.

AND GAVE HIM A NICE WARM HUG

Brooklyn, 1944

The store was hot and smelled like the doctor's office. Ladies in bathrobes were walking around with shiny paper in their hair. Aunt Rae had a big green can on her head with wires coming out of it. "Look who came to visit," she said, holding out her arms.

"Are you sick?" he asked.

"See how he worries," she said. "No, darling, I'm making myself pretty to visit Uncle Bernie on his army post."

"Sit still, Rae, you wanna catch on fire," a lady said. She had a blue dress like the lady in the doctor's office.

"Where's he stationed?" a lady under a can asked.

"Fort Dix. You have to take two buses. They look at you like you're a prostitute and make you to show your marriage license at the gate..."

"And meanwhile the real prostitutes bribe the MP's and go right in," Mommy said and the ladies laughed... "That's the Army for you..."

"Where's Benny?" a lady asked Mommy.

"He was at Belvoir, but he shipped out last week," she said. "He thinks the Philippines."

"How long's he been gone?" the lady in the blue dress asked.

"Two years now. He was six months in California so we never got to see him..."

"Well, you've got your little man to keep you company."

Mommy hugged him hard. "Yes, he takes good care of me..."

Bubbe was in the kitchen pouring soup into glass jars, and putting a "holly" bread in her bag. "Can you stay by yourself while I walk Bubbe to the subway?" Mommy said.

"Where are you going Bubbe?" he asked.

"To Coney Island to take care of Tante Annie. They had to cut open her stomach to take out her gall bladder."

"Mama please, you'll upset him," Mommy said.

He walked down the hall with them. But as soon as they closed the door he saw a big man standing near the kitchen waiting to cut his stomach open with a big knife. He scrunched in a dark corner by the door so the man wouldn't see him. When Mommy came in he hugged her legs so tight. "There's a man going to cut my stomach open."

"Where?" She laughed and bent to kiss his head. "What an imagination..." She picked him up and carried him to the coat rack. "See, it's just Aunt Rae's jacket hanging. Look, now I'll take it off... No more scary man..."

In the morning Mrs. Ackerman was in the kitchen stirring a pot with Bubbe's big wooden spoon. "Hello cutie pie, ready for breakfast?" Mom came in dressed for her job. "Mrs. Ackerman's going to stay with you while Bubbe's with Aunt Annie." She looked in the pot. "You can put in some mashed banana to make it sweet..."

"I make Cream of Wheat for my grandson Maxie every morning," Mrs. Ackerman said.

"Don't forget his cod liver oil," Mom said.

"I'll give him, I'll give him..."

"Put a little water in his orange juice so it won't burn his mouth. And a splash of coffee in his milk to warm it up, with a little sugar..."

"Go already, Stella," Mrs. Ackerman said.

He walked Mommy to the door. She hugged him with her nice smell. "I'll be home early sweetheart and we'll have franks and beans and chocolate chip cookies, okay. Go, I'll wait until you're safe in the kitchen before I leave..."

Mrs. Ackerman forgot to give him his cod liver oil. She put a big spoon of sugar in his Cream of Wheat. It was cold with bumps in it. She stood over him and shook his shoulder. "Eat, it's good for you." She gave him cold milk with no coffee. It made his stomach hurt like when he couldn't make. She put the radio on, loud. All the people laughing. She was laughing, too, but looked at him mad. "Go play…" He ran so fast one of his slippers fell off, but he was afraid to go back down the hallway to get it. He hid behind the bed with his rifle like the soldiers in the movie. Through the glass door he saw Mrs. Ackerman sitting in Bubbe's chair and eating candies out of her candy dish. Walking around the room picking things up. He looked at his book about the ducklings and the policeman with the big fist who helped them cross the street. Turned the pages over and over…

Mrs. Ackerman opened the door. "Look who's come to play…"

Maxie was blinking and coughing with all the green sick stuff coming out of his nose. He got afraid again. Maxie always jumped and yelled to make him run away. Tried to pull him off his bicycle in the park. He put his soldiers on the bed, facing each other, but Maxie pushed him and made shooting noises "boom, bam." Threw the soldiers up in the air and banged them on the floor.

He sat on his bed and looked at the duckling book to feel better. Maxie picked up his ball with clowns on it so he raised his hands to play catch like he did with Mommy. Maxie threw it hard at his head. It didn't hurt so he threw it back in Maxie's face. Maxie cried and the red boo boo stuff dripped out of his nose. Mrs. Ackerman came in. "You play too rough," she said. And squeezed his shoulder to make it hurt. She took Maxie's hand. "Come Maxileh, you want a cookie?"

He put his soldiers back in the box and hid in the closet. It was nice in the dark. Nobody could find him. He stayed until he heard Mommy and Mrs. Ackerman calling. Mommy sounded scared, too. "Was he upset about something?" she asked.

"Maybe an upset stomach from all the cookies," Mrs. Ackerman said.

He scrunched in a corner under Aunt Rae's big black coat. Mommy was in the bedroom, calling him, "where are you?" He jumped out. "Boo!"

Mommy laughed with a happy look and picked him up. "I thought you had run away to join the Army. Mrs. Ackerman says you ate all the cookies we were saving for dinner."

"I didn't eat cookies," he said.

Behind her Mrs. Ackerman shook her head. "Look how young they start to lie..."

After Mrs. Ackerman left Mommy looked at his lips and smelled inside his mouth. "Did you have fun with Mrs. Ackerman today?"

"She hurt my arm when Maxie came to play," he said.

Mommy looked like she was going to cry. "Oh darling, I'm so sorry..." She hugged him and smoothed his hair. "Mrs. Ackerman won't come here anymore. Now let's get some more cookies for our special dinner..."

He liked the franks all smooshed up with beans. Mommy cut off the hard part of the bread. She gave him apple juice and cold water from the ice box. Sat close, her arm around him. "Just eat a little fruit." And fed him sweet peaches from the can...

The doorbell was ringing. "Who can that be?" Mommy said. "Maybe Bubbe came home early... Be right back..."

But she didn't come. She was at the door, talking to a man in the hall. "I got the price of admission," he said.

"Just for a second," Mommy said. The man had a brown face and shiny black hair and was dressed up like the men in the magazines. He took a can out of a big bag "Ta da," he said.

"Is that real coffee?" Mom said.

"Didn't I tell ya?" the man said. "And there's more where that came from..." He took out another bag... "Five pounds of filet mignon, prime... And this, five pounds of hotel butter, not margarine..."He gave her a big box. "And here's Hershey Bars for the little prince."

"Black market?" Mommy said.

"What do you care?" He gave her some tickets. "Ration cards, real, not phony..."

"So you're a goniff now," Mommy said.

"Every family should have one, especially in war time." He gave Mommy a big white cake box. "Babka. Your mother will love it..."

"To what do I owe the honor?" Mom said.

"I saw your sister in the street all dolled up to see her husband. She told me your aunt was dying in Coney Island. So, as the officer in charge of morale on the home front... "

"Every yente in the building will know you were here..."

"Nah, I went to the roof next door. Came down the stairs. I can leave by the fire escape."

"You know all the tricks."

"But I only play 'em for you..." He gave him a candy bar. "You like chocolate, Slugger?"

Mommy took it away. "It'll keep him awake... This is Morris, a friend of daddy's..."

"Are you in the Army, too?" he asked.

"The Army doesn't want me," Morris said. "I had a sick heart when I was a little boy like you..."

"Spare him the diagnosis," Mommy said.

"I don't want him to think I'm a draft dodger... Or you, neither..."

"Show Morris your pictures and your soldiers, sweetheart," Mommy said.

He walked down the hall to the table with the army pictures. "This is Daddy and Uncle Bernie. And Uncle Sammy with his friends on the tank..."

"I know your Daddy," Morris said. "I knew your mama, too, when she was a little girl. And not such a little girl," he said loud like he was talking to Mommy.

He took out his box of soldiers and lined them up on the supper table. Morris put the big guns behind them. "This is your artillery," he said. He moved the tanks up and put the soldiers behind them. "The tanks go first and the soldiers follow them." He put the Jap soldiers behind the fruit bowl and under the tablecloth. "The Japs are hiding. We have to shoot a lot and bomb them. Do you have any airplanes? I'll get you some... Is it alright if I bring

207

the kid some toy planes next time?" he called.

"What next time?" Mommy called back.

The kitchen had the good coffee smell like in the morning. Mommy gave him a little piece of Morris's cake with some chocolate in it. Morris put his arm up on the table. "Wanna arm wrestle? C'mon, pull my arm down to the table." Morris's hand was big. He pulled it so hard his arm hurt. "Oh, oh, I can't hold on," Morris said. He made a face like he was trying hard. "I can't beat this guy." And his hand slammed on the table. "I give up, you're too strong for me," Morris said.

"No I'm just a boy, you're a man," he said.

"Smart kid, can't put anything over on him," Morris said. "Like his mother…"

"Say good bye to Morris," Mommy said.

They walked to the door. Morris tried to kiss Mommy's hand, but she pushed him out. and closed the door loud. "Okay, that's over with," she said. "What book should we read tonight?"

"The one where the policeman helps the ducklings cross the street." he said.

"That's my favorite," Mommy said.

He woke up in the nighttime. So black he couldn't see his room. So quiet. But there was a squeaky sound like someone walking. Whispers like the bad people on the radio.

The floor was so cold. The shade was over the door like when he had to take a nap in the day. He ran fast to Mommy's room and pulled hard on her door. "Mommy, Mommy…" He heard her. "Oh God, he's awake…" The door opened and Mommy ran to him in her bathrobe. Behind her he saw the man get up from her bed with a big knife.

"Are you okay?" Mommy said. She picked him up and carried him fast into his room. She wasn't wearing her long sleeping dress and her hands were cold.

"Is that scary man here?" he said.

"Yes, but don't worry, I'll chase him away right now. Just stay here nice and safe…"

Mommy closed the door so loud. He heard her in the big room fighting the man. "Get out!" she screamed. The man was talking, but Mommy screamed again so mad it made him scared and try not to cry. "Get out. Get out! Get out!"

Mommy came in. "It's okay, the scary man is gone." She carried him back into the big room. "See, nobody here," she said. She walked down the hall. "Nobody in the kitchen. Nobody by the door…"

"He's in your room," he said.

"Well, let's see." Mommy carried him into her room. "See, nobody's here… Wanna climb in with me?" Her bed was warm with her nice smell. She got in next to him and put the covers tight around them. "Just the two of us," she said. And gave him a nice warm hug.

HE'S IN THE MOVIE, TOO.

April 1963

Can't wait to get to work. Sleepless in the dark, heart pounding. Normal morning routines of washing, shaving and dressing seem to go on forever.

At eight in the morning I walk up the subway steps onto Rector Street. I feel like I'm in a newspaper movie. Yellow *New York Post* trucks roar out of the garage with the first edition. Pressmen wearing paper hats trudge across Washington Street to the Exchange Bar for a shot and a short beer between press runs.

Run up to the second floor three steps at a time into the city room. Big and noisy like a railroad station. Smoke curling at the ceiling. Phones ringing, people shouting, rushing in and out of the composing room. Grimy windows, always closed. Radiators clanging out steam heat. Hallways are freezing, ice floes in the toilets, but they say it swelters in the summer. Typewriters clacking, voices calling "Copy!" Dayshift people brush by me with their coffees. Night rewrite guys come out with their papers, looking for their bylines.

The *Post* turns out seven new editions a day, each timed to a delivery schedule or to the closing of the stock market. Urgency ramps as the next edition is readied for press. Breaking news is updated, new stories, new headlines, new pages, new front page, even if the story hasn't changed. Rewrite men toss their stories to city editor, Johnny Bott, who does a quick read, raises the story over his head and calls "Copy!" Just like in the movies. I grab it like a baton in a relay race and walk two steps to hand it to the news editor, Jack Blaylock, who redesigns the pages for the next edition and hands the stories to the copy readers for editing and headlines. Then a copy to Al Davis, the managing editor and Paul Sann, the executive editor. (They read every story that goes in the paper.) Between editions the copy goes in a pneumatic tube to the composing room. On deadline they call "Copy!" and I grab the story and the headline and run it out to the linotypists. Later I'll run edited proofs, trims, new leads, adds and last minute rewrites to the printers.

The paper is put together on the dark factory floor of the composing room. Rows of linotype operators drop burning hot type into trays, which go to compositors to place in forms and on to stereotypers to make into molds and down to the pressroom where presses roll out inked sheets, which are then put together and sent by conveyor belt to the mailroom where mailers assemble packages for delivery, tied with twine and dropped down a chute to the garage where drivers load their trucks and speed out to newsstands all over the city.

In the mailroom I pick up a hundred copies of the latest edition for distribution to the city room. The mailers are thick-lipped and leering, look like they come from the same demented family. "Send that copy girl down here, the one with the big tits." (That girl, Phyllis C. tells me "they're all talk, they can hardly look at me...") Upstairs to the columnists' floor. Max Lerner, liberal pundit, a dwarf with a leonine mane of white hair. Gossip columnist Leonard Lyons, another Jewish midget with a gigantic nose who looks like a Nazi poster. James Wechsler, famous for his defiance of Joe McCarthy, red suspenders, bottle of Heaven Hill bourbon next to his Underwood. Earl Wilson, gossip columnist, out all night he sleeps during the day. His assistant Gene is yelling on the phone like Tony Curtis in *Sweet Smell of Success*. Elevator to the penthouse office of publisher Dolly Schiff. Perfunctory smile from her blonde secretary. Quick shot of Dolly in an office papered with photos and plaques. White-haired lady, German-Jewish banking money. Teetering on flamingo legs. Across the hall to the treasurer, Robert Gray's office. Movie star handsome, Robert Taylor style, rumored to be the latest in a long line of Dolly's lovers, which include FDR. Grab the elevator back to the city room. More pencils to sharpen, more "books" to make—three pieces of copy paper, sandwiched between two carbons. Out to a dark corner of the composing room to the proofreaders, white-haired, pink-faced old men, in vests, bent under lamps, in green visors, cuff guards to protect their white shirts. They find typos, errors in spelling, punctuation and grammar errors in stories that have been read and reread by three sets of editors. Never a word of greeting. Never see them in the luncheonette downstairs or the bars where everyone goes when the day is over. A bunch of Bartelbys. Never see them arrive or depart. Maybe they never leave.

Four morning papers. *The Wall Street Journal*, the business paper, never see anybody reading it on the subway. *The New York Times*, the paper of record, you can believe every boring word. *Herald Tribune*, the paper of feature writers, Tom Wolfe, Jimmy Breslin; can't believe any of it, but it's fun to read. *The Daily News*, paper of the people. Two million of them line up outside candy stores and newsstands every night at eight waiting for the first edition, but not for its scathing right wing editorials, witty headlines or crack police coverage. They want the "handle," the last three numbers of the amount wagered at the track that day to see if it matches the number they bet for a five hundred to one payoff.

Two other afternoon papers, *The World-Telegram* and *The Journal-American*, each strongly identified with its loyal readership—conservatives for *The Telegram* and Hearst right-wingers for *The Journal*. I ask Oliver Pilat, City Hall reporter why, in a solidly Democratic town, all the papers except the *Post* are Republican. "The unions make people vote Democrat, but they think Republican," he says.

The liberal *Post* won't poach any readers from the right-wing papers. The goal is to be smarter and better. The worst thing is to be beaten by another paper.

I make hundreds of books and stack them for the reporters. Sharpen hundreds of two H pencils. They quickly lose their points and become like crayons. No editor will use a smeary pencil that is half its length so I drop the stubs in a glass and resharpen a few hundred more. After a week the blisters on my thumbs and forefingers are so bad I need double Band-Aids. After a month I can light a kitchen match on my calloused fingers to amuse my friends in the Figaro.

I run up to the library—it's only called the "morgue" in the movies—to get "clips" for the reporters doing research. Rows of filing cabinets take up most of the floor. Envelopes bulging with stories, yellow, crumbling to the touch. Three librarians working full time, cutting newspapers and magazines apart and adding to the collection. Happy little guys clicking long, shiny scissors. Human repositories of information, can't stump them on names or dates.

The paper is divided between the New York boys who started as copyboys and the old pros, who have knocked around as itinerant reporters. Ted Poston, tall, professorial, horn-rimmed glasses, covers civil rights, anger barely contained between the dispassionate lines of his stories. One of the first Black reporters hired by a major newspaper, he has been with the *Post* since 1936 and was an adviser to FDR during World War II. Gene Grove, worked on all the big Ohio papers; Norman Poirier, French Canadian from Kerouac's home town Lowell, Mass., worked around New England; Paul Capron, West Point grad, wears the puttees of a World War I Calvary officer, worked and drank his way across country several times, picking up jobs on small town papers along the way. They're the elite. Only the best reporters get to work on a New York paper.

Among the ex copyboys: Al Ellenberg, who gets sly jokes into news stories, looks like a kid's eighth grade graduation picture; Pete Hamill who writes eloquent features like one of the tough Irish kids in the schoolyard; Anthony Scaduto who covers crime and police like

Clark Kent looking for a phone booth.

Each reporter has a unique typing style. Grove, long legs crossed, suit jacket on, like he just dropped in. He's famous for writing a story in which the first letters of every new paragraph spelled out F-U-C-K-Y-O-U-B-I-T-C-H. Scaduto, pipe clenched, coiled over the typewriter like a cat ready to spring. Stan Opotowsky, looking upward for inspiration, like a piano virtuoso, fingers flying over the keyboard. They never seem to be thinking. Write as fast they can type, clean copy, no typos. Could I ever be that fluent? It takes me two hours to write a postcard.

The most important departments in the paper are entrusted to junior reporters. The TV listings, the first and only page many readers turn to, are put together by Bill B., a young, effusive guy from North Carolina, who works out of a cubicle by the coatroom. He was a copy boy for years and when the former TV editor died (nobody seems to retire), he inherited the job. I am amazed at his cheerful efficiency. He assembles the daily listings and edits a page of feature stories every day, writing up interviews, choosing photos. Meanwhile, he is compiling the coming week's schedule for the Saturday paper, writing a feature for the weekend entertainment section and rushing to interview some TV celebrity. He's starstruck, the perfect guy for a puff piece because he loves the people he's writing about. He's self-effacing, almost apologetic, and takes an anxious breath before he crosses the city room to hand his copy to the editors.

The *Post* 's famous sports page, which goes out all over the country, is put out by another junior reporter—night sports editor, Vic Ziegel. Downtrodden, abused by the editors—Al Davis once called him a "fat, four-eyed, depressed, bald-headed Jew," he prowls the empty sports department in perpetual motion, checking the wire machines, answering phones, running back and forth to the composing room. From twelve to eight he edits the stories of all the beat reporters, writes headlines, lays out pages, chooses photos, writes roundups on all the games and boxing matches, rewrites wire stories, assembles box scores and racing results. He's the complete newspaperman. Like Bill B. he put in years as a copyboy before he got this job and will have to wait years until someone retires or dies before he gets promoted to covering a team.

The bosses come in at five in the morning to put out the first edition. Davis, managing editor, was famous as an investigative reporter with scores of scoops to his credit. Paul Sann, executive editor, quit school at seventeen and has been working for the *Post* ever since. Johnny Bott, city editor, crippled from a childhood bout with polio, coffee in a jelly jar, chewing on a cigar holder. News editor Jack Blaylock has a tremor, not from booze or Parkinsons, but the constant abuse he gets from Davis, who sits a few feet away, yelling, "play that bigger, hurry up, that's wrong…" He waves a piece of yellow paper lined with six columns where he has laid out the stories. We run that out to the composing room so the compositors can reconfigure the pages. Blaylock passes the copy over his shoulder to Fred McMorrow, called the "slot man," because he sits in a slot in a round table in command of five editors. A heavy, perspiring redhead, eternally hungover, he chews on his Guardsman's mustache, occasionally yelling "Copy!" and raising a plastic cup, which we fill at the water cooler and bring back to him. He slides the copy to an editor who writes a headline that fits perfectly over the story.

Davis was appointed managing editor when his predecessor, also thirty-six, dropped dead at his desk. Death on the job is part of *Post* folklore. There's the famous story of Dexter Teed, a reporter who staggered drunk into the city room and slumped over, dead, at his typewriter. He was covered with newspapers and a rewrite man started to write his obit, yelling, "Get me the clips on Dexter Teed." In my time I will see Mark S. a hugely fat news editor, droop, head on chest. After a few minutes with stories piling up, a copy boy will have the nerve to shake him and cry out, "He's not sleeping, he's dead." Sidney Zion, a reporter will be wheeled out on a gurney after passing out. "Don't hold up the paper," he'll call. Ike Gellis, the sports editor, rigid with a stroke, will be buckled into his chair and wheeled downstairs to an ambulance. A proofreader will go down with his head on the desk. A pressman will be hit by a truck. There will be several heart attacks on the toilet. "That happens a lot," I'll say, and the other copy boys will laugh, "How do you know?" until Davis who hears everything that's going on in the city room will holler from his desk, "He was an undertaker..."

Sann, short and trim with a dark green shirt that looks like an army blouse, iron gray hair, strides through the city room, cowboy boots knocking on the wood floor. Davis, goggling behind thick glasses, hunches and hurries, chewing on the wet stub of a fat cigar, spitting shreds as he talks. At five in the afternoon, after the Final Market with Wall Street's closing prices has been shipped out, I'm sent to the liquor store on Washington Street for Beefeater Gin and Boissiere Vermouth. One day the owner tells me, "We're out of Boissiere, call 'em and see what they want." I remember the Martini and Rossi umbrellas in the Paris cafes and bring back a bottle. Davis explodes. "Copy boys aren't allowed initiative, go back and get Cinzano." As I run out, Joe Kahn, a star reporter, looks up from his typewriter to commiserate. "If you had brought back Cinzano he would have sent you for Martini and Rossi..." I run both ways, come back in a sweat. Davis and Sann have the first of many martinis. Sann laughs a little louder, Davis's face gets redder. He looks angry, but it's just the booze.

By six, the city room is empty except for a few reporters working on overnight features, Mort Shiffer, the night city editor, is there to call the bosses if some huge story breaks. A janitor wearing surgical gloves and a cap folded out of newspaper wheels a huge trashcan, dumping the leftover lunches, containers, ashtrays, IN and OUT trays, sweeping scraps, lids, butts, tear sheets into a dust pan. One bent old Black guy to clean up the careless droppings of a hundred and twenty people. He's in the movie, too.

THEN EVERYBODY WILL GO

May 1963

Writers drink, drop acid, get psychoanalyzed, drive themselves crazy trying to find the philosopher's stone. But the secret is right there on the newsstand.

Who? What? When? Where? The first line of every newspaper story is also the first line of every masterpiece.

Dostoevsky: "On an exceptionally hot evening early in July a young man came out of the garret in which he lodged…"

Cervantes: "Somewhere in La Mancha in a place whose name I do not care to remember a gentleman lived long ago."

Kafka: "When Gregor Samsa awoke one morning from unsettling dreams he found himself in his bed transformed into a giant insect."

The *Post* is an afternoon paper, which means it has to find fresh news in stories that were already reported. These are called "second day leads." They can be as simple as continuing the story—"Detectives descended on this narrow street in Greenwich Village looking for clues to the murder of…" to adding a feature twist—"Elizabeth J… came to New York looking for a job in fashion. Her search ended in a garbage can in a tenement basement…"

So engrossed in the form, I'm missing the content. The world is erupting out of those neatly structured paragraphs. Civil Rights is the big story. Freedom Rides, demos, sit-ins, lawsuits to compel integration. Students in Birmingham, Alabama are attacked by police dogs, high pressure hoses and club-wielding cops. Mild response from JFK; he is trying to keep segregationist Southern Democrats in the fold

217

for the next election. Martin Luther King Jr. denounces his civil rights initiatives as "tokenism."

In the northern cities the struggle is to improve the public schools and integrate the craft unions. Busing kids to the all the white schools is bitterly resisted. Parents demand more control of their schools. The Teachers Union is hated by right and left.

Anger everywhere, black and white, worker and hippie, cops and radicals. Black guys spit as I walk by. I remember my grandfather telling me, "In the old country we would spit when we passed a church." Scuffles on the streets, people turning to curse each other. Cars screeching to a halt, doors swinging open, as drivers barrel out, screaming threats. Lurching junkies, sprawled in the cold, nodding in the park, clawing at their faces, cramming sugar packets into their mouths. The subways are a horror show. Muggers find easy pickings in women alone, elderly workers in empty cars. Crazies acting out. Hostile drunks bashing each other with wine bottles, pulling kitchen knives.

I'm a "camera eye," like Dos Passos. Observing without reacting. Turning everything I see into a news story. Shrieks jolt me out of a subway doze. A naked guy is waving his dick at a cowering girl. Heroes pushing him away, I sit there, composing: "A naked man running between the cars caused havoc on the GG train yesterday." On the D an elderly woman jabs at me with a hat pin, screaming, "Women should not be touched..." I sidestep, noticing the *Watchtower Magazine* in her satchel. "Passengers scattered on the D train yesterday as an elderly female Jehovah's Witness screaming 'women should not be touched,' pushed through the rush hour crowd wielding a foot long hatpin." I'm impatient with literature. Long expository paragraphs, explanations of character and motive. I understand Hemingway's trick: write fiction like a news story.

Max Lerner sends me upstairs to the library for copies of *Life Magazine* going back to January '61. *Life* along with *Time* and *Fortune* is a right-wing Luce publication not read in my house so I've only seen it in barbershops. It has a cover photo of two American soldiers and a company of Vietnamese with the line: "We are in the midst of a raging, tearing controversy about our role in Vietnam..."

Lerner is discovering the war, but *Life* has been covering it all along. As far back as October '61, its cover shows an American soldier training for jungle warfare, captioned, "Vietnam, our next showdown." Another *Life* from January '63, has a photo of Vietnamese soldiers guarding Viet Cong prisoners on a boat in a swamp and is captioned: "We sink deeper into the Vietnam War..."

Everybody is afraid of the Hydrogen Bomb, three-headed-babies-in-the-ruins kind of war. They thought it might start in Berlin. Or Cuba. But *Life* magazine knew in '61 that it would be in Vietnam and now the world is catching up. A reporter somewhere calls it "the little war that just sneaked in." All of a sudden there are sixteen thousand "military advisors" in Vietnam. Kennedy has increased the draft call. Only married men will be exempt except in time of national emergency. Then everybody will go.

"...THE PRESIDENT OF THE UNITED STATES IS A DOUGHNUT"

May 1963

The wire room is so narrow I can stand in the middle and touch both walls. So small I can make it from end to end in two jumps. Lined on both sides with AP teletype machines, printing out stories, sixty words a minute, International, National, State and Local. The same machines that were installed in 1943, during World War II, each with a different colored paper so the editors can see at a glance what they're getting. The *clackety-clack* and the bright *ding* of the bells drowns out the racket in the city room. The paper comes out of a box in fifty-pound rolls under the machine. Stories fly off so quickly that they have to be torn off or the paper will bunch under the overheated machines. A copyboy was fired when a mountain of copy burst into flame and the city room had to be evacuated.

It's an oven, over a hundred during the summer, so the other copy people are glad to let me cover it. I love to stand over the machines, watching the words appear, the story take shape. The job involves a modicum of news judgement—the wire room copy boy decides which stories to bring to the editors. The decision is made easier by the bells that ring with every story the AP deems important. When URGENT is printed a few times across the page you tear the story off the machine in "takes," run it out to the city desk and run back as the next take comes off the machine. Bring a useless story and you'll get a calm rebuke from Bott, the city editor, "I don't need this." But the foreign editor, Arthur Hurwitz, under pressure from Davis, frantically pasting tear sheets together to make a story, will crumple a pile of useless copy into a beach ball and throw it at you "Get this crap out of here!"

Events are overtaking each other so quickly that the machines are in constant URGENT mode, bells ringing, editions being changed, front pages being "replated" in mid press run.

Martin Luther King Jr. and Malcolm X are following each other around the country, giving speeches, radio and TV interviews, meeting with students and local leaders, engaged in a running debate. King is in Detroit, telling 25,000 civil rights marchers that the "Negro and his white allies recognize the urgency of the moment..." Saying he has a dream about white and black joining hands, quoting the Bible— "justice will roll down like waters, and righteousness like a mighty stream..." A few months later Malcolm tells a rally in Detroit, "I don't see an American dream, I see an American nightmare," and predicts that "every effort to force integration upon the white man or to force the so-called Negro into the White society... will meet with bloodshed and destruction."

King has allied himself with pediatrician Benjamin Spock in the Ban the Bomb movement, saying, "I am a strong believer in disarmament and suspension of nuclear tests... It's not a choice between violence and non-violence, but non-violence and non-existence." Malcolm disdains any alliance with whites for any cause. "We don't have time for the white man," he says. He wants to carve a Muslim country out of thirteen southern states. "We're for separation, not integration."

In early June the URGENT bells start ringing for a new crisis. Buddhist monks have gathered in Hue, South Vietnam, to protest discrimination by the ruling Diem family. Soldiers pour tear gas chemicals on their heads, blistering their faces and lungs. Photos of the writhing monks in orange robes, smiling soldiers standing over them, appear all over the world.

Diem, a dogmatic Catholic, has taken a vow of celibacy and is quoted as saying, "Christ has come to the south." He has banned

Buddhist flags and all emblems of Buddhism and put Christians in positions of power. It is revealed that the US supported the Diem family's military coup and abrogation of free elections, that the US has been financing ARVN, Diem's army since 1961 at a cost of a million dollars a day. When Buddhists protest in front of the Government House in Saigon, Diem's soldiers open fire and kill ten. A week later Quang Duc, a monk, sets himself on fire on a busy street in Saigon to protest the shootings. "A homunculus in a fiery womb," somebody writes. Self-immolation has been a standard method of Buddhist protest for centuries. "Before closing my eyes to Buddha," the monk had written, "I respectfully plead to President Ngo Dinh Diem, asking him to be kind and tolerant toward his people and to enforce a policy of religious equality."

David Halberstam of the *New York Times* is the only reporter on the scene and scoops the world with an eye witness account. AP photographer Malcolm Browne gets a photo of the monk's body curling like a piece of charred paper in a ball of flame. JFK acknowledges: "No news picture in history has generated so much emotion around the world as that one."

The Buddhists claim that Quang Duc's heart remained intact in his incinerated body, making him a *bodhisattva*, or an "enlightened one." But Madame Nhu, Diem's sister-in-law, mocks the immolation as a "barbecue," and invites more Buddhists to immolate, saying, "We will clap as they burn." US diplomats say she "is a dragon lady," and the true ruler of South Vietnam. She has closed bars and brothels, public performances, dances, banned opium smoking, criminalized adultery. Photos of her in clinging satin, slit to the thigh, plunging neckline, teasing smile. A sexy zealot.

Viet Cong guerrillas, supported by Communist North Vietnam, Russia and China, have routed a South Vietnamese Army division, equipped and trained by the US. Kennedy is sending "advisers" to help the Diems, adding to the sixteen thousand American troops already on the ground. Questions in Congress about our support for the Diem regime.

URGENT bells on the A wire. Alabama Governor George Wallace has vowed to stand in the doorway of the University and block entry to two Negro students, a mild-mannered boy and girl, neatly dressed, who want to integrate the all-white school. The burning Buddhist is banished to the back pages as Kennedy tries to arrange a compromise and is attacked by the South for his tyranny, the liberals for his vacillation. Forced to act, Kennedy calls out federal troops. Threatened with arrest, Wallace backs off and the students enter. More URGENT bells as Kennedy makes a stirring speech, acknowledging the hundred-year injustice against Black Americans and declaring that, "no American will be free until every American is free." The next night Medgar Evers, head of the Mississippi NAACP, is gunned down in his driveway. Civil rights leaders and liberal politicians hurry south for his funeral. Malcolm X refuses to attend, saying, "When I go to Mississippi it won't be for the funeral of a Black man."

Kennedy embarks on a fence mending tour of the Southern states. Plans to meet in Dallas with John Connally, Governor of Texas. But that story is bumped when he makes a surprise appearance in Berlin, scene of Cold War standoffs with the Russians. "He'll go anywhere to get George Wallace off the front page," Davis says. Kennedy stands in front of the wall dividing the Communist East from the West and declares to an audience of hundreds of thousands *"Ich bin Eine Berliner."*

An argument at the copy desk. "Should have said *Ich bin Berliner,* I am Berliner," says Danny Goldberg, a survivor born in Germany. "A *Berliner* is a doughnut made in Berlin. When he said *Ich bin Eine Berliner* he was saying I'm a doughnut..." McMorrow disagrees. "He's using the article *eine* as emphasis. The people are cheering. They know what he means." Danny won't relent. "They're laughing because the President of the United States just called himself a doughnut."

"THEY MAKE FUN OF EVERYBODY"

August 1963

Everybody's organizing trips to the March on Washington. Signs on the trees in Washington Square Park for buses, vans, cars. A kid giving out leaflets from the Socialist Workers Party. "D.C's gonna be the place to be..." Malcolm X is leading a Nation of Islam contingent. "Just to show white people what will happen if they don't listen to Mr. King," he says.

I walk from the deadline frenzy of the *Post* to the serene, Bach-inflected world of the Figaro. Smudge marks on my forehead and ten copies of the paper I do the movie newsboy bit, going from table to table, "Extra, extra read all about it... Paper, mister?" Figaro chess players are oblivious. Excitement swirls around them like rapids around a mossy rock. The hipsters turn to the Sports page. "Only thing in this paper worth reading since Murray Kempton left..." There is a table of older guys, threadbare suits, cigar holders, who gather for chess and espresso. Their Mittel European accents confer authority. They speak with knowing cynicism about the March. King is the "acceptable insurrectionist," someone says. "Religious agitators always stop short of social change. Look at Christ..."

"Who are these guys?" I ask Burt, the night manager. "They teach at the New School," he says. "The tall guy is married to the woman who wrote about Eichmann."

Peggy rented a bus for the March and is trying to fill it. "Chip in what you can," she tells me, but gives back my ten. "Five'll be fine." We meet at six a.m. at the Port Authority. Naomi runs up. "Am I late?"

Her thick brown hair is tied in a bun. Skinny with long, graceful fingers. Tight turtle neck, her breasts seem to rise over her ribs and end under her shoulders. I try to sit next to her, but someone brushes by me, "excuse me, brother..." It's Ray, Naomi is saving a seat for him in the back. Two Black guys behind me: "Is Ray hittin' that?" Peggy pats a seat next to her. "Sit here." Four hour ride. We sing "This Land Is My Land," and "We Shall Overcome" over and over until I tell her, "This is how they brainwashed the prisoners in Manchurian Candidate..." She laughs and looks at me fondly.

Buses are backed up on the off ramp leading to the city. "They say there's a million people here..." Marshals greet us at the staging area. "Make sure you know the name and location of your bus so you can find it on your way back."

Groups push in to get closer to the Lincoln Memorial. Ray turns to a crowd of kids in high school jackets. "Anybody got a good arm here?"

A few "yeahs..." " I'm a pitcher..."

"Think you could pitch a grenade up there and blow Abe's head off?" Ray asks.

Laughter. "Yeah, I could..."

Picket signs, school jackets, union caps. Mostly black people, pushing us aside. "It's their thing, we shouldn't be here," I tell Peggy. "We need white people," Ray says. "Stop 'em from firing into the crowd." Naomi laughs. "They see you with a white woman, they'll shoot you down like a dog..." He jumps back in mock alarm. "Shit, baby, you're right..." Throws his arm around her. "But you're worth it."

Snatches of songs and speeches, echoing off the PA. Caught in the surge like in a breaking wave. Folk singers. Peter, Paul and Mary sing "If I Had a Hammer." Bob Dylan is on the platform. Joan Baez sings a song in honor of Medgar Evers. I have the jazz fan's horror of folk music, but Peggy loves it. "The folk song is the purest expression of the people's will," she says.

"It's bourgeois pop," I say. " How about some jazz guys? Miles would be too cool to come, but they could get some of the old-time blues guys. Did they ask Louis Armstrong or Count Basie? Duke Ellington comes from D.C... Maybe some rock and roll guys, too, like the Coasters. The Dell Vikings are an integrated group... Just no white guy whining about blowing in the wind..."

"It's his struggle, too," Peggy says. "It's everybody's struggle. We're all making history today."

I hear a familiar name—"Rabbi Joachim Prinz—" and push past Naomi. "He hears Rabbi and all of a sudden he's interested," she says to Ray.

"The most urgent, the most disgraceful, the most shameful and the most tragic problem is silence," Prinz says. Polite applause. His words break up and drift away. Somebody announces, "The Reverend Martin Luther King Jr..." A roar. The milling slows. People shouting to King. His voice comes over loud and clear.

"I am happy to join with you today in what will go down in history as the greatest demonstration for freedom in the history of our nation..." The crowd is stilled... "Five score years ago when President Lincoln signed the Emancipation Proclamation..." A million people are on tiptoes... "I have a dream..." It's what they've been waiting for. Some cry and answer... Others hang back, shyly. But soon the rhythm of the cadences affects them all. Peggy is jumping, waving her arms... "I have a dream..." The same speech he's been making all over the country. "Great God Almighty I'm free at last!" The crowd roars as one.

Peggy clutches my arm, tears streaming... "Isn't he wonderful?"

People on the mike urge everyone to disperse peacefully. Back at the bus Ray is talking to Naomi. "Man's got power. He coulda had all them people about-facin' and marchin' on the White House..."

"Maybe he will someday," she says.

"Never happen," I say, playing the hardboiled anarchist. "The civil rights movement is about incremental compromise within the status quo…"

Ray squints. "Say what?"

"Incremental compromise within the status quo, Ray, pay attention," Naomi says.

"King's strategy is to make the power structure take baby steps until he's walked them into a new reality and there's no turning back," Peggy says to me, like she's talking to a child.

"Religious agitators always stop short of social change," I say. "Look at Christ…"

"Christ?" Ray says. "How did he get into the act?"

"On a white donkey, didn't you see him?" says Naomi. They walk away, laughing.

Peggy pats my hand. "Never mind them, they make fun of everybody…"

SHLEPPING STIFFS

October 1963

The Viet Cong is overrunning villages in the South. The AP reports they have killed eighty American "advisers." In a nationally televised press conference, JFK reiterates his intention to support the South Vietnamese. "What helps to win the war, we support; what interferes with the war effort, we oppose. We are not there to see a war lost."

I step into a vacant storefront and light up before work. Marijuana is not good for repetitive tasks. I freeze at the sharpener, pencil poised, forget why I'm there.

The bosses eat the same breakfast every morning. Davis gets a buttered roll, cottony dough pulled like excelsior out of its center, and fresh squeezed orange juice with no pulp or seeds. Saul, in the downstairs luncheonette grumbles, "I have to drop everything for him?" as he squeezes OJ through a strainer.

Sann gets Instant Sanka, black—he doesn't want it brewed—"well done" rye toast with cream cheese. Saul puts it back in the toaster for another minute to get it well done and scrapes off the burnt parts. Sanka smells vile and tastes like my Grandmother's Postum. The cream cheese sits like a sooty slush drift on the brittle rye toast. Sann bolts it down, coughs out the burnt bits and lights a little cigarillo. How can he eat this disgusting shit and then smoke that stinky cigar? His mouth must taste like a garbage can. He looks up, one morning, and catches me in full revulsion. "Why don't you try another breakfast?" I say. "An egg sandwich or something…"

Sann's assistant, Pete S. is up before he can answer and grabbing my arm… "Get over here…" Walks me down the hall away from Sann's desk. "What do you care what he eats?" Shoves me into the wire room. "Stay here. Don't let him set eyes on ya or ya won't make it through the day."

The AP machines are ringing like crazy, literally shaking… URGENT: DIEM UNDER SIEGE…

I rip the copy out of the machine and run it to the city desk. Bott takes a look and waves it. "Give this to Paul." I run to Sann's desk. "Diem attacked." He grabs the bulletin and runs out to the composing room to change the front page.

Reams of copy are curling out of the wire machines. Breaking news: URGENT DIEM DEPOSED… "South Vietnamese President Ngo Diem was toppled in a military coup today…"

DIEM FAVORED CATHOLICS… BUDDHISTS CHEER… LODGE SURPRISED BY COUP… "Henry Cabot Lodge, American Ambassador expressed shock at the coup that deposed President Ngo Diem, today…"

KENNEDY WARNED DIEM… "The [Diem] government has got to get in step with the people, if they are to win the war in this very essential struggle," the President told Walter Cronkite."

DIEMS FLEE SAIGON… "Sources are reporting that Ngo Diem and his brother, Ngo Nhu have fled the Presidential Palace through a secret tunnel…"

The AP is sending photos of the Diems. Madame Nhu in a slit dress. Monks on fire. Davis stands over Opotowsky as he types one paragraph "takes" at breakneck speed and the copyboys rush them out to the composing room.

And then just as the paper is about to go to press a flurry of bells announces another URGENT BULLETIN: DIEMS ASSASSINATED… Diem and his brother are found dead on the floor of a church in the Cholon district of Saigon. What does this mean to the war effort? Will the North attack the South? Who will take over in South Vietnam?

I'm exhilarated. This is where I want to be, middle of everything. Then a cold, dark, plunge into depression. I blew it. Shot off my marijuana mouth to Sann. They'll fire me. I'll be back at Riverside... Shlepping stiffs...

"WE BEAT THE WORLD!"

November 22, 1963

The union won't let them fire me. They'll just ignore me, pass me over for tryouts. Blame me for every mistake until I quit.

Week before Thanksgiving. The city's pulse slows. People yawning on the subway. Christmas lights going up in Brooklyn. Salvation Army Santas, ringing bells. The papers run holiday features. Who's giving out turkeys? What movie star will be serving oldsters or disabled vets? What ballplayer will make what polio kid's dream come true?

JFK has begun televising his press conferences live. Declares his "object" is to "bring Americans home" from Vietnam.

Leonard Lyons has an item about Joan Crawford, in Dallas with her husband Alfred Steele, Chairman of Pepsico, for the annual convention; Richard Nixon is the featured speaker. Dallas cops have posted a twenty-four hour guard outside the Steeles' hotel suite to protect Joan's multi-million dollar jewelry collection.

JFK is arriving in Dallas to host a fund raising luncheon. Crawford is an old friend of Joe Kennedy Sr., the President's dad, but she's also a loyal Republican and smiles sweetly when asked if she'll attend. "I don't think so..."

I am addicted to Sauls' grilled cheese, bacon and tomato—he puts mayo on the sandwich before he grills it. I like it with a light coffee, three sugars and a Winston to finish it off. I'm licking the hot mayo as it oozes out of the bread when I hear the URGENT bells on the "A" wire going crazy in the wire room.

231

Rudy, the composing room foreman, always calm and unhurried, strolls into the city room. "When we gonna replate?" he asks.

"Why?" he's asked.

"Because the President's been shot," he says, turns around and strolls back.

There are three of us, standing by the city desk, but Bott looks accusingly to me: "Who's covering the wire room?"

No time to wipe the mayo off my face. "I'll check..." It's Mike W., a pothead from Syracuse, who's always late and complaining about how hard the easiest chores are. He's head down on the table in the executive conference room, sleeping it off. I run into the wire room. Every machine is shaking and ringing, copy curling on the floor. I find the first bulletin:

PRESIDENT KENNEDY WAS SHOT

Rip it off and run it into the city room. "President's been shot..."

Sann vaults his desk.

I run back for the second take...

"AS HIS MOTORCADE LEFT DOWNTOWN DALLAS... MRS. KENNEDY GRABBED HIM SHE CRIED..."

Davis slams down the phone. "Johnson okay? He was in the follow car with Ladybird..."

I run back as the next take comes off with Jackie's quote.

"OH NO..."

I run back...

REPORTER JACK B. ASKED KENNETH O'DONNELL, THE PRESIDENT'S ASSISTANT IF HE WAS ALIVE. NO ANSWER...

"Where is he?" Davis asks.

"PRESIDENT TAKEN TO PARKLAND MEMORIAL HOSPITAL..."

Davis: "Do we have a stringer in Dallas? Don't bother with the hospital or the cops... Call the Catholic Church. Ask if they're giving last rites..."

Now that the first bulletins have been sent the AP starts putting together a story.

PRESIDENT KENNEDY AND TEXAS GOVERNOR JOHN CONNALLY WERE SHOT FROM AMBUSH TODAY IT WAS NOT KNOWN IF EITHER OF THEM WAS KILLED.

Mike W., is rubbing his eyes. "What happened?"

"President Kennedy was shot," I say.

"Shit! Fuck! Are they pissed?"

They wheel in a TV. "Put on CBS," Davis says. Stan Opotowsky is writing the story. I run in a correction. "Three shots fired, instead of two..."

Davis is riffling furiously through the wire copy. "They say he was face down on the back seat, covered with blood, but still breathing..."

Circulation manager comes in. "What are we gonna do?"

Sann has to decide whether to run a front page declaring KENNEDY SHOT or wait until we find out he's dead. The other two afternoon papers are facing the same dilemma. If they call the President wounded and he dies they'll be peddling old news. If they declare him dead and he lives it will be the worst journalistic blunder of the century. If they delay the press run the other papers will be out with KENNEDY SHOT. Even loyal *Post* readers will buy the other papers.

I run back to the wire room. No arrests, no suspects. A Secret Service man threw Lyndon Johnson on the floor of his limo and sat on him. Opotowsky hasn't stopped typing for a second.

I'm watching the machines. The President is in surgery. Connally in critical condition.

Then the bells start again:

TWO PRIESTS WALKED OUT OF THE EMERGENCY ROOM AND SAID THE PRESIDENT WAS DEAD...

Sann comes back from his desk with the new headline: JFK SHOT TO DEATH.

Editorial has done its job. Now the rest of the staff has to work as quickly. Linotype operators, compositors, mailers, drivers. The whole cumbersome process of putting out an edition has to function at top speed to get the papers to the newsstands before the competition.

I'm running copy out to the composing room, dodging people like a half back. Sann and Davis laugh. "Run 'em over, kid," Sann says.

I run down to the mailroom for the new edition. Headshot of Kennedy. Big, bold Roman font on the front page, screaming JFK SHOT TO DEATH. "Wrap one in cellophane," a mailer tells me. "It's gonna be worth plenty one of these days…"

We get a photo of Lyndon Johnson being sworn in aboard Air Force One with Jackie looking on. It goes inside the paper. No one wants to touch that historic front page.

"Go home," Davis tells me. "Come back at four a.m."

We're on the street with JFK SHOT TO DEATH. Everyone is buying the *Post*. The other papers, with their old news, sit untouched on the stands.

Back home, the Lenvins, old friends of my parents from DC, are up for Thanksgiving. In the living room, coffee cups and ashtrays, watching Johnson arriving at the White House.

"Kennedy needed a Southerner on the ticket," my father says. "But everybody was surprised that Johnson took the job. He had less power than when he was Majority Leader and now he's President."

"He's been strong on Civil Rights," my mother says.

Still high on the excitement of the day I give them copies of the *Post*. "This is the absolute latest…"

They read, shaking their heads. Mrs. Lenvin dabs at a tear… "Poor man, he was under such pressure."

"We got the whole paper out in fifteen minutes," I say. "I was running back and forth, adds, new leads, corrections. This rewrite man, Stan Opotowsky, you never saw a guy write so fast… The story flows like a poem…"

Awkward silence. My mother is shocked by my bragging, embarrassed in front of her friends. "It's a terrible day for the country."

I know. I'm supposed to nod, gravely and echo the pieties. But I can't contain my glee. "We beat the city, Ma. We beat the world!"

"CARRY THEIR LUNCH IN A PAPER BAG"

Hectic weekend, the story changing every hour. Lee Harvey Oswald, arrested for shooting a Dallas cop, is now charged with murder. He declares his innocence to reporters. "I didn't shoot the President."

Reams of detail coming out of Dallas. Who is this guy Oswald? Commie? Right-wing nut job? Double agent? Every trickle of info makes us desperate for more.

Sunday morning Jack Ruby shoots Oswald in Dallas Police Headquarters. A photo so perfectly captures the moment that it looks like a staged movie scene. Even the hardened newspaper guys are stunned. And then suspicious. "What's goin on down there?" Ruby owns a strip joint, knows all the cops, has been linked to the Chicago mob. Visited Cuba...

Eddie, at the switchboard, has been hanging up on crank calls for two days, but this one seems real. "I've got a guy on the line who says he knows Oswald's probation officer in the Bronx..."

This is almost laughable. "Oswald was in the Bronx?"

"Must have roomed with Trotsky," Danny G. says.

I fill out my time sheet, putting in for forty extra hours at triple time. F. gives it back to me. "Put in for straight time," he says. "Don't make money off a national tragedy..."

Chuck Caruso, the make-up editor, comes out of the composing room, his white shirt smudged with type. He's in charge of getting the page layout right, making sure the newest leads, adds and corrections are on the pages. A sallow, beardless, moonfaced guy with sad beagle-brown eyes and a waddle walk. "Who can drive me to Brooklyn? I wanna get to the bar before last call."

"I'll take you."

On the way he quizzes me.

"Where ya from?"

"Seeley Street..."

"Oh yeah around Prospect Avenue... You know Danny Marino?"

"He's the toughest guy in the neighborhood..."

"He's a lot more than that. Know Johnny Boy Columbia?"

"I know his little brother, Andrew. They own a fish store."

"They own a lot more than that. Yankee fan?"

"I hate the Yankees."

"Just checkin'. Like the Rangers?"

"I don't follow hockey..."

"Best sport in the world..."

The tunnel toll is thirty-five cents. Caruso gives me a dollar. "Tell him to keep the change..."

"Never saw anybody tip a tunnel guy," I say.

"Toughest job in the city. Two hours on patrol in the tunnel, breathin' gas fumes. Some drunk hits a wall, cars speedin' around a curve and you gotta stand there with your hand up, stoppin' traffic, hopin' some other drunk don't run into you... After four hours you switch off to the toll booth. Have to touch all that dirty money. Slobs, blowin' their nose, wipin' their ass. Some people put dog shit or piss or snot on the money for a gag. Throw the money at ya or throw a slice of pizza or a Trojan or just drive through, give ya the finger. Drunks try to pull you outta the booth"

"That would make a great feature," I say.

"Here's another one: Night counter guy at the Rikers Diner on 45th. Go there at four in the morning. You gotta deal with bums and drunks and psychos. Pukin', brawlin', junkies nodding in the bathroom, tryin' to beat the check... All for a dollar an hour..."

"It could be a series," I say. "The hardest jobs in the city…"

"Bank it for when you're a reporter and lookin' for a story on a slow news day."

"I'll never be a reporter. Sann doesn't like me."

"He thinks you're a wiseass… There's worse things…"

He's looking out the window, watching me in the reflection. He's in the news meeting every morning. Did they say something about me? Is he trying to tell me something?

"Pull over, we're here," he says.

A no-name bar under the El on MacDonald Avenue. "Park in front," Caruso says.

"It's a pump…"

"We don't get tickets."

Dingy joint. Small bar, a row of booths. No juke box, no flashy girlfriends, no cops. Just tough guys talking quietly. TV showing the news, but nobody's watching.

"Don't they care about what happened?" I ask.

"Only if they can make a dollar out of it," Chuck says

The bartender looks like Skipper at the Caton Inn—sleeves rolled up on his white-on-white, Gold Rolex, ruby pinky ring… Chuck hands him a paper and he goes right to the Sports page. "West coast tracks stayed open through all this… Degenerate horse players don't care about nothin'…" Pours Seagrams Seven in a glass and squirts in a splash of cola for Chuck. "What can I getcha?" he asks. My father keeps a case of J&B in the hall closet. "J&B on the rocks," I say.

"Know what the nice people call J&B?" Chuck asks me. "Jewish Booze…"

"Nice people?" Is that their name for mob guy?

"Everybody thinks it's because Jews drink it at Bar Mitzvahs," he says. "It's 'cause Jewish bootleggers make it in basements. See that guy over there?" Puts his finger against his chest and points toward a booth… "The little guy with the Dodgers jacket? They call him Slivovitz Sam. Makes plum brandy for the Polish trade in Greenpoint

237

and Riverhead..."

"My grandfather drinks Slivovitz."

"It's kosher for Passover. Made with fruit only. The nice people trust Sam because he did time and didn't give nobody up. They got a special mechanic who builds him a still in an empty store next to the Silvercup Bread plant in Williamsburg. The bakery smell masks the smell of the alcohol. You need tons of sugar to make alcohol and the Feds are always watching the wholesale market to see who's buyin' in bulk so Sam sends runners, kids like you, out to supermarkets. Buy out the five-pound boxes, leave a few on the shelf for show, pay cash, case closed. Hundreds of pounds makes ten gallons of pure alcohol..." Leans in and lowers his voice... "They got a guy in the Domino Sugar factory who ships them a truckload every coupla weeks when he can chisel enough outta the inventory. They drive the alcohol to a garage in Little Italy where they cut it and add color and flavoring like they did in the old days. J&B is popular so they knock it off and Sam makes it taste like the real thing. They got a bottle factory in Queens and a print shop that runs off any labels they want..."

"I thought they stopped bootlegging after Prohibition," I say.

"They just started," he says. "Counterfeiting all these name brands. Distributing to all the bars and restaurants. It's a million dollar business..."

"How do you know this stuff?" I ask.

"These guys talk to me. Everybody wants to tell their story."

"You should be a reporter."

"Too much pressure," he says. "I'm good where I am."

"Hey Baby Gould!"

It's Rizzo! Pinching my cheek so hard he almost pulls me off the stool. He's wearing a black and white checked sports jacket, green silk shirt, blue stone pinky ring, horn-rimmed glasses... "Where ya been, ya bum? Big shot newspaper guy now, too good to visit your friends? Your father's real proud of you. I told him you should write my life story..." Gives me a noogie that makes my eyes tear. "Tommy boy, give these bums a drink..."

Caruso watches Rizzo go back to his booth and turns to me.

"You know this guy?"

"He's a hearse driver at Riverside."

"That's just his cover job to show income." Lowers his voice. "He's big. He buttons 18th. Avenue for Don Giovanni..."

Rizzo who always has a piece of swag jewelry wrapped in tissue paper. Who sells steaks out of the trunk of his car on Friday. Who brags about his sexual escapades. Plays the buffoon, the butt of jokes and accepts the ridicule without complaining.

"You think these guys are Bogie in a dinner jacket?" Chuck says. "This is a way of doin' business that goes back to Sicily. Simple guys who don't draw attention. Live in a small apartment with the same old wife. They do more business in a day than Rockefeller does in a month. Go to the same corner or park bench every day. Carry their lunch in a paper bag..."

"DON'T EMBARRASS US"

January 1964

Amazing how quickly news goes stale. JFK had three front-page years. Bay of Pigs, Cuban Missile Crisis, Berlin Wall, Freedom Rides, University of Alabama, March on Washington, killing of the Diems, war in Vietnam. All these momentous events have receded into memory. Even the assassination is pushed to the inside pages by the arrest of Oswald, which is then chased by the mystery of Jack Ruby.

In a speech to the Congress Lyndon Johnson reminds the country that he's stronger on civil rights than Kennedy.

"I urge you again," he says, "...to enact a civil rights law so that we can eliminate from this nation every trace of discrimination and oppression that is based on race or color..."

Check the mail every day. Nothing from the Draft Board. Have they forgotten about me? Did the building burn down?

The bloom is off the rose. The job I once rhapsodized about has become unbearable. Same maddening routine. I no longer compare the papers coming off the press to fresh baguettes, warm from the oven. Can't wait to light up after work and go to the Village.

Some of the copy people are talking about trying for jobs with small town papers like the Bergen Record or the Middletown Journal and working their way up. But that could take years and stories about pancake breakfasts and high school football won't impress big city editors.

John C. tells me that *Newsday*, a Long Island paper, is looking to expand its New York coverage. I write to City Editor Arthur G. A few weeks later I get a printed form, scheduling an interview. I call in sick and take the railroad out to the *Newsday* offices in Garden City, a cloistered white enclave in the ethnic shambles of Queens. The city room is small and calm compared to the sprawling chaos of the *Post*. Sunlight sparkles through squeegeed windows onto blue metal desks. Young, neatly dressed reporters tap at new Royals.

I'm sent to a cubicle. Arthur G. short and thick with a shock of comb-breaking white hair, Marine Corps tattoo on his forearm, takes off his glasses, squints and tilts his head. "We've met before…"

"Don't think so…"

"We definitely have…" Suspicious look at my resume. "Brooklyn College. Class of '61?"

Got that lie covered. If he checks I'll say I had to complete a few courses and was a January grad.

"Worked rewrite at Agence France Presse in Paris… Not much use for French around here," he says.

"Maybe at the UN," I say.

"I don't think you'll be covering international diplomacy for a while."

Still glaring like he's trying to figure out how he knows me. "

"Ever have a real job?"

"I worked at Riverside Chapel in Brooklyn," I say.

Snaps his fingers. "That's where I saw you. My father-in-law's funeral. You were saying the prayer for the dead…"

I'm going to hear it now. Like Mamanna says: "an undertaker never gets compliments, only complaints."

"My father-in-law was the only survivor of a Nazi massacre of his village in Galicia," G. says. "He kept a record of every Jew, where they lived, what they did, what happened to them and their families. Wrote it with a nub of pencil on a piece of torn shirt and carried with him through the war, in the forest with the Polish Home Army, DP camps, in a hospital where he almost died from sepsis…"

Was this one of those funerals where the guys broke me up? Or the family caught us popping lit cigarettes out of our mouths?

"The Israeli Consul brought that piece of torn shirt all the way from Jerusalem," G. says. "Survivors came from all over. The head of the Milliners Union. Abe Stark, Borough President of Brooklyn. But the manager wouldn't let anybody speak... You mumbled the prayer so fast like you were trying to get it over with."

"You're commanded to say the prayers as quickly as possible," I say.

"But not skip words. Not rush through the service. Speed through traffic, the hearse driver going through red lights..." His voice breaks. "You desecrated a hero's memory."

I can only manage a lame excuse. "We had to get to the cemetery before it closed."

"As long as you're here..." He flips some copy across his desk. "You've got fifteen minutes..."

Not much point in taking the test, but I look it over. A cop was shot on Thursday, his assailant arrested in a shootout on Friday and arraigned on Monday. The trick is to start with the arraignment and work backwards.

Shit, I can do this. I'll show him what he's missing.

I write a vivid lead: "Emmett Waters confronted a blue wall of rage in a Suffolk courtroom today as he was dragged cuffed, bruised and screaming defiance to be charged for in the cold-blooded execution style shooting of Patrolman Dennis O'Hare last Thursday.

"A hundred of the slain officer's fellow officers watched in angry silence as Waters, a career criminal, was denied bail by Justice Stanley Shackleton and put on a 24-hour suicide watch..."

The rest of the story is a recap of the facts. I try to write clean like the guys at the *Post*, but strike words and sentences, writing corrections in the spaces above them until the page is like an abstract drawing of crossouts, arrows, scribbles in the margins.

"Expect me to read this?" G. says. "What's a blue wall of rage?"

"It's the cops," I say. "I explain it in the second paragraph."

"Then say it in the first... What does cold-blooded mean? That he was shot by a frog?"

"I guess it's a cliche," I say.

"It's worse than a cliche, it's meaningless. 'Blue wall of rage' is worse than meaningless, it's nonsense..." A look of disgust. "Slain officer's fellow officers? Never repeat a word in a paragraph, you did it twice..." Reads a little more, shaking his head. "Adjectives are only for movie reviews and cooking columns..." And then like he hates to say it: "But it's got a sense of drama. What are you doing about the Army?"

I lie without blinking or thinking. "I'm in ROTC..."

"Take a writing class... You'll hear from us..." And points to the door.

Head down, drenched in flop sweat. I was so confident while I was writing this shit. "Blue wall of rage?" Seemed like a great metaphor. "Cold-blooded execution?" One of those automatic phrases you just write without thinking.

Friday afternoon I'm leaving after the last edition. Davis screams, "Gould!"

Quiet in the city room. Everyone's gone home. Davis is wrestling with a jar of olives. Hands it to me. "Open this, my hands are wet..." Twist the cap as hard as I can. Moment of panic when it doesn't budge. But finally a click as the vacuum is broken. The cap spins off spills olive juice on my pants.

"Arthur G. called me for a reference," Davis says. "I told him you were a heroin addict."

Can they fire me for applying to another paper?

"Think you're ready to be a reporter?" he asks.

"I won't get any readier sharpening pencils," I say

"Own a suit?" Davis asks.

"Yes..."

"Wear it on Monday... You're going on the street. Don't embarrass us."

AND I DIDN'T HELP THE HORSES

I'm on tryout. I have to break a big story in thirty days or I'm back to being a copyboy.

Everyone is at their copy tasks Monday morning when I show up in my black suit. I've leapfrogged people who've been waiting years for a tryout, but no one seems to mind. Eddie at the switchboard, "Good luck..." Mike W., sharpening pencils, bleary from the weekend, "Go get 'em man..." Only Mike B., the clutzy sports copy boy, comes at me with a vindictive smile.

"This is just a trick to get rid of you. I heard Davis say you were a disloyal wiseass. They'll give you a month and then flunk you out."

I find a desk in a corner and sit behind a paper, hoping nobody will notice me.

"Where are you hiding, Gould?" Bott calls. Gives me a press pass in the shape of a badge with my name typed on it. "Go over to the police shack and keep Artie company."

The shack is a two story "taxpayer" on Broome Street behind Police Headquarters that houses the press offices of all the papers and wire services. Most of the beat reporters are old timers, who watch the police ticker and alert their papers to a big story. Only the *Daily News* has a real bureau, three full-time reporters, who have secret connections to the cops. The *Post* has a desk with one chair and a phone. Artie Rosenfeld, the senior man, has been covering police for forty years. Remembers the Lindbergh kidnapping, the Lucky Luciano trial. He carried a gun during World War II in case he came across Nazi saboteurs in the Bronx. Never leaves his desk. Never takes his fedora off, although he will push it up past his hairline on hot days.

The ticker is spitting out reports of murders, muggings, fires, sit-ins, anti- and pro-war demonstrations, tenant strikes, racial conflict, drug busts, gruesome murders. Everything looks Page One to me...

"Bank robbery in the Bronx. Guy slipped the teller an envelope. Got away with seventeen hundred and fifty dollars..."

"We get two or three of those a day," Artie says. Gotta have a fatality to make the paper."

The fire bell rings. The beat guys can tell by the number of rings where the fire is and how serious. "Sounds big," I say. "Toastin' marshmallows," says Artie.

A body floating in the East River, another under a tree in Crotona Park. A shirtless guy with a cleaver threatening people outside Macy's. "Here's something different," Artie says. "Police horse hit by a cab in Madison Park. It'll be a feature if he dies..."

On the 4 train I'm writing the story in my head. Grief-stricken cop wants to fire the fatal bullet for his fallen equine partner of many years.

Gray and drizzly. A huge chestnut stallion is lying in a maroon puddle in the middle of Fourth Avenue, traffic crawling around it. Its foreleg is bent under it, a piece of bone protruding. A cabdriver, old guy in a Florida windbreaker with palm trees and birds, is giving a statement to a cop. A sergeant in a patrol car, talking on the radio. "Cabbie was speedin' to make the light on Fourth Avenue. Hydroplaned in a pothole, lost the wheel and hit the horse. Officer taken to Manhattan General with a possible broken leg..."

"What's gonna happen to the horse?" I ask.

"They'll take him to a guy in Jersey who puts old police horses out to pasture..."

"Bullshit," somebody mutters behind me. An old Black guy with a floppy newsboy hat. "They stand the horse up in a narrow pen and shoot him between the eyes with a .22 rifle. Sell the meat to Canada and overseas. Use the blood for glue. Hooves, tail, every part until there ain't nothin' left. Horse is worth more dead than alive."

"But they have to kill it with a broken leg," I say.

"Cop's got a broken leg, they ain't gonna kill him," he says. "They don't wanna say he's so old, probably twenty, his bones just broke under him so they'll say he got hit by the cab…"

"Did you see it?" I ask.

"I seen enough workin' at Belmont for twenty-seven years. Happens to people, too. Ever see an old lady walkin' on the street go down like her leg buckled? They don't shoot her with a .22, do they? Give her a wheelchair."

He's got a heckler, another old guy using a shopping bag as an umbrella. "They can't give a horse a wheel chair."

"They can tape him up, wait'll he heals, give him somethin' for the pain…"

"Horses don't feel pain," the heckler says. "Jockeys whip the shit outta horses…"

"They wouldn't whip 'em if they didn't feel it," the old man says. "Try whippin' a cow, she'll moo in your face. Horses got thin skin. That's why they don't make horse skin coats. They know the only way to stop the whip is to run faster. Look at his nostrils, all wide, ears flattened. He's screaming inside, but won't show pain while there's people around. Look in his eyes. He knows he's gonna die today."

I call Nathanson, assistant city editor. "This is a cover up. An old guy in the park who used to work at the track says they work these horses until they collapse."

"Go to the hospital and talk to the cop," Nathanson says. "Get the horse's name and age. See if you can find out how many police horses there are on the street, their average age. Find out what happens when they can't work anymore. Call the SPCA, I'll bet they know about it."

I go to the Emergency Room. The cop is in surgery, they tell me. Won't give out his name or condition. I call Headquarters. They tell me to speak to the Mounted Unit. Call them, but the Captain is gone for the day.

I call the Nathanson. "Couldn't find anybody," I say. "I could paint a picture of the scene. The dying horse, the wise old race track guy..."

"But it won't help the horses," Nathanson says.

The city room is empty when I get back. I write a dynamite lead: "A police horse lay dying in Union Square yesterday and life went on around him..." New paragraph: "Traffic was rerouted and passersby stopped for a quick look before going on their way. The dying horse watched with glazed, impassive eyes..." The story flows with no corrections until the last portentous sentence: "He knows he's gonna die today, the old man said." I stare at these words, transfixed by their understated beauty. Hemingway couldn't have captured it better.

Next morning I run to the newsstand. There's a photo on the front page, a high shot like it was taken from the top of a car. The horse is lying on the street, surrounded by cops. The overline reads: FREDDIE'S LAST RIDE... Look at it again and realize: Schmuck! It's the *Daily News*. They beat my understated beauty to the streets with the official police version.

"Sad story, huh," the newsstand guy says. He thinks my moan was sympathy for the horse. It's for me. If I had called the SPCA I would have had a story to go with the photo. But I was more anxious to show what a great writer I am. So I got spiked. And I didn't help the horses.

"MY OWN MOTHER BETRAYED ME"

February 7, 1964

"Be invisible," the anarchists say and I'm trying. No bank account so Jack, the shylock in the *Post* composing room, cashes my paychecks. No legal residence. Benny's cousin Iggie is the super in a building on Barrow Street in Greenwich Village. He rents me a sub-basement for $53, plus $15 to use his phone and hook up to his electricity. It's gloomy and the pipes sweat and mice are humping in the makeshift shower, but I'm next to the boiler room so it's warm in the winter.

"Don't let nobody know you live here," Benny says. "They'll change your draft board. Nobody enlists in the Village and all the rich kids get shrink notes that they're queer or strung out. They gotta make their quota so they'll grab your ass right away."

I call my mother: "If you get a letter from the Draft Board, just write 'no longer at this address' and put it back in the mail box."

I can barely see the street from my window. A sliver of sunlight tells me it's time to get up and call in.

"The Beatles are coming to town today to be on the Ed Sullivan show," Nathanson says. "Need a story on the police detail at the airport—how many cops, who's in command, will they get a motorcycle escort... Call in every half hour. Oh yeah, your mother called."

The Beatles have exploded in the US with their new style that some are calling "pop'n'roll." A month ago they were an obscure English band. Then they released "I Wanna Hold Your Hand" followed by "She Loves You" and the next day they had millions of adoring fans. Their coifs, their attitudes, everything about them is a revelation. Their harmonies are so advanced they've sent the Beachboys back to the drawing board. Now they're making their first trip to the US for their official anointing as teen idols.

It's only been a few months since JFK was assassinated and the cops are nervous about crowds. They tried to keep the time and place of arrival a secret, but Murray the K, a New York DJ, leaked the flight number and the airport is reporting thousands of screaming teenyboppers swarming the Pan Am lounge.

There are almost as many reporters as fans. Flashbulbs popping, radio reporters and TV guys, fighting for space. Norah Ephron, is covering it as well. She'll do a feature while I get the numbers. I count thirty-six cops holding back a surging crowd (official count, three thousand) of little girls screaming "I love you Paul, George you're the cutest... John, are you really married?" Ringo's fans aren't as articulate and can only sob his name. One girl pleads with me: "please ask Ringo if he's Jewish."

I see a little girl alone, clutching a photo of John Lennon like a missal. Tells me she's thirteen, but looks eleven. "My stepmother made me stay in my room," she says. "I waited until she left for work then snuck out. I'll have to get back before she comes home."

I prompt her. "She'll beat you..."

"She'll just shake me real hard. Make me stay in my room all weekend."

I call in. "Little girl defies her wicked stepmother, knows she's going to be beaten, but she had to come." I tell Nathanson.

"Is there a glass slipper in this somewhere?" he says. "Your mother called again."

Probably something I have to do. Or didn't do... Or did badly...

Later that night, the Beatles stop at the Peppermint Lounge, a twist bar on 45th. The street is closed off. Giant police horses snort clouds of breath. Fans run shrieking through the barricades. Willie Caine, the veteran AP police reporter sees me trying to get quotes. "Forget the Bobbysoxers, kid," he says. "This is a mob joint. Johnny Biello runs it for the Matty the Horse. Who steered these kids to a mob joint is the real story."

I call F., the night city editor. "The real story here is who steered the Beatles to a mob joint," I say.

"The real story would be if it weren't a mob joint," he says. "Get some fan stuff. Your mother wants to talk to you. She called three times..."

I fight my way inside the Peppermint Lounge, but the Beatles have already slipped out a back door and all that's left is a hundred reporters interviewing four go-go girls.

I find a beehive blonde. Bunny tail and fishnets, ready for her big break.

"Gonna put my picture in the paper?"

"If you waited on the Beatles."

"I couldn't get near them, their bodyguards pushed me away..." Shows me a bruise on her arm. "Look what they did..."

I grab Pomerantz, the *Post* photographer. "Take this lovely lady's picture."

Her name is Phyllis and a long last name she has to spell twice. "What paper this gonna be in?" she asks.

"The *Post*," I say and she makes a face. As the only liberal paper in town we're a definite underdog. She cheers up when I tell her I'm on the show biz beat. Know all the columnists and press agents. I casually suggest that she give me her number so I can drop off the prints. She shoves her cast iron bra into my shoulder and whispers, "got a joint to get me home?"

I have a couple of roaches in a matchbook. Go into the bathroom, empty a cigarette and re roll a joint. She grabs it. "Don't worry, I have more at home."

I call in the go-go girl story. "Your mother's worried about you," F. says. "Better call her."

It's one in the morning. Is somebody sick? Did somebody die? Will I have to shlep out to a funeral in Brooklyn on my day off? Can't call now, that stoned out go-go girl is waiting for me. I run to a booth. A man answers. "Gray's Papaya..." I ask for Phyllis. "No Phyllis here, this is Gray's Papaya, asshole." Bitch took my last grass and gave me a wrong number.

Back to the Village. On Barrow Street a guy in a doorway is pleading into an intercom, "Lemme in, I'm freezin'..." I descend two flights of clammy cement steps to my sub-basement. The lamppost drops a splash of light, on an envelope outside my door. An order from Selective Service to report for physical examination on December 20th warning that I face "imprisonment of up to five years and a ten thousand dollar fine" if I don't appear.

Busted! There's only one way they could have found me. I call home and wake up my mother. "Ma, they changed my draft board. Did you give them my new address?"

"I had to. This was the second letter..."

"Ma... all you had to do was write ADDRESS UNKNOWN and put it back in the mail box."

"You think you can hide like a mole in that cave and the world will forget about you?" she says. "They'll catch up to you and it'll be worse..."

"You betrayed me," I say. "My own mother betrayed me."

SISYPHEAN QUEST?

A breaking story tells itself. What they want from me are the stories that no one needs and no one will miss. The toy shows and rodeos, the dying police horses. Stories that earn their way into paper with great writing.

Frantic for a big story. I'm waiting for the call "Gould!" and the kiss off. "We're not going to hire you, but you can finish your tryout..."

"A guy hung himself in Hotel Christopher," Nathanson says. "Go find out who he was."

Ten floors of dismal brick on the West Street. Cramped lobby with a clerk behind a glass window. Little guy in a green visor. Checks the register. "Room 815. Checked in as Christopher Street... So full of booze it took three days before he started to stink..." Sees me writing this down. "That's not his real name, kid. He looked at the sign outside and registered as Christopher Street, get it?"

Elevator, narrow as a coffin. An old guy pushes in, staring straight ahead, toothless jaws chewing air. Door creaks open on a long, dark hallway, fixtures blinking on and off, walking in and out of pools of light like a private dick in a B movie. Who's behind these varnished doors with the faded gilt lettering? Old drunks with dirty secrets? Palsied divas with scrapbooks of former glory? A hundred ruined lives... Make a great TV series... Call it Hotel Tragic...

The door to 815 is ajar. Lumpy bed, blotchy spread. Mattress slashed, looking for a miser's stash? Dresser drawers pulled out. An empty bottle of Gordon's Gin on the floor. Sash cord tied into a noose. Fixture hanging from the ceiling. Must have come loose as he was hanging, but not enough to crash to the floor and save his life.

I knock on 817 next door. Shuffling footsteps. A lock clicks, a chain slides. Try 818 across the hall. Click, slide. Breathing on the other side of the door. Waiting for me to go away. If this was a B movie they'd be murdered after they talked to me. Cops would grill me. Gangsters work me over in an alley.

The clerk sends me to the Sixth Precinct on Charles Street. Turn of the century dungeon. Vaulted ceilings. Lumpy tile floor. The desk sergeant opens a spooky ledger right out of a horror movie. "Ambulance call. Try Saint Vincent's…"

St. Vincent's morgue. They find a John Doe in the log. "Suicide by ligature strangulation," the attendant says.

"Any attempt to establish identity?" I ask. "Dental records? Fingerprints?"

"They don't call the FBI for a floater, pal. They dump him in a meat wagon and bury him in Potter's field, case closed."

A great story is taking shape. I call Nathanson. "A nameless man checks into a hotel. Polishes off a quart of booze and hangs himself. An unfeeling city disposes of him. Cops, morgue attendants. Nobody even tries to find out who he was. Buried in a pauper's grave in Potter's Field…"

"It's a story if he turns out to be the black sheep son, heir to millions," he says. "The circus is in town. Go up to the Garden. Cover the clown auditions. Make it a happy story. Whose dream will come true?"

The clown audition is a parade of grotesques. I count a hundred and eleven. In seedy motley, creepy make up, juggling, tumbling, screeching—scary, weird… Not funny.

"Whose dream will come true?" I ask the PR guy. "Nobody's," he says. He points to Regina, a double-jointed fat lady who can do a complete split; a Black guy with huge feet and red lips who calls himself Flippy the Funny Postman; "Tex Weinstein, the Cowboy Clown," a wizened dwarf in chaps and a ten-gallon hat, who bowlegs around shooting a cap pistol. "They audition every year and never get hired."

Jerry E. a diminutive photographer climbs on my shoulders and yells to the three of them. "Come right into the lens. Do your routine..." Regina touches the top of her head with a swollen foot. Flippy bares horse teeth over his thick lips, Tex waves his oversized Stetson. "Yipee ky yoo..."

Later, in the city room, Jerry shows me a photo. Ugly, yet endearing faces in a fisheye distortion. "It's an expressionist masterpiece," I tell Jerry. "Like a still from *Freaks* with a dash of Fellini." He's worried. "Think it's too artsy-fartsy?"

Takes me an hour to write the lead. Finally: "The circus is in town and nobody has awaited its arrival more anxiously than Flippy, the funny Postman, Regina, the double-jointed fat lady or Tex Weinstein, the Cowboy Clown. Spirits undimmed, embarking on their annual Sisyphean quest..."

Nice... Got a Nathaniel West feel to it.

Next morning the story is on the "slop" page, a filler which is dropped after the first edition. Simple headline: THE NEWEST CLOWN. They threw out my prose poem about all the sad grotesques in all the furnished rooms and used the AP copy about the farm girl from Nebraska who made it to the big top on her first try. Ran an AP photo of a young girl in clown pajamas balancing atop a circus ball.

I'm looking for a wall to bang my head against. Nathanson said he wanted a happy story, a dream come true. All I had to do was give it to him. But I had to make a statement. I had to be profound. Instead I was sophomoric. And I got the metaphor wrong.

Prickles of cold sweat as I imagine the night editors roaring with laughter.

"Sisyphean quest?"

WHAT DID I DO WRONG?

Next morning Nathanson puts me on the phone with Ted Poston. "There's a building in Harlem infested with rats," he tells me. "The man has been struggling for months to get his family out of there."

A four-floor walkup on 132nd off Lenox. Jerry E. is taking pictures in a crowd of clamoring kids. We trudge up the four flights. A door is open on a railroad flat, rooms on each side of a long, narrow hallway. A little boy rides out of a room on a tricycle. "Down here in the kitchen," someone calls.

His name is Garland Cherry. He's a young guy in gas station overalls. "Just came home from work." His wife, trembling with shyness, whispers her name, "Deborah..." She's wearing blue scrubs. "I work in a salon." Garland's mother, housecoat, large, veined hands, sits at the kitchen table, knitting. There are two little boys, a toddler in a crib. "We bring the baby to whatever room we're in," Garland says. "Don't like to leave her alone."

Jerry is impatient. "Can we start the show?"

"Everybody gotta stand on a chair," Garland says.

We climb on kitchen chairs. Garland lifts the two little boys onto the kitchen table. "Nobody say nothin'..." Pulls the chain on the kitchen fixture and the room goes dark. Quiet for a moment, but then there is a scratching sound on the linoleum floor. "They're comin'," a little boy says excitedly... "Shhh," says Garland. Pulls the chain and the light comes on.

The rats look around like okay you caught us. Big brown rats. Five, maybe six on the kitchen floor.

"It's a family," Garland says. "That's Big Dog"—points to a rat the size of a dachshund nosing around the refrigerator—"and that's Blondie"—a smaller one with a yellow tuft on its back. A baby rat climbs up the leg of the crib. "Call her Trixie," says Garland. "Watch, she'll try to get in the crib to play." The baby reaches through the bars of her crib. The rat jumps across to her, but can't grip the mattress and falls to the floor.

"She can't get a good jump off the linoleum," Garland says. "So she'll try to climb up again. Once they get it in their head to do somethin' they figure out a way."

"Aren't you afraid they're gonna bite the baby?" I ask.

"They don't bite people," Garland says. "But they'll bite food right outta your hand."

"How'd they get in?" I ask.

"Dug a hole under the sink. I closed it with a metal plate and they dug under it. They can chew through concrete or metal, copper wires... Hold their breath underwater. Come up right through the toilet." He jumps off his chair. "I'll show you..."

Jerry has already shot a roll and is reloading his flash. I'm paralyzed, watching the rats crawl around my chair.

"They won't bite you, I promise..."

I step down. The rats scurry through my legs. We follow Garland down the hall to the bathroom. "Don't turn the light on," Jerry says. He drops to one knee in front of the bathroom door and pushes it open. The flash freezes the rats. One on the toilet bowl. One sliding into the sink. Another falling off the shower curtain.

I've seen water bugs in my mother's kitchen, but never rats.

"How do you use the bathroom?" I ask.

"Just start runnin' the sink or the tub. They don't come around when we're here and they leave when we come in. Fat as they are they can squeeze through the drain."

"How can you sleep at night?" Jerry asks.

"We got the fort room," he says. He takes us into a bedroom.

Mattresses on the floor, toys and coloring books. A fourteen inch TV with tin foil on the antenna. "No pipes around here and they don't like the radiator. We never bring food here…"

"Why don't you just put rat poison down?" Jerry asks.

"The babies might put it in their mouths," Garland says. "Put a cat in here, they'll eat it. Can't kill 'em, can't do nothin'… It's their apartment, too…"

"Why don't you move?" I say.

"No place to go," Garland says. "We went on a rent strike so the landlord put an eviction notice on us. We're on the waiting list for the projects. Meantime, nobody'll rent to us because we got this court order. There's a lotta hustlers. Move in and don't pay the rent. Takes six months to get an eviction notice, few more months while you go through appeals so they get a free apartment for almost a year. We're not playin' that. We just don't wanna live with rats."

Write my lead on the subway.

"Garland Cherry isn't asking for much. He just doesn't want to live with rats."

Rewrite it in the city room. "Garland Cherry isn't asking much. He just doesn't want rats crawling in his baby daughter's crib…"

The kid on the tricycle, Grandma knitting, baby in the crib. Rats in the bathroom. Four hundred words barely cover it.

"Call the Department of Finance and see if you can find out who the landlord is," Nathanson says. "Call the Board of Health and see if they've been to the building…"

Jerry E. comes up from the darkroom with glossy shot of rats on the floor, the baby reaching between the bars to a rat clawing at the mattress. Rats in the bathroom. A rat standing on its hind legs looking into the lens.

I go home surprising my mother. She made meat loaf, mashed potatoes and peas. I'm ashamed of her clean kitchen.

"Did you have rats in your apartment when you lived in Harlem?" I ask.

"Cockroaches. Horseflies in the summer. There were rats outside the stables on St. Nicholas Avenue..."

"I saw some pretty big rats when I was collecting rents in Harlem," my father says.

I'm shocked. "Funny job for a Communist."

"My first job. I had four buildings on Seventh Avenue. People would have rent parties on Friday. I went around on Saturday morning with my book. They paid in nickels and dimes."

"Did they hate you?" I ask.

"I was the Jew who came for the money. But they were polite. Some of them even offered me coffee and cake..."

Next morning the story's on Page Five with a big photo layout. So happy I made the paper it takes me a second to realize I get my first byline. **By HEYWOOD GOULD.** I get chills looking at it.

Davis peers over his glasses. McMorrow gives me a thumbs up. Nathanson calls me over. "Go thank Ted for giving you the story."

Poston is on the phone. I scribble "THANKS FOR THE STORY" on a piece of copy paper and drop it on his desk. He looks at it and nods, then goes back to his call. I didn't expect applause, but he's dismissing me.

I see Gil M. making books. He's a Freedom Rider, hosed, cattle prodded and arrested in Birmingham. He'll want to talk about the story. But he gives me the briefest, coldest nod of acknowledgement.

I reread the story. It's vivid, heartrending. Children trapped in an apartment full of rats. Rent strikes and eviction notices. Struggles to get an apartment in a segregated city. Blackballed by landlords in their own neighborhood. My first byline. Eloquent, full of concern. Might even do some good. Everybody likes the story but the two Black guys.

What did I do wrong?

"CAN WE BRING PASTRAMI?" HE ASKS

Shit's happening every day. Civil Rights, Ban the Bomb, Stop the War. Free Love, Free Speech… All the fuses that were lit in the fifties are exploding in the sixties.

Senator Morse makes headlines with an anti-war speech. "There are no Russian soldiers in Vietnam, no Chinese soldiers. American soldiers are the only foreign soldiers in Vietnam."

Pediatrician Benjamin Spock, leader of SANE (National Committee for a Sane Nuclear Policy), has been reluctant to associate with the anti-war movement, fearing them to be wild-eyed anarchists and hippies. But now he includes peace contingents in his demonstrations against nuclear armament. And begins making statements criticizing US involvement in Vietnam.

President Johnson had withdrawn a thousand troops from Vietnam a month after JFK's assassination. But there are conflicting reports that he has reinserted the thousand and added thousands more. The War Resister's League, a few hundred strong, marches from the *New York Times* to the UN. People screaming at them, "rotten Commies, go back to Russia…"

All this stuff going on and I can't get a story in the paper. No byline for days. Two weeks to go in my tryout and it looks like they've written me off.

Bill B. says, "Try the loony desk." It's at the entrance to the city room. People gather there every morning to pitch stories. Forlorn eccentrics, hoping for an interview.

An old woman hunched in a long overcoat, digs her nails into my arm. "They're torturing my son in Matewan..." It's a prison hospital for the criminally insane. Her son was a bookkeeper at Chase Manhattan Bank, she says. He discovered that the Chairman of the Board, David Rockefeller, was writing checks to himself from defunct accounts and called the Attorney General. They fired him, said he was deluded, but "he wouldn't give up," she says, proudly. To get him off the case they rigged evidence and charged him with embezzlement. They forged extortion notes in his name. Bribed psychiatrists to say he was a dangerous psychopath so they could keep him locked up forever. She has a bundle of letters, ink-smeared screeds describing how they rape and torture the inmates. "The Rockefellers are trying to drive my son crazy... Put people outside his cell, screaming and playing the radio all night. People in the bathroom eating their own BM's. He does his business in the toilet paper and tries to flush it, but they say he is dirtying his cell and lock him in solitary..."

I ask Nathanson. "Is this possible?"

"David Rockefeller doesn't need to embezzle," he says. "But I could believe the torture part."

A tiny man with a chapped red face and a fringe of white hair over a pink scalp. Looks like a demented cherub. Has a worn leather briefcase filled with documents. "Conclusive proof that the Russians are buying up all the property in New York..." Using front companies, he says. Buying small parcels so as not to attract attention. Alleys between buildings, odd lots, some no more than a few square feet. Phone booths, newsstands on city property that they can get cheap. "The Soviet Union will conquer America one square foot at a time..."

I check with Don Forst, the Business Editor. He chews his stogie. "Could be a plan."

Everybody's got their revelation in a shopping bag, a satchel or battered briefcase. Mr. Belmont carries a scroll like the Hebrew Torah. Bill B. knows him. "Oh boy, you're in for it now..."

He's an ancient in a dark suit, tieless, white shirt buttoned at the neck. Starts his spiel with the familiar "This is conclusive proof..." And continues... "that Jerusalem was the landing zone for Jews who arrived from outer space. Moses landed on Mount Sinai, the Jews just made up that story about the bullrushes. He fathered a new race of aliens in the desert and conquered Canaan. Christ rose up to resist. They killed him but couldn't kill his message. They dispersed, lived among us, pretended to assimilate, all the while planning to return to Jerusalem. The Czars and Kings and Popes, the greatest oppressors of Jews were actually Jews themselves creating the myth that Jews were helpless victims. Hitler, the second greatest Jewish conspirator after Moses, started the World War as a means of generating sympathy so a guilty world would restore the Jews to Jerusalem where they could establish a base for their master plan of conquest. But..."—he raises a finger— "that was their big mistake. The Christian nations have a secret plan of their own. At the moment when all the Jews in the world are assembled in Jerusalem, a land and sea blockade will be set up so they can't escape. They'll be marched onto rocket ships and launched into outer space from the top of Mount Sinai... It will be the greatest coordinated effort in the history of mankind..."

I tell Nathanson. "There's an old man who says the Jews are going to be put on rocket ships and launched into outer space."

"Can we bring pastrami?" he asks.

NOTHING COMES OUT

The Final Market, last edition of the day comes in a little after five in the afternoon. The day shift gets a "Good Night," rises as one and tucks their papers under their arms... "Shall we repair?" McMorrow says. And off they march up the block to the Page One bar. Everyone is invited, regardless of station. Still, I hover around the entrance for a week, watching the boisterous goings on before I finally get up the nerve to push open the door.

No beers here, the drink of choice is a martini. "No fruit, no vegetables," McMorrow says, no olives or lemon twists. Ronnie, the bartender, sleek dark hair, green silk jacket with black lapels, pleated white shirt and black bow tie, lines up rocks glasses and passes a bottle of Noilly Pratt dry vermouth over them. Then fills the glasses with Beefeater Gin. McMorrow holds his glass to the light—"Ah yes..."—and takes a deep, thankful draught. I order a Screwdriver, but Ronnie shakes his head. "The acid'll eat your guts." He fills a rocks glass with ice and pours a trickle of Harvey's Bristol Cream over it. "This'll keep you in the game."

Ronnie stands at the register, arms folded. No jokes or small talk. Won't let anybody buy him a drink. A drunk reaches over, "Hey pal..." and he smacks the guy's hand. "I'm not your pal, pal..."

The evening always starts on a festive note. The regulars drink themselves bright-eyed and witty. The banter flows. The jokes, the war stories.

One night they're toasting Ronnie. "Winner of the Vic Damone look-alike contest..."

Lou, the owner, desperately amiable, afraid of Ronnie's temper. "Ronnie could sing rings around Damone…"

"Afraid not," Ronnie says.

"Ah, Damone's just a pretty boy, he's no Sinatra…"

"He doesn't swing like Sinatra, but he actually has a better voice," I say, sounding like the pedantic jazz bores I hate.

I'm shouted down. Sinatra replaces God in all bars after eleven o'clock. A run to the jukebox for the anthems, "Angel Eyes," and "My Way…" "Is this not the greatest voice in the world?"

Ronnie slides me a drink. "Damone's a choir boy, classically trained," he says. "I just picked it up, imitating Dean Martin, Eddie Fisher, Tony Martin—crooner style. Sang with the house band at the Elegante on Ocean Parkway. We used to do two, sometimes three, sweet sixteens a weekend. We'd have a procession with the sweet sixteen and her friends in their gowns. Then a dance with the dad to some shmaltzy song like *Enamorata*. It was a neighborhood place, Patsy Menino, the owner lived a block away. Booked local talent, a lotta people got their start. My dream was to get on the Sullivan show. But then the Scandora brothers took it over. They were connected to people in the city and they started gettin' all the headliners, you know, Jerry Vail, Alan Gale. Big time comics, Totie Fields, Jack Carter… Judy Garland was booked for a weekend. Rented the biggest house in Bergen Beach… A pick-up band came out from the city. No rehearsal, they played the book like they'd been doing it forever. You watch people like that and you go, am I kiddin' myself or what?"

The Wall Streeters in front of the bar like to brawl when the booze kicks in. The *Post* guys just sit in the booth, licking their lips, trying to get their mouths to work. They get plates of snacks—cocktail franks, bar nuts, fried shrimps—then stare at the food as if they're not sure what to do with it. After a few rounds the eyes go glassy. The stories become monologues. A lot of mumbling, sucking on cigarettes. They're all married, living in Queens or on Long Island. Every night they stumble into cabs and go to Penn Station where they get on the

Long Island Railroad for the hour's ride to Baldwin or Manhasset. Grab a cab at the station. Roll into their houses at midnight. Are the wives asleep? Or waiting up with screaming accusations?

McMorrow comes to work on crutches. His wife put a wrought iron porch chair in front of the door so he would bang his shins. "Neat trick, huh. She puts tacks on the bathroom floor, glue in my toothpaste... "

It's a men's club. No woman can keep up. One night Nora Ephron brings two of the copy girls in for a drink. It's early and effusion still reigns. In her short time at the *Post* Nora has become a star with her light features. She's deferential around these old pros. Careful to say the right thing. But after five drinks everything you say is wrong. Like my father when he's loaded, they're waiting to pounce on the most inoffensive remark. Lucy K... takes a sip of a martini and shudders. "How can you drink these things?"

Poirier slides down the bar, a dapper, silver-haired French Canadian, equally renowned as a reporter and ladies man. Lucy smiles at his approach.

"A martini is like anal sex," Normand says. "At first it disgusts you. You try it once just to be a good sport. Then you can't live without it..."

Lucy didn't expect this. She's searching for a comeback, but Ronnie intervenes.

"Go home, Normand. Party's over..."

Normand draws himself up like an offended aristocrat. "Are you ejecting me?"

Lou comes down the bar. "Whatsa matter Ronnie?"

"People don't insult women in my store," Ronnie says.

"Such delicacy, such fine sensibilities," Normand says.

Lucy doesn't want a scene. "It's okay, Ronnie," she says, "I'm not insulted..."

Lou takes Normand's arm. "Lemme get you a cab." Normand shrugs him off. "I can raise my hand and whistle by myself, thank you…"

Nora holds him up. I walk out behind them, ready to grab him if he falls. I hear Ronnie telling Lou, "This is how I run my bar. If you don't like it…"

Outside, the streets are slick. Nora steps out into the rain to hail a cab. "Insidious bitches," Normand says. "Castrate you with kindness." He shakes an awning rod. A sheet of water streams off the awning, drenching Nora. Sopping wet, her mascara running. "You bastard," she says.

Normand slips off the rod and lands on his ass in a puddle.

"Taxi," he calls.

Puts his fingers in his mouth and tries to whistle. Nothing comes out.

"YOU JUST CLARIFIED THEIR THOUGHTS."

I'm sent out to the press shack at Brooklyn Police Headquarters on Bergen Street. The *Post* equivalent of Siberia. Irving Lieberman, the beat reporter, has been there for forty years, but his ambition is unquenched. He's jealous of every petty crime that's reported. "I'll take that," he tells me and calls his mysterious sources, hand cupped over the phone so I won't hear. A fussy little guy, stickler for details, he badgers the cops—"how many cars responded? You've got two ages for the alleged perpetrator. What does the middle initial *T* stand for?" He sits across from Sam Rubinstein *Herald Tribune,* another driven septuagenarian who scooped him on the arrest of the Nazi saboteurs at the Brooklyn Navy Yard in 1944 and won't let him forget it. They compete for every story as it if were their first day on the job. Sam jumps at the sound of the fire bells. "Three alarms already. Could spread..." Irving is dubious. "It's a one-story taxpayer. They're just being careful." But then sneaks across the street to check with the Fire Department, while Sam calls a source at the local precinct.

There's a *Comida Criolla* down the street. I eat *chicharrones* with red beans and yellow rice. Get a thick shake at the Carvel on Flatbush Avenue. Collapse on the dusty leather couch outside the office. In my *comida* coma I hear Lieberman.

"Wake up, they want you to go to Bensonhurst..."

Faced by a court order to integrate the public schools the Board of Ed has been sending busloads of Black kids to white schools all over the city. The reaction in the white neighborhoods has been furious, accusing liberals of supporting busing while sending their children to private schools. Vito Batista, head of the United Taxpayers Party and perennial losing candidate for Mayor, has seized on the issue. Short, squat and occasionally unkempt, he is comic relief with his pencil mustache and fiery, populist rhetoric. But his outspoken opposition to busing has struck a chord with a white middle class that feels overtaxed and undervalued.

Batista is leading a demonstration at P.S. 101 in Bensonhurst on Bay 34th, a mixed, Italian-Jewish neighborhood a few blocks from 86th, the main shopping street of Bensonhurst. About a hundred people are marching in front of the school, some carrying signs reading, "KEEP OUR SCHOOL PURE..." "NO BUSING..." NEIGHBORHOOD SCHOOLS FOR NEIGHBORHOOD CHILDREN..." Mostly women, some pushing toddlers in strollers. A few older guys in union jackets, Laborer's International, Building Trades, Teamsters Locals. Chanting, "No Busing in Bensonhurst. Keep our schools pure..." Police cars parked in front of the school. Cops chatting and smiling with the protesters.

A grandma type, a normally benign face, twisted in hatred "This isn't their neighborhood. They don't belong there..."

A young woman carrying a baby. "They mess up their own schools so bad they can't go. What do you think they'll do here?"

"I'm not gonna send my daughter here with these animals."

I try to provoke a quote. "The NAACP says you're just like the White Citizens Councils in Mississippi," I say.

It works. "White Citizens Councils are trying to protect their children just like us," somebody says.

Batista is surrounded by admirers, carrying signs, "BATISTA FOR MAYOR!" "TAXPAYERS REVOLT!" He beams into the mikes and cameras. "My position is no forced busing of students," he says. Cheers all around. Chants of "Batista for Mayor..." Standing behind him a local hood hoists a sign: "NO NIGGERS IN OUR NEIGHBORHOOD..."

Batista hastens to explain. "This is not a race issue. You will find Negro homeowners in St. Albans and Springfield Gardens who know I'm fighting for them as well..."

An old man standing outside a house. "Those poor kids..." I try to plant another quote. "Looks like Mississippi..."

"Yes, like Mississippi... You'd never think it would happen in New York."

"Can I use your phone?" I ask.

A tiny apartment cluttered with family photos and *tchotkes*. An old woman watching a soap opera. "He's gonna put me in the paper," the old man says. He takes me into the kitchen. Linoleum, oilcloth and the hovering aroma of last night's brisket. I call the paper. Nathanson is irked. "You're cutting it close to deadline..." He puts me on with Normand Poirier. I'll give him the facts, he'll write the story. But I have the lead:

"Waving signs reading keep our schools pure and screaming no niggers in our neighborhood, a mob gathered in front of PS 101 in Bensonhurst, this morning, to prevent bused in Negro students from entering the school..."

I describe the people, "grandmotherly type, face contorted, young woman with a fussing baby, union members who were given the day off to attend..." All I hear is breathing and typing.

Nathanson comes back on. "Get some reaction from the students and the teachers..."

Lunchtime, I grab a few students. They just parrot the grownups, "we don't want them here," etc. One girl, blinking, nervous. "I feel sorry for them, not having any friends in school and everybody ignoring them..." The other kids jump on her. "Why don't you go out with one of them if you feel so sorry..."

Where are the Negro students? I ask. They eat in the auditorium, someone says. They're scared to come out for lunch.

I walk into the school. The stage lights are on in the auditorium. The Black kids are in the front row. Anxious faces in the front row turn toward me.

Run back to call Nathanson. "Got an add for the story... Kids afraid to come out for lunch. Eating in the dark auditorium. Huddled together in the front row..."

Outside, Tony Calvaca, senior photographer, white hair, black suit, is toting a Graflex, moving people around like it's a wedding photo.

"That's it, everybody get behind Mr. Batista. Hold your signs up... Little higher..."

At 2:45 a yellow Board of Ed van that transports Special Ed kids, pulls up. The cops form a double line. The Black kids come out. I count five boys and two girls, walking the gauntlet. Calvaca pushes cops out of the way and drops to one knee—"heads up, let's see your pretty faces"—like it's a cheesecake shoot. But it works. The kids look up. A girl even smiles.

The protesters walk behind the police lines, shouting: "Go home. Go back where you came from..." Chanting. "No forced busing... Keep our schools pure..." for the TV cameras. A very old man, withered skin, hanging off trembling arms, teeth bared in skeletal grin, wincing with every breath—I've seen healthier people on the embalming table. "*Vergonia*, shame on you," he says, voice trembling. "Shame what you're doing to these children..."

The people turn on him, decrepit as he is. "Shut up, what do you know about it?"

"That's Larry's uncle from the old Stoneworkers Union..."

"That was a Red local. It got decertified..."

The van rumbles through the crowd, kids clustered at the window, people running alongside screaming insults. One of the hoods bounces a rock off the hood. Another rock cracks the side window—the kids duck for cover.

At the teacher's entrance three women are running to a waiting police van. I chase them. "Do you support the students or the demonstrators?"

This is too much for one teacher, heavy and brunette, streaked with gray, wingtip glasses on a string. "You can't force people to come together. Everybody wants to be with their own kind."

I've got quotes, color. I call it in to Poirier. He cuts me off. "I got enough for a book."

At five I pick up a copy of the Wall Street Special. It's there, on Page 3, PARENTS PROTEST BUSING IN BENSONHURST. The byline reads "By HEYWOOD GOULD AND NORMAND POIRIER. It runs through late editions. I see people reading it on the subway back to the city. In the Page One, Ronnie has the paper spread over the bar. "That's my old neighborhood," he says.

Poirier waves me over to his booth. "Good work, today…"

"I kinda put some words in people's mouths," I say.

He smiles like he knew that. "You just clarified their thoughts…"

"I FUCKIN' LOVE YOU..."

In a few days my month will be over. Unless I break a story I'll be back sharpening pencils and getting coffee. Worst thing is I won't be able to stand the humiliation and I'll have to quit.

A kid grabs a waitress on Thompson Street in the Village and tries to drag her into a basement, but two garbage men jump off their truck to her rescue. The kid's Legal Aid lawyer says it's a frame. "She was loaded. She sees a Negro guy walking behind her and in her drunken stupor thinks he wants to rape her. He was just trying to calm her down. My friend's an intern at St. Vincent's. I'm gonna get her blood count. Check back with me later..."

I write an eloquent plea against injustice. "L. is an unemployed Negro laborer with a police record. His accuser is an aspiring actress, working as a waitress. When he goes on trial for attempting to rape her it will be his word against hers. Who will the jury believe?"

The lawyer calls the paper later that night asking for me. I'm out celebrating my eloquent plea so he gives the story to a rewrite man. Turns out she was way over the legal alcohol limit and has dropped the charges. My story is spiked. No big deal, happens all the time. But I needed the byline.

Next day. East River CORE is picketing the Plumber's Union headquarters on Fourth Avenue. The day before, the plumbers, an all-white father and son union, had walked off a job when four non-union Blacks and Puerto Ricans were hired. Forty-three picketers, the usual mix of Old Left, militant black and white college kids. A group sits down in the doorway. Union officials step over them to get into the building.

Organizer, Blyden J. light-skinned, straight hair, who looks like he belongs in Cab Calloway's band, accuses: "This is George Meany's local. President of the AFL-CIO. Big shot in the Democratic Party, friend of the President. His union won't admit Negroes and Puerto Ricans into their apprentice program so they can never get their licenses. The height of liberal hypocrisy…"

Maybe but picket lines are what McMorrow calls "ho hums." Unless there's a riot or a civil rights celebrity shows up it'll be four paragraphs on page 40.

A plumber pushes through the line to the doorway. A girl lies down in front of him. He steps on her face going in. The crowd cries out. "Hey man, what are doing?"

A familiar voice behind me. "You gonna let him get away with this?"

It's Ray. He runs off the line. "Hey tough guy, c'mere, step on me…"

He's held back. "Ray calm down… The girl is up. "I'm okay, Ray…"

"Hey Ray," I say.

He squints, then remembers. "Oh yeah, the undertaker…"

I follow him across the street. He calls to a group of Black kids. "You guys stay close to me. Don't let nobody break you up. When we get into the office just sit down on the floor. Don't talk to nobody. Resist when they try to bust you. Resist, man…"

Ray runs into the alcove where eight older people are staging a sit-in. A portly, dignified Black man in a gray suit grabs his arm. "It's happening, brother. We're making headway. Don't give them an excuse…"

A chunky cop, kinky red hair, comes through the door and tramples the sit-ins. Jumps in front of Ray. "You try to get into the business offices you'll be arrested for trespassing…"

Ray shoves him. "Get outta the way, pig. "

The cop flicks his wrist and a blackjack appears in his hand. He backhands it across Ray's head. Doesn't look like much of a blow but those blackjacks are filled with buckshot. Ray buckles and goes glassy. The cop grabs him by the back of his shirt and drags him out to the street. The picketers are shouting, Police brutality!" A chubby white girl runs off the line, crying, "Ray..." Two cops push her back... Two more come to help the red-headed cop hustle Ray to a patrol car from the Fifth Precinct. They throw him in the back seat and peel out, sirens blaring. I follow, yelling. "Ray, what's your last name?"

"His name is Ray W..." Blyden says.

I've heard how cops take people to abandoned buildings and work them over. Ray will show up tomorrow all beat up. But it will be too late for me. I need a police brutality story now.

I run to the Fifth Precinct on Elizabeth Street, a stitch spearing my side. The desk sergeant doesn't even check the blotter. "We don't have a Ray W. here..."

Back at the scene the reporters are gone, TV units are pulling out. I call in and try to dramatize what I have. "CORE member Ray W. was blackjacked and dragged to a patrol car. Attempts to locate him were not successful and..." Normand interrupts me. "Yeah, I got it..." At six I grab the last edition. My story didn't make it. They go with an AP piece out of D.C. about how President Johnson met with George Meany and Labor Secretary Wirtz to resolve the problem.

Two days to go.

Nathanson throws me a press release. Another ho hum. The NYPD is instituting a pilot project to teach Spanish to the cops. The class is at the 24th Precinct on 100th.and Central Park West, down the block from what is called a "predominantly Hispanic" housing project. A bunch of white cops, grumbling because they were called in before their tours. Big asses squeezed into grade school desks.

It's a PR push. TV, radio, everybody's there. David Halberstam of the *Times* recently expelled from Vietnam for his anti-war reportage, is the main attraction. Reporters paying homage, almost groveling. "First

day on city side, David? New York's more dangerous than Saigon…"
He sits in the middle of the room with a legal pad on a clipboard. A
young social worker explains the situation to him. There's a problem
with communication in this mostly Hispanic area, she says.
Complaints of police brutality from the people in the projects.

The teacher, an earnest little guy, has written a group of everyday
phrases on the board. "You don't have to be a linguist," he says. "Just a
few words in their language shows respect and makes interaction a lot
easier."

He hands out a mimeographed sheet. Brief history of Puerto
Rico. Names and addresses of agencies the cops can recommend to the
local people. Tries to get a response. "How many of you studied
Spanish in high school?" One hand, half-raised. "How many of you
think this will help you do your jobs?" No hands raised. They're hating
this.

After a few more questions get no response, Halberstam has seen
enough. He rises slowly, tall, imposing, with horn rims. For a guy
who's covered palace coups, firefights and assassinations this isn't much
of a story. The TV people aren't thrilled, either. It'll be a thirty-second
spot showing the cops taking notes if it runs at all.

The cops turn and watch the press leave.

"Any questions before we have the next tour in?" the professor
asks.

Angry stirring. One cop who's been writhing like he's in pain
raises his hand.

"What if we're transferred to Greenpoint? Do we hafta learn
Polish?"

Hoots.

"How about Williamsburg. Hafta learn Yiddish?"

"Oy vey…"

The teacher tries an appeal to reason. "It wouldn't hurt to pick up
a few words, would it?"

The cops ignore him and try to top each other as they walk out.

"How do you say hey Pablo pick up that beer can that you just threw in the gutter?"

"What's the everyday phrase for stop pissin' in the street, Haysooze?"

"I don't see no sentence for garbage goes in the garbage can, not on the sidewalk, Jose..."

"This is America, right? They're supposed to learn English."

"They're supposed to know how to talk to us..."

"How do you say put that blade down, Ruben?"

Next day. Halberstam's story is all sweetness and light on the front of the Metro page. The earnest professor. The attentive policemen.

My story is on P. 24. Single column next to a Modell's ad.

"The Police Department thinks it would be a good idea for the cops on the beat to know a little Spanish.

"The cops at the 24th Precinct don't agree..."

I quote the teacher's phrases. Describe the cops, sullen as the cameras roll, then sounding off as soon as they think the press is gone. Their salty, bigoted wit that entertains even as it appalls. A very different version of the same event.

I'm done for. They'll believe, Halberstam and think I was making it up.

The last day of my tryout. I call in for my last assignment. "Come into the office," Nathanson says.

Davis is yelling at the copyboys: "Where are the proofs?" Sann is reading the first edition, boots up on the desk. Pete, his assistant, waves me over to his desk and hands me a folder filled with forms. "Fill these out."

"What for?"

""Union stuff. Insurance. We gotta change your classification."

"Back to copyboy?"

"Up to reporter."

Is this possible? Did I make it? "I thought they were calling me in to give me the bad news," I say

"Sometimes you get good news, too," he says.

"Is it because I beat Halberstam" I ask Pete.

"Not my department," Pete says. "All's I know is Mrs. Schiff called down this morning and said to put you on staff."

"Mrs. Schiff makes those decisions?"

"It's her paper."

Something spins me around. "I have to call my mom."

I flash to all the tryouts I failed. Teams I didn't make because I messed up at the last minute. The time I lost the borough spelling bee because I spelled "truly" with an "e" when I knew that was wrong. Lost the geography contest because I couldn't say where Soldier's Field was, even though my mind was screaming CHICAGO! I thought I had choked again, but this time I got lucky. If Halberstam had stuck around he would have gotten the story.

Triumphant march through the city room to my desk at the door. Loonies waiting patiently to tell their stories. McMorrow, chewing his ginger mustache, raises his drink cup. Davis spitting a cigar shred. The copy people mumbling congrats. Can't blame them for rooting against me, I would do the same. "Normand really stood up for you," Mike B. says. "Nathanson, too. I heard them telling Davis what a good reporter you were. And he was saying yeah, yeah, I know he's good..."

I feel a rush of love for this kid, bearing up under his own bitter disappointment to tell me something he knew I would really want to hear. "I love you for telling me this, man," I say. I shake his hand so hard his glasses drop over his nose. "I fuckin' love you..."

MINUS "DREAMLIKE"

After a few months I'm still getting a ping! of pleasure every time I see "By Heywood Gould."

A pang of resentment when I've been rewritten.

The night editors won't let me use similes to convey the tension of the moment, the crosscurrents of grief and rage, swirling under the placid surface of a judicial procedure. "Spectators filing into the courtroom like the audience in a theater" is cut. "The black-robed judge enters with a stern look..." Gone...

Adjectives are out. Parents whose daughter died in an illegal abortion, her body stuffed in a trunk by her boyfriend and dumped in the Hudson, "hold hands sit in silent grief" as the prosecution describes the last tormented night of her life. Next day "silent grief" is out, replaced by "grieving parents clasped hands as..."

I describe a man blinded in an acid attack by a spurned mistress, "trembling on his cane, dark glasses hardly hiding his scarred eye sockets." The "cruel irony" of a wife who has to care for the husband who was cheating on her. The "pathetic delusion" of the accused mistress wearing a tight low-cut dress and high heels against the advice of her lawyer. Next day no "cruel irony." It was my pathetic delusion that they would keep "pathetic delusion."

A fifteen year old boy is accused of raping a nine-year-old girl on the roof of a Brooklyn project and throwing her fourteen floors to her death when she threatened to tell her parents. Detectives testify that he took them to the scene of the crime and showed them how he did it. I call in a description. "Skinny, eyes bulging defiantly, large hands sticking out of the sleeves of his dark suit." Next day "defiantly" is out, the eyes just "bulge." The victim's father, restrained by solicitous relatives, jumps over the rail… "Screaming curses he wrapped his hands around the defendant's skinny neck and tried to throttle him," I dictate. Somebody changes "throttle" to "choke."

Assigned Counsel Abe Brodsky says the boy was bullied and deceived and wasn't advised of his rights. "Tan and pin-striped, flashing a gold watch as he grills the detectives." Gone… Catch him joking with cops during recess. "It's understood that he's putting on a good show for a guilty client," I write. "Giving the state its money's worth." Gone. "You're not a columnist, " Nathanson tells me. "You don't have the right to an opinion."

The only eyewitness is an eight-year-old friend of the victim who saw the defendant dragging her into an elevator. The courtroom "buzzes" as she is called to the stand. Another cliche. What are they, a bunch of bees? Is there another word I can use? "Murmurs?" "Stirs?"

"The prosecution's star witness was so small she had to be helped onto the witness chair," I write. "Her voice was so soft she had to be coaxed to speak louder…"

"Chairs creaked in the hushed Brooklyn courtroom as spectators leaned forward to hear…"

Hate to use "hushed," but "silent" is somehow wrong and can't think of another word. The little girl was the one who pointed the defendant out to a traffic cop on the day after the murder. I write that she is "unshakable" under Brodsky's gentle cross-examination. "Shakes her head decisively." Putz! You can't say "shakes" if you just said "unshakable." Always drop the adjective in favor of the verb. Just have Brodsky ask "Are you sure it was James? Could it have been somebody else?" And have her "shake" her head. "It was James…" It's got an elegant Hemingway elision about it.

Next day the DA passes me a note with the correct spelling of his name. More spectators in the courtroom. Did my story draw them?

A rumpled guy in his fifties with copy paper in his pocket slides into the bench next to me. "Homer Bigart," he says. "They told me to follow you around." What a compliment! Bigart is a Pulitzer Prize-winning war correspondent of the *Times*. Expelled from Vietnam he's been covering civil rights and union struggles in the south. His stories are far from objective, referring to "peckerwoods" and "rednecks;" the *Post* would never allow those loaded nouns.

The prosecution has arranged a bus trip to the scene of the crime for the jury. Brodsky rises, shouting, "Objection Your Honor. This will prejudice the jury." Objection overruled, of course, but Brodsky seems sincerely outraged. "This case is replete with reversible error," he tells the DA.

Two yellow school buses, one for the jurors, the other for the press. Police and court personnel in their official vehicles. "Quite a convoy," Bigart says. The right word, I was thinking "cortege" from my time in the funeral business. We drive into Bedford Stuyvesant, the heart of Black Brooklyn. Farragut Houses on York Street. Four brick buildings rise out of a landscape of weedy lots and chain link fences. "Looks like the housing blocks in Soviet towns," Bigart says. I wonder if he'll use that in his story. A court officer turns. "They were built after the war for returning veterans, but the colored moved in first and they couldn't get whites to sign up."

Gray stone floors, green walls and low hanging fixtures in cages. "To keep the muggers from pullin' the lights out," the court officer says. "See they made the elevators big just like in schools or office buildings, so these guys hide in the shadows and jump people as soon as the door close. Take your life in your hands just tryin' to go into your apartment. Old people lock themselves in for days…"

Court officers chase the residents out of an elevator and escort the jurors in. A rickety ride like in a freight elevator to the fourteenth floor and then a single file climb up a clanging flight of metal stairs to the roof. Tar buckling, low parapet, Manhattan skyline shimmering in the distance. I understand what Brodsky meant when he said the jurors would be "prejudiced." The ten middle-aged white office workers have never been to a project. The two Black ladies, stiff and proper, are mortified. They pick their way through broken bottles, cigarette butts, glassine envelopes, discarded shoes and underwear, ready to believe anything could happen there.

Good story. The bus convoy through Bed Stuy. Jurors on the roof, watching the DA retrace the defendant's steps. Skyline of Manhattan shimmering "dreamlike" in the background. It runs all day. Minus "dreamlike."

"WE SCARED THE HELL OUT OF NEW YORK CITY"

April 1964

Civil rights press conferences have become another ho hum. Announcing another a picket line that will peter out. Sit-in that will be broken up, cops dragging limp bodies across the floor. I'm yawning as I enter the conference room at the Hotel Theresa on 125th and Seventh.

"Oppression is so boring, isn't it dahling?"

It's Gladys, the Freedom Rider I met in Washington Square Park. "Same old story over and over," she says. "Imagine how we feel…" Hair straightened, clingy dress, high heels. "But this'll grab you. We're gonna shut down the World's Fair."

On the dais, people hold signs reading NEW YORK'S WORST FAIR, SEGREGATED SCHOOLS FOR NEGROES AND PUERTO RICANS and WE WANT A FAIR WORLD NOT A WORLD'S FAIR.

Brooklyn CORE leader Isaiah Brunson announces a plan to stall cars on the highways to create a mammoth traffic jam and prevent people from attending the opening day of the 1964 World's Fair. Tall and awkward, he speaks deliberately with an almost hillbilly inflection.

"We are having the stall-in to shut off traffic at the World's Fair because the city and the state have seen fit to spend millions and millions of dollars to build the World's Fair, but have not seen fit to eliminate the problems of Negroes and Puerto Ricans in New York City."

Brunson says he already has commitments from eighteen hundred drivers to stall their cars on the major arteries leading to the fair site in Flushing Meadow, Queens. That should be enough to shut down the Fair and more are coming. There is also a plan to lie down on the Long Island Railroad tracks to stop the trains, and another to jam subway cars so tightly that fairgoers cannot squeeze in. He hands out a leaflet urging supporters to "drive awhile for freedom" until their cars run out of gas and clog the highways.

The World's Fair is being hyped as the biggest event in the city's history. Its theme is "Peace Through Understanding," a celebration of "Man's Achievement on a Shrinking Globe in an Expanding Universe." It is predicted to bring in hundreds of millions in tourism, create thousands of jobs. Parks Commissioner Robert Moses, who ran the 1938 Fair at the same location under Mayor LaGuardia, has signed up scores of major corporations, and over twenty countries. Raised millions from private investors to develop the land, build new access roads, erect national pavilions. President Johnson is scheduled to give the keynote address on opening day.

Moses is arbitrary, dictatorial, notorious in Brooklyn for denying Dodger President Walter O'Malley's requests for a new stadium, forcing the team to move to Los Angeles. He has positioned the Fair as a sacred cow, above criticism, and the press has toed the party line, printing handouts and puff features. But not *Post* reporters Sid Zion and Joe Kahn. They've been working secretly on an investigative series uncovering misuse of public land, bribery, influence peddling, extortion, and Mob penetration reaching from the construction site right up to Moses's office. They plan to run it in five installments the week before Opening Day. "We caught everybody with their hands in the till," Sidney tells me. "Everybody's dirty."

The series never runs. Rumor is that Moses called Dolly Schiff and it was killed at the last minute. Instead of exposing the Fair, the *Post* condemns the stall-in: "The projected traffic tie-up can win few converts to the civil rights banner. It will provide new ammunition for racists—here and in Washington..."

Joe Kahn isn't surprised. "Dolly would have lost a half million or more in advertising if she ran our series." He is philosophical about it. But Sidney is furious and quits the paper.

We're bombarded with stories about the great pavilions. Disney, IBM, Space Park. International pavilions, Africa, Asia. The marvels of technology and "human progress." Entertainment, food, music, culture. The message is hammered home: Any attempt to sabotage this important national event would be tantamount to treason.

Black leaders sense that the stall-in not a popular cause with white donors. James Farmer, head of National CORE says it will "merely create confusion and thus damage the fight for freedom." He expels Brooklyn CORE from the national organization when they refuse to desist. Roy Wilkins, executive director of the NAACP, says the plan is "pure Brooklynese," which they proudly confirm—"we are definitely Brooklynese." Martin Luther King Jr. calls it a "tactical error," but adds: "What's worse, a stall-in or a stalled Senate." Only Malcolm X, now broken with Elijah Mohammad, announces his support and lets CORE use his offices at the Theresa.

The political establishment reacts strongly. Mayor Wagner says CORE is putting a "gun to the city's head." He plans to deploy eleven hundred cops and hundreds of tow trucks to keep the highways clear and prosecute all demonstrators. Traffic Commissioner Henry Barnes warns that "a stall-in will paralyze the city. It'll take a week to untangle the mess." He threatens to arrest any driver whose car runs out of gas on city streets. Queens DA O'Connor gets an injunction against Brooklyn CORE, which its leaders plan to defy and go to jail if necessary. In Washington, Hubert Humphrey, the floor manager of the Civil Rights Bill in the Senate, cautions that "illegal disturbances, demonstrations which lead to violence or to injury will strike grievous blows at the cause of decent civil rights legislation."

The "Brooklynese" argue that the Civil Rights Act may benefit Negroes in the segregated south, but won't help the northern urban Negro whose struggle is for employment, education and housing. They charge that Manhattan and parts of Queens have been spruced up in anticipation of the millions of tourists who will come, but nothing has been done in Negro and Puerto Rican neighborhoods. Thousands of jobs are being created, but none for the hundreds of qualified Negro and Puerto Rican plumbers, carpenters, electricians who are barred from the unions.

Gladys and the Harlem chapter are participating. Bronx CORE joins as well. Some labor unions announce their support. District 65, Retail, Wholesale and Department Store Workers, which my mother had secretly organized for in the thirties. Sanitation Men's Union President John J. Delury says his ten thousand members will refuse to tow stalled cars. "We're not going to scab on anyone fighting for their rights."

Gladys keeps me posted on the pressure they're getting from liberal politicians. "Trying to bribe me with a city job," she says. "I tell 'em, that the best you can do?" George Johnson, large, black and boisterous has chosen the role of comic relief. "Let 'em pass me a bag of money so I can hold it up at a press conference and say is this the thirty pieces of silver y'all are always complainin' about?"

I get a good story out of the stacks of hate mail—"dirty niggers, go back to Africa." CORE Press Officer Arnold Goldweg is getting "die you dirty commie kike" notes. George Lincoln Rockwell's neo-Nazi National Renaissance Party firebombs picket lines in the Bronx and threatens an attack on the stalled cars. Cops raid their headquarters and find a cache of weapons.

Opening day is April 22. The *Times* has a story about drivers in Philadelphia and Baltimore heading for the city and concludes: "No power on earth can stop [the stall-in] now."

Gladys invites me to spend the night at the command post in the Hotel Theresa. Her colleagues Marshall and Roy object. "He might hear something he shouldn't." I tell them I won't print anything they say is off the record. Offer to leave the room if they want to talk privately.

I already have the lead: "Hoping to bring attention to their struggle with one dramatic act of social sabotage, the members of Brooklyn CORE stalled thousands of cars on the highways leading to the World's Fair today... "Afterwards, I'll write a piece for the Marxist *Monthly Review* about my night "at the nerve center of the direct action which stopped the capitalist juggernaut in its tracks..."

The evening begins with Chock Full o'Nuts donuts and coffee. Amazing how teetotal these people are. No beer, just soda. Nobody's sneaking out to get high. Across the room George wags his finger. "No funny ciggies here unless you brought your own." And laughs. "I know who you are, honey. I get down to the Village once in a while."

Everyone is gathered around a TV, watching the cops and tow trucks lining up along the Long Island Expressway. Police Commissioner Michael Murphy, a burly, scowling street cop, shaving chafe on his pink jowls, declares: "These so-called civil rights protesters are denying everyone else their civil rights..."

Footage of people piling into cars in Baltimore and Boston. "They should each be drivin' their own car," somebody says.

"They can't afford cars. That's what we're fighting for..." More laughter.

I take down their euphoric predictions.

"This action will change the course of the Movement..."

"From now on we won't be supplicating, we'll be dictating."

One phone with two extensions keeps ringing, buttons flashing as convoys call in. Gladys has a chart with names and numbers of vehicles.

"Gloria E. from Cambridge, Maryland has promised at least two hundred cars."

"We're gonna have two thousand, minimum..."

"Two thousand will shut it down for sure."

After midnight scouts begin reporting back.

"A few cars on the Grand Central."

"People wanna know where to stop."

"As close to the entrance as possible."

"With all them cops standing around one car'll be scooped up right away."

"Let them go a few exits down, pull off to the side and wait until they have enough cars to block the road."

"Cops won't let 'em pull over…"

"We shoulda had walkie-talkies…"

The TV has signed off for the night. Next news will be on the morning shows. The phone rings sporadically. A few cars leaving. A school bus full of people.

"Why are they in a bus? They should be in as many cars as they can get."

I call the city desk. "Any news?"

"A few stories about cars taking off from various spots in the South."

Groans… "They're just leaving now? They were supposed to start yesterday morning."

Phone calls to the Brooklyn organizers. No cars showing up yet. A feeling of foreboding. I scribble some notes. "An unseasonably chilly blustery April day… On 125th Street, garbage trucks plied the dishwater dawn. Night workers, cringed against the shivery drizzle…"

Hours pass with no calls. The morning papers are predicting thousands of cars, massive jams. My story is about the planners watching the clock, working the phones and gradually realizing that the stall-in is a bust. It's confirmed by the TV news showing rain blowing across empty highways.

Opening Day is still a few hours away.

"Still time for something to happen," someone says.

But the mood has changed.

"This was just an idea off the top of Lou Lomax's head."

"Should've had a practice run…"

Gladys hangs up the phone. "They're turning back. Say they don't wanna get towed and their cars busted up for no reason. We forgot how much people love their cars."

It stays rainy and cold all day. The fair opens to sparse attendance. In the first few hours it's mostly dignitaries. In an election year, this was supposed to be a triumphant campaign visit for LBJ to a solidly Democratic area. Instead he is greeted by protesters, heckling so loud that they drown out his speech. Stung by this reception, he tries for a tolerant tone. "I feel sorry for these people," he says. "They're misguided..." Mayor Wagner, a loyal machine Democrat is furious. "This is a great humiliation for the city." Cops in yellow slickers drag people face down on the clammy pavement to paddy wagons. Officials discount the effect of the stall-in. They blame the weather and promise a big day tomorrow.

I hitch a ride with Gladys and George. Police cars are lined up on the right lanes in both directions. A few tourist buses leaving the Fair. Helicopters overhead. No people. We cross an empty Triboro Bridge into Manhattan. Hear the official attendance on WINS News. "Two hundred and fifty thousand people were expected. Seventy-nine thousand showed up, many of them invited guests."

"Seventy-nine thousand?" George says. "I didn't see seventy-nine people."

"That's the official count," I say. "They inflated the number."

"I guess we were carried away by the vision of thousands of Negroes"—a sardonic glance at me—"and a few well-meaning whites in a five mile traffic jam honking horns and singing "We Shall Overcome" in front of their tacky little carnival."

"It's a flop," Gladys says.

"No it's not," I say. "Fifteen people bluffed out the whole country..."

She squeezes my hand, eyes shining, ever hopeful.

"We did, didn't we? We scared the hell out of New York City..."

"THE WORST B-MOVIE I EVER SAW..."

The Post is running a daily column of heartwarming tidbits. Nobody wants tales from the dark side of the Fair.

We dutifully troop to the press building for the debut of the world's first automatically opening doors. An engineer explains how an electric eye triggers a motion sensor. We each take a turn walking up to the door. Transparent, all glass, no knobs. "You don't have to slow down, it'll open," an engineer says. Later that day a *Journal American* photographer is running to a story. He doesn't see the door and crashes into it breaking his nose. That evening a pizza guy from the Vatican pavilion makes the same mistake from the outside. I write up a paragraph: "The world's first automatic door broke two noses and a pepperoni pizza in its World's Fair debut, yesterday." It's bumped by a story about how Belgian waffles are the favorite snack of the Fair.

I do a piece about the how many times the word "largest" is used. The lead is: "Bet you don't know what a carillon is. It's a set of bells in a tower, played by keyboard. The World's Fair has the largest carillon in the world, atop the 120-foot Coca-Cola Tower...

"The Fair boasts the largest globular structure ever built by man—the 12-story-high stainless steel Unisphere, symbol of the fair. It has the world's most powerful searchlight beam. The world's largest fountain. Largest projection screen in the world. Largest outdoor photographic prints...

"Uniroyal has built the 'world's largest tire' to be used as a Ferris Wheel. One afternoon it stalled in mid air, stranding a hundred riders, and broke the record for the world's largest flat tire.."

Chortling as I type. Night Managing Editor, George T. looks up suspiciously. When I hand in my five paragraphs he's ready with the 2H pencil.

"I don't like your snide tone," he says.

"I'm using the quotes right off the handouts," I say.

"I know what you're doing," he says, leaning on his pencil as he crosses out my satire.

I try to ingratiate with a piece about all the different license plates in the parking lot. I count one from every state, Quebec and Ontario. All the different vehicles—vans, jeeps, dune buggies, old Packard hearses, motorcycles. An elderly couple rode a bicycle-built-for-two all the way from Indianapolis. "Are those people real?" George T. asks. "I wanna see a picture…"

Jackie Kennedy brings Caroline and John John on a visit to the Coca Cola Pavilion. It's been five months since the assassination and she's escorted by a phalanx of Secret Service, city cops, officials, local pols.

Jackie is stylish in a short, white coat. Two women behind me disapprove.

"She should still be in mourning."

"You'd think Oleg Cassini would make her something nice in black…"

I go with the adorable kids stuff and leave the ladies out. Six syrupy paragraphs. Who would want to read this? Everybody, it turns out, even the Village hipsters.

"Did you get to talk to her?"

"She's got guts coming out in public. Who knows what could happen?"

Peggy alerts me. "We're having a big anti war demo on the steps of City Hall. Twelve kids are going to burn their draft cards." I call Nathanson, "Let me cover it. I know a lot of people in the movement."

"We'll have Ollie (City Hall beat reporter) on it. You go to the Florida Pavilion. See if you can get some quotes from the cockatoo."

The Florida Pavilion is hyping the performing porpoises, talking cockatoo and tropical aviary in its Miami Jungle exhibit. Two flamingos, ankles manacled, are on a patchy sward at the entrance, shivering so hard the feathers fly off their coats.

I call Nathanson. "Flamingo abuse in the Florida pavilion."

"You'll need the ASPCA or some city agency to start an investigation."

I try to con a confession out of the press guy. "The ASPCA says these flamingos are dying every day and you fly up new ones to replace them."

That is completely untrue," he says. "We have the same flamingos we started with. The cold doesn't bother them."

"Then how come they're shivering?"

"They're not shivering, they're quivering. Didn't you ever see a fuckin' flamingo before?"

Robert Moses, fervent zealot of corporate capitalism is trying— and failing—to keep politics out of the Fair.

The NAACP schedules a protest against the minstrel show at the Bourbon Street Pavilion, but is threatened with arrest if they throw up a picket line. They cancel the demo.

The American-Israel Pavilion wants to remove a mural about Palestinian refugees from the Jordanian Pavilion. It's a poem next to a picture of an Arab mother sheltering a child. Tells how for centuries Jews, Christians and Muslims lived in peace on the land until "strangers from abroad...Terror's victims who became terror's fierce practitioners..."

The Israelis say it is anti-Semitic propaganda. That the Arabs created the terror by defying the UN resolution creating two states, one Arab, one Jewish, and invading Israel. The Jordanians vow to close the Pavilion if forced to take it down. King Hussein says, "We are against Israelis, not Jews," which could be true as he is dating Jewish actress Susan Kohler. Paul O'Dwyer, a pro-Israel left-wing City Councilman, sponsors a resolution condemning the poster and calling for its removal. Moses refuses to intervene. "I will not dictate what should be in the pavilions." Both groups threaten to counter picket each other. Moses warns they will be arrested and expelled from the Fair. The Arabs back down and demonstrate in front of the Israeli Embassy in New York. But Dr. Joachim Prinz, president of the American Jewish Committee, defies Moses's ban and shows up with twelve picketers. They are arrested by the World's Fair Pinkerton Police and charged with "disorderly conduct."

"Good story," I tell Nathanson.

"Go see the Burundi dancers," he says. "They're the hit of the Fair."

Burundi, a tiny, impoverished African country, has one of the largest pavilions. The King's Royal Drummers and Dancers are a troop of Watusis, tall, graceful, loincloths and flower necklaces. Hoisting spears, crouching with menacing chants, jumping high in the air with warlike shrieks, bells jingling at their ankles. The elderly tourists are underwhelmed. "Looks like they're wearin' the same leis as them hula dancers at the Hawaiian pavilion."

I ask for an interview. The PR guy seems nervous. "They only speak Kirwani, their native dialect.

"That's okay," I say. "I'm fluent in Kirwani..."

Backstage, I find somebody to translate. The dancers give me the official story. How they are chosen as children for their talent and grace. Learn the hunting dances, war dances, marriage, etc. Travel the world for the King...

But as soon as the PR guy steps away, they surround me, all talking at once in English. "We are slaves here." They tell me that the royal family takes all their appearance money and gives them nothing. They are all sharing one room at the Hotel Bryant, a fleabag in midtown Manhattan and have to sleep on straw mats. They are not permitted to attend parties at the other pavilions. And worst of all, the Coca Cola pavilion sent over ten cases of Coke as a present and the princes took every bottle.

The story comes out fast and fluent like a good jazz solo. I describe the performance: "spears and loincloths, drums pounding jungle rhythms... flashes of tropical color... leaping in traditional war dances..." Ending with the heartfelt cry, "We are slaves in this great country..."

George T. squinting in pain, slams it down on the spike.

"This is worse than the worst B movie I ever saw."

"DID YOU MAKE THOSE BOY SCOUTS UP?"

July 1964

"Do the weather," Nathanson says. "Crowds at the beaches. Emergency room admissions for heat stroke or sun burn. Board of Health advisories…"

It's a non-story. No highways buckling or hurricanes approaching. No spike in crime or elderly deaths… The heat hasn't broken any records.

But it's been hot enough to try the patience of Patrick Lynch, a janitor for three luxury townhouses on East 76th, the Silk Stocking District, richest neighborhood in the city. A bunch of Black kids from the Bronx are in summer school at Wagner Junior High. After class they hang out on the steps of one of Lynch's townhouses. He tries to chase them, but they jeer and refuse to move. He grabs a hose, shouting "I'll wash you niggers clean." (He later denies saying this.) The kids throw bottles, rocks and garbage can lids at him. James Powell, a skinny twelve-year-old, chases him into a basement.

Off-duty cop Thomas Gilligan has been watching from a flower shop across the street. He runs over, flashing his shield and drawing his pistol just as Powell emerges, laughing, from the building.

At that point the narrative gets contentious. Gilligan says Powell pulled a knife and slashed him, showing a cut on his knuckle as proof. Others say there was no knife and Gilligan must have deliberately cut himself. Gilligan fires a warning shot that shatters the window of one of the townhouses. Lowers the gun and fires twice, spinning the slight five-five Powell around and dropping him prone. In days to come everyone will have a different version of what happened. But everyone will remember the big white cop, gun in hand, standing over the body of the little Black kid.

(Later, a knife is found in the gutter a few feet from Powell's body. Witnesses accuse the cops of planting it.)

Hundreds of middle school kids, pent up from five hours in hot classrooms, stream onto the street, blocking vehicles and throwing bottles and trash at police trying to secure the crime scene. The Tactical Patrol Force, an elite unit charged with controlling disturbances, rolls up in buses. Big white cops, wearing motorcycle helmets and wielding metal batons instead of the standard wooden billy club, they move in a wedge, breaking up clusters of kids until order is restored.

Ted Jones of the *Times* has a page one story next day. NEGRO BOY KILLED; 300 HARASS POLICE: Teen-Agers Hurl Cans and Bottles After Shooting by Off-Duty Officer.

Harlem CORE calls for a March Against Police Brutality. Two hundred protesters show up outside the school, carrying signs, "KILLER COPS MUST GO..." "END POLICE BRUTALITY..."

The funeral has been set for the next night at Delany's Funeral Parlor in Harlem. Tension in the streets. Speakers on street corners. Black Nationalists, Muslims, local leaders. At five, Nathanson sends me home, but I hang around. An angry crowd forms outside the funeral parlor. Police set up barricades and admit only invited guests. Reporters, fearless, or maybe just oblivious, in pursuit of a story, become targets. "Get whitey..." "Kill whitey..." I push through the crowd waving my press card and saying, "just doing my job," as if that will earn me sympathy. An old man grabs my arm. "Better get outta here, son," and says, "let this fool go."

Cops step back to let a limo ease to the curb. James Powell's mother is carried out, convulsing in grief. The crowd presses in on the cops. A photographer tries for a shot of the mother. Somebody shouts,

"Get him, break his camera..." Two other reporters are cursed and shoved. They shove back and are quickly surrounded, pushed, pummeled. "Lynch the white motherfuckers..." Junius Griffin, a Black reporter for the *Times*, fights his way through and pulls them behind the police lines.

Protesters confront the line of cops. "Go home," a cop says. Shouts of derision. "We are home, baby." A bottle crashes at a cop's feet. He picks up a jagged piece and throws it back into the crowd. Rocks and bottles rain down. I seek safety behind the police line under a shower of lethal debris. Try to run around behind the protesters, but am knocked aside by a line of charging cops, swinging wildly. People are trampled. Cops drag bleeding kids by the shirts. A cop is sitting on a crate, blood streaming under his helmet and down his face.

"They're marching on the precinct," someone shouts.

A CORE rally against police brutality, led by Black Nationalist James Lawson and local pastor Reverend Nelson Duke, has moved down Lennox, picking up people as it goes until it's several hundred strong in front of the 28th Precinct on 123rd and Eighth.

A Captain shouts through a bullhorn.

"The shooting incident is being investigated by the District Attorney's office."

The crowd won't be mollified. "Killer cops must go... Punish the murderers..." Snipers on the rooftops keep up a steady barrage of bricks, building tiles and bottles. Cops rush into the buildings and up to the roofs. They grab a few bombers, but others move to adjoining roofs and down back stairways.

(The next day the *Times* reports that the same orators who incited the mob now tried to calm them. Too late... "Harlem is burning," someone shouted.)

Police brass at the door of the precinct. Tactical Patrol Force buses arrive, sirens screaming, lights strobing down the street. Cops wade in, trying to break the crowd into smaller clusters. Groups run down 123rd, breaking windows, torching cars.

"They're burning the Theresa," someone shouts.

Must be a thousand people streaming up Seventh to 125th. I try to hide in the shadows against the buildings. A patrol car mounts the curb, scattering people as it bumps down the sidewalk. A white cop rolls down his window.

"Better get the fuck out of here, kid. I'm not runnin' into a crowd of crazy niggers to save your ass…"

Flames rise in the night. Word spreads along Seventh Avenue, people shouting. "They torched a police car…"

Sirens shrieking, shots cracking. I wait outside the 125th subway station until the stairs are clear and duck into a phone booth. People rush by, rocking the booth, banging the door. Jumping the turnstiles, breaking into the gum and candy machines on the platform. A tense ride downtown. Glares and threats. More white people come on at 96th. Uneasy looks…

I get off at 14th and walk down Seventh Avenue. A hundred and fourteen blocks away from Harlem, Greenwich Village is an island of tranquility. Bach, chess and burgers in the Figaro. The Black regulars aren't here, though. Up the street the Port of Call, the Black hangout, is almost empty.

Patrol cars on every corner. Jimmy, the mounted cop, riding up and down MacDougal. No mixed couples. No black guys on the street.

The riot rages all Saturday night and into Sunday. Malcolm X warns that if all the "armed men" in Harlem confront the police there will be "total war." Mayor Wagner asks Martin Luther King Jr. to speak to the crowd outside the 28th Precinct. King is cursed and bombarded. Ducking bricks and bottles, he has to retreat.

Molotov cocktails are thrown at the cops. The *News* runs a photo of a burnt out patrol car. Cops are given permission to fire if threatened. An ammunition truck is brought down from the Bronx to keep them supplied. Witnesses say cops drove down the side streets, firing out of their windows. One man is found dead on a roof, shot with a .38, the police bullet. Police are reporting nineteen injuries.

Hospitals, disputing this, say hundreds were treated.

Usually, on summer Sundays, the best young basketball players in the city, mostly Black, gather to play at the Village courts on Waverly Place and Sixth Avenue. Coaches and scouts come down to watch. Today, the only show is me and Benny taking on all comers at handball. Played at top speed with a hard black ball. I learned it in Coney Island while cutting Hebrew school. We roll up our pants over our knees and take our shirts off. My body is a scrawny, stoop-shouldered, embarrassment, but I play with vengeful energy and no one can beat me. The "parkies" hook up a hose and we run cold water over our heads. Uptown girls, go-go boots and mini skirts, swinging shopping bags from the cool Village stores, watch us through the fence. Lust swirls in the summer air.

Later, a veal parmigiana hero and a slice at Whitey's on Sixth Avenue. The riot is on the TV over the bar. News footage from behind the police lines. Rocks, bottles, the occasional Molotov exploding. Groups running down the street, throwing rocks through windows. Cops cuffing looters.

"Fuckin' animals. They're destroyin' their own neighborhood."

"Fuckin' landlords must be celebratin'. They gotta put up with all these deadbeats and junkies. Now they just collect their fire insurance, case closed..."

"Whaddya wanna bet some wiseguy hired some bums to burn down his store..."

Monday morning I'm back at the Police shack. I ask Artie Rosenfeld: "anything like this ever happen before?"

"In '43," he says. "Colored troops were back from the war and they wouldn't take any guff. A cop shot an Army Lieutenant in a hotel lobby and that started it. Burning and looting, buncha people killed. La Guardia sent a coupla thousand cops and National Guard and then walked the streets himself, calming things down. Everybody loved him, even the colored..."

Nathanson calls. "Take a walk around Harlem. See what's going on."

I take the 2 train to 125th. The streets are empty. Dept. of Sanitation street sweepers gathering debris and broken glass with extra wide brooms, shoveling them into cans and dumping them into garbage trucks. Store owners hosing the sidewalks. Acrid smell of quelled flames. In front of the Theresa a tow truck driver is hooking up the burnt hulk of a police car. A few kids jump in my face. "You better get your ass outta here." An old man spits on the sidewalk as I walk by. "Wash the spot where the white man walks," and brandishes his cane. A police car rolls alongside. Black cop leans out of the window. "Want a ride to the subway?"

"No thanks…"

He offers me a white crash helmet. "Better take this then. They're still up on the roofs…"

The helmet will make me look like a chicken shit white boy.

"I'll be okay…"

He shrugs and drives away.

I walk past glares and insults to Delany's Funeral Parlor. The building is dark, but the door is open. Red plush carpet. Fragrance of rotting flowers. A heavy old man in pinstripe trousers and black suspenders. "Whaddya want?"

I tell him I worked for Riverside and he brightens up; undertakers love to talk trade. "Family wanted the Asian Mahogany casket, eleven hundred. People pledged money to help them pay for the funeral. Watch, I won't see a dime…"

I ask if embalming a body with bullet wounds is a problem.

"If it's a head wound you gotta putty it in and get the skin tones right. This boy was shot in the torso. We found one bullet in his lung. The other went right through his stomach and out his back. Thirty-eight makes a small hole…"

On the way out I see Ted Jones and Junius Griffin of the *Times*. They walk on either side of me, smiling at each other. Do I look scared? Do they think they have to protect this chickenshit white boy?

"I'm gonna go walk back to the park," I tell them.

Something whooshes. A water balloon crashes at my feet, drenching my pants. Kids laughing out of a window drop another one. I jump out of the way. "Walk in the middle of the road," Jones calls. Pass a few old men sitting on a legless sofa outside a barber shop. "Keep goin', young man. Next one might be a brick and I don't want it fallin' on me..."

At the park entrance two Black Boy Scouts are showing a map to a big Irish cop. Smiles, and trusting looks from the kids. The cop points them in the right direction and says something that makes them laugh as they walk away.

I phone in a first person story of what just happened. Headline reads: A WHITE MAN'S WALK DOWN A HOSTILE STREET. The story runs all day. That night Joe M... challenges me:

"Tell the truth. Did you make those Boy Scouts up?"

"THINK HE EVER LAUGHS?"

August 4, 1964

SLAIN CIVIL RIGHTS WORKERS FOUND. Three young guys, two white and one black, who were in Mississippi to help register black voters, disappeared in late June. Today their charred bodies were found in a burnt out station wagon in the woods. The white kids had been shot once in the heart. The black kid was beaten beyond recognition and shot multiple times.

The kids were from New York. I call Gladys and ask if she knew them. "Andrew (Goodman) and Michael (Schwerner) went down on a CORE project," she says. "Their mistake was riding with James. If it had just been two white boys they might have gotten off with a beating and a night in jail.

Naomi, the radical, is at the feminist table in the Figaro. Sleeveless blouse cut at the midriff. No visible means of breast support. Dungaree shorts like bikini bottoms. She walks toward my table. Ignore her until she is standing so close that if I turn my head I'll nose her bellybutton. "Can you give me a ride to Union Square?" she asks. "I'll chip in for gas."

I'm in a tight chess game with Pierre, a French draft dodger. Could take an hour. "We can call it a draw," he says. I stick by Lenny Frankel's motto—"eager don't get beaver"—and nonchalant it. "Just let me finish the game."

But then I rethink. What if she promotes another ride? There are guys in this place who would carry her to Union Square.

"Okay, we'll call it a draw," I say.

"I don't accept," Pierre says, knowing I want to leave.

"Okay, I resign…"

Naomi follows me across MacDougal to my car. "You've got a ticket."

"That's from yesterday. I just leave it there to fool the cops."

"Cool trick."

Which never works, but there's no need to tell her.

"You're looking pretty teasey for a woman's libber," I say.

"Dressing down is playing into the male stereotype that feminists must be dowdy and ugly," she says. "If men are insecure about a strong, sensual feminist that's their problem."

"What's happening at Union Square?" I ask.

"I'm meeting someone," she says.

"Ray?"

She laughs. "You kidding?"

"What's wrong with him all of a sudden?"

"Ray's the biggest little boy I ever met."

"Bigger than me?"

"You're not a little boy," she says. "You're an old Jewish man… Look how you sit?"—she pulls my shoulders back—"Like you've got the weight of the world on you… I'll bet you say Oy when you have an orgasm…"

"Play your cards right and maybe you'll find out," I say.

"And you're addicted to jokes like an old Jewish man," she says.

"What's wrong with jokes?"

"Bourgeois technique to soften the blows of oppression. Encourage people to laugh at their lives and they won't want to change."

Union Square is a meeting place for radicals of every stripe. On the perimeter orators mount benches and makeshift podia with indictments of Capitalism, American Imperialism, Communists, Atheists. Crazies cackle in the shadows under the trees. Dope dealers step off for private conversations. Dead-eyed muggers watch the crowd like predators looking for a straggler.

Naomi grabs my hand. "C'mon and meet the only man in my life…" She glides through the crush to a rickety bridge table where a bald old guy with a battered fighter's face, sleeves rolled over brawny forearms is hectoring the passersby. "Britain freed its slaves in 1807. If there had been no so-called American Revolution slavery would have been abolished in the colonies and there would never have been a Civil War…"

"Ben," Naomi calls.

He holds out his ink-stained hands. "Nochkele."

"Are you related?" I ask.

"He's the biological father of my mother," she says. "But since bourgeois morality compels women to lie about their sensuality, who knows?"

She runs up for a hug. "Ben, this is Heywood. He works for the *New York Post*."

"The *Post* is a dangerous paper," Ben says.

I'm surprised. "Only liberal paper in town…"

"Fascists starve the workers. Liberals keep them begging for crumbs…"

"Ben fought in Spain with the International Brigades," Naomi says proudly.

"My father was in the Lincoln Brigade," I say. No point in adding he never got to Spain. "He was treasurer of the Bronx Communist Party."

"Half the people in the Party were FBI informers," Ben says. "The other half were robots who couldn't think for themselves."

"Ben planted mines in Madrid," Naomi says.

"I was with the FAI, Anarchist units," Ben says. "We could have beaten the fascists, but no one wanted us to win, least of all our Communist comrades." Hands me a leaflet, THE BETRAYAL OF SACCO AND VANZETTI. "This might interest you coming from a

Communist household. You see Sacco and Vanzetti committed the robbery as a direct action..."

"You mean they were guilty?"

"Guilt and innocence are constructs of bourgeois repression," he says. "Direct action is propaganda by deed, meant to inspire others to sabotage the wage system. The so-called American left portrayed this as a case of false accusation to be corrected by the so-called liberal judiciary."

"Was shooting the guard part of their deed?" I ask.

"The guard was defending the cash nexus," says Ben. "He should have dropped his gun and joined them."

"But they claimed they were innocent."

"At that point it became more important to join with the lesser evil against the greater threat of fascist dictatorship. America was days away from Revolution. If the Capitalists and Communists had not connived with each other to create the so-called New Deal allowing the patrician FDR to save his own class with toothless reform we would be in a very different world today..."

"A worse world," I say. "There would have been no New Deal."

"More crumbs for the masses," he says with magnificent disdain. "The people have no power in the statist system."

"They have the vote," I say.

"Emma Goldman said if voting changed anything they would make it illegal." He points to a livid scar above his eye. "Gurrah Shapiro's goons gave me this, the day the gangsters were voted control of the Bakery Workers in the name of the workers. The same day Stalin was starving the Ukrainians in the name of the Revolution and Eleanor Roosevelt was having tea with Sidney Hillman, the so-called union leader who betrayed the workers to the counter-revolutionary Democratic Party..." The words flow like he's said them many times. "Communism is an oligarchical conspiracy disguised as a revolution. The state is its oppressive instrument. Stirner says the state is a chimera, there is only the individual... Anarchists don't seek personal power. We strive for the administration of things, not people... In the words of Gramsci, we live without illusions, but are not disillusioned..." He shoves a pile of pamphlets in my chest. "Educate yourself. Free your mind."

We leave him, haranguing a few winos as if they were a cheering multitude.

"He's wrong about Capitalism and Communism," I say. "They're deadly enemies."

"Coercive systems tacitly collaborate with each other to maintain power," she says. "Kennedy and Khrushchev are puppets. The Cold War is an invention. The Hungarian Revolt, the Bay of Pigs were all meant to fail."

No place to park, even the hydrants are taken. There's a space in front of a storefront on Cornelia Street. Blackened windows mean Mob club, park at your own risk, but I pull in anyway.

A few winding blocks to Barrow Street. I want to get her into my place before she changes her mind. "I live like an anarchist," I say. "There is no official record of me anywhere."

"Except for your byline," she says. "They could find you in a second..."

She feels her way down the metal stairs to my sub-basement. "This is a magic place. You could plot great deeds here..." Brushes my hand away from her shoulder. "Do you have to play the chivalrous rapist?" Pushes me down on my unmade bed. Cool, dry lips against my neck. Warm breath in my ear. "Can you imagine yourself a female? Welcoming? Receiving?"

I can. No problem.

In the morning Naomi scours the food-crusted pots on my stove, washes my underwear in the shower and makes me get out of bed so she can soak my sheets in the super's work sink. "Don't confuse this with an atavistic domestic tendency," she says. "I enjoy cleaning."

A gust screeches through the window, scattering her grandpa's pamphlets. I watch the supple curve of her back, breasts stirring as she reaches under the bed to retrieve them. Looking for a relevant quote she finds Prince Kropotkin, Russian aristocrat turned Anarchist.

"America shows how all the written guarantees for freedom are no protection against tyranny and oppression. In America the politician has come to be looked on as the very scum of society."

"True," I say, "and we're not going to change it."

"Yes we will. We'll mobilize the best minds of our generation…"

"Like in Alan Ginsberg's line, *I have seen the best minds of my generation?*"

"Ginsberg was talking about a bunch of suicidal drug addicts… I'm talking about galvanizing people like you into collective action. You could do a lot of good by just inserting subtle anarchist messages into your stories…"

"You kiddin'? The editors catch one word of anarchist propaganda and I'll be covering toy shows in the Bronx."

"You're hopeless," she says. Pushes me back on the bed. "You're just a common garden variety frivolous male. A full stomach and empty gonads is all you aspire to."

We make a date to meet at Union Square at six-thirty. I grab her at the door. "Before you go can we empty my gonads one more time?"

She kisses me on the forehead. "Get some sleep, frivolous male…"

I awake in the dark. Seven-thirty, I'm an hour late. I run to Cornelia Street. A few neighborhood guys are sitting on bridge chairs in front of the club. All of my tires have been flattened down to the rims. They stare at me, arms folded.

I run to a garage on Sixth Avenue. The owner is mystified. "Why'd you park in front of a mob club? I'll have to get their permission to tow you."

I run all the way to Union Square. A weary white-haired woman holding a thermos is watching Ben fold up his bridge table. "My granddaughter went straight back to Sarah Lawrence," she says. "She's a graduate assistant there you know…"

So that's what it was. Con the infatuated schmuck into writing anarchist propaganda. Dump him when he balks.

In the movies the jilted lover gets drunk and pours out his heart to a friendly bartender. I get a slice and a sausage sandwich at Whitey's almost every day, but they act like they don't know me. A bunch of neighborhood guys are at the bar watching the Mets get clobbered.

I blink and the Mets are gone. "Live from the White House," an announcer says. Then a reporter: "Three Communist patrol boats attacked the destroyer USS Maddox in international waters off the coast of North Viet Nam Sunday with torpedoes and gunfire. The Maddox, joined by U.S. Navy jets, fired back..."

The announcer in heraldic tones: "The President of the United States," and it's Lyndon Johnson behind a desk...

Renewed hostile actions against United States ships on the high seas in the Gulf of Tonkin... Air action is now in execution against gunboats and supporting facilities in North Viet-Nam..."

"What's goin' on?" I ask.

"The gooks took a coupla potshots at one of our destroyer and we're bombing the crap outta them."

"Fuckin' hillbilly wantsa start a war..."

"Look at the puss on this guy. Think he ever laughs?"

"REPRESS THE PELVIS AND YOU CONTROL THE WORLD"

August 1964

Front page, *New York Times:* RED PT BOATS FIRE ON U.S. SHIP ON VIETNAM DUTY. U.S. FIRES BACK, SINKING THREE BOATS.

LBJ tries to rally the country. "We must make it clear to all that the United States is united in its determination to bring about the end of Communist subversion and aggression..." He submits a resolution to Congress condemning the "aggression of the communist regime of North Vietnam..."

Oregon Senator Wayne Morse opposes it, claiming to have "inside information" that the attacks never took place. Morse says it's a violation of the Constitution to give the President the power to go to war without a formal declaration from Congress. Senator George Aiken, Republican of Vermont, agrees but says: "As a citizen, I feel I must support our president whether his decision is right or wrong." To which Morse angrily replies: "Since when do we have to back our president, or should we, when the president is proposing an unconstitutional act?"

Morse is joined by Senator Ernest Gruening (D.Alaska) who urges Congress not to "send our American boys into combat in a war, which is being steadily escalated..." And warns: "Someday this will be considered a crime."

Radical journalist I.F. Stone says it's all just a pretext to widen the secret war we've been waging against North Vietnam since 1954. Cites foreign diplomatic sources who say the Tonkin Gulf attack never happened. "If there was an attack and if we sank three patrol boats why was no flotsam or jetsam offered as proof of the wreckage?" he asks

Liberals who have been warning about American involvement in Vietnam now endorse it. Walter Lippmann, known as "the dean of political columnists," writes, "President Johnson cannot be counted on not to be provoked if the provocation is continual and cumulative..."

Max Lerner says the resolution is necessary because TV coverage would reveal too much to the enemy. "In the era of the electronic battlefield congressional debate on a declaration of war would represent a surrender of secrecy and surprise."

Both houses pass the resolution. Morse and Gruening are the only "Nay" votes.

The *Times* is optimistic. "This should and will end the incident if North Vietnam and Communist China want it to end."

LBJ claims "overwhelming support" in the polls but Gruening disagrees. "American public opinion, judged by my mail, is overwhelmingly committed to a policy of peace," he says.

Barry Goldwater, the Republican presidential candidate, proposes dropping "low yield nuclear weapons" on North Vietnamese supply routes to "defoliate" the jungle and make the area impassable. He's an ex-Air Force pilot and the press worries he'll nuke Hanoi if elected.

Draft talk in the Figaro. People comparing shrink notes.

The War Resisters League draws a crowd in Union Square. "There is no such thing as a just or necessary war," the speaker says.

"World War II was necessary," someone says.

"Only because the United States had entered World War I. If we had let the Kaiser win, there would not have been a Hitler."

A poster on a lamppost advertises a "teach-in" at the Jefferson Bookstore, a few blocks away. Owned by the American Communist Party, the store has been firebombed several times. It wears its scars— blackened door frame, taped window, cratered doorstep—like badges of honor. The manager, a Jewish guy from Brownsville, usually sits among his shelves of Marx and Lenin with only a few old Commies for company. But tonight the place is packed. The crowd has overflowed onto the street. The speaker is a pudgy, blotchy-faced, bald guy—looks like a high school teacher—in a rumpled denim jacket, white shirt and tie.

"Defeated at Dien Bien Phu, Malaysia and Indonesia, the Imperialists have chosen to make their last stand in Vietnam," he says. "They will use this so-called attack as a pretense..."

Shouts...

"The military-industrial complex needs this war..."

"War is the health of the Police State."

"This is a distraction to get the Black struggle off the front page. They are going to take hundreds of thousands of brothers away from the front lines of the Revolution and send them to the jungle to die..."

Someone shouts, "Watch out for the FBI agent, people. He's the one screaming the loudest, the one who organizes everything. Always has plenty of money to rent the hall for the meeting, print pamphlets, travel to demos. Always has a petition to sign so they can have your name and address."

A kid with tinted glasses à la Godard. "FBI's in that building across the street. Cameras behind those dark windows. Raise your collars and shield your faces going out..."

"Check out *I Led Three Lives* to see how the FBI infiltrated the CP in the fifties..."

"They think they're heroes. That they're risking their lives moving among us..."

The blotchy guy pops up. "If you find an agent or an informer, expose them to the world. But no violence. They're looking for an excuse to launch a mass round up of radicals like the Palmer raids in the twenties..."

"Sexuality is their real enemy."

An old guy. Shirtless, flabby old-guy boobs under overalls,

shouting: "They want to divert your natural aggressive urge for sexual gratification into the brutal sadism that sends you rushing onto the battlefield howling for blood…"

"Reichian crap!" someone shouts.

The guy squints into the crowd, jowls atremble. "Wilhelm Reich is the only true martyr of the Revolution…"

"What about the Rosenbergs?"

"The Rosenbergs were unwitting instruments of the coercive bureaucracies. When they were no longer useful to the Marxists they were turned over to the Capitalists. Reich was defamed, persecuted and secretly assassinated behind prison walls because he had discovered their secret weapon…"

"What weapon?"

"Pelvic repression."

Jeers…

The old man howls like a spurned prophet. "Listen to me… The pelvis is the seat of pleasure, of relief, of reproduction, and thus of ultimate redemption. The repressed pelvis causes hemorrhoids, impotence, constipation, frigidity, anxiety, all the ills of modern life. It is the somatic metaphor for the dogmas of patriotism and mystical religion…" He walks through the crowd like he's searching for somebody and finds her: a busty blonde in a work shirt. Puts a swollen hand on her shoulder, panting like a dog in heat. She recoils, nose wrinkling at his stinking breath as he shouts: "Repress the pelvis and you control the world."

"WE NEED A VICTORY"

September 1964

In Chicago, a Black woman tries to sneak a bottle of gin out of liquor store and is tackled by clerks. A few hours later people are dead and the whole block is burning. The store's been there for generations with no problem. Its white owner is perplexed. "These are my people," he says. "When they can't pay I take a shirt or something in trade…"

Outbreaks in Jersey City, Paterson and Elizabeth, New Jersey. They start with a police shooting, a protest that gets out of hand, then torching and looting. Smaller cities, smaller riots. No dead, minimal damage in the downtown areas. The photos which were so shocking a few weeks ago are now a commonplace. A gutted building. Black protesters screaming rage into the deadpan faces of burly white riot cops. Somber white mayors at press conferences. The same quote in a hundred stories. "How can they destroy their own neighborhoods?"

The riots are Page One around the world. Somebody calls it "the long, hot summer." A twelve-year-old kid takes the BBC on a tour of the burnt out buildings of Harlem. The German newsmagazine Der Spiegel runs photo spreads of white cops beating Black men. An Austrian paper says: "There can be no doubt that the events [riots] must be blamed on the basic attitude of part of the American society as it was expressed at the Republican convention with the nomination of Arizona Senator Barry Goldwater…" The London Daily Telegraph says, "Goldwater's nomination has already incited Negro terrorism in reply." Martha and the Vandellas, on tour in London, are confronted by reporters shouting the lyrics of their hit single. "Summer's here and the time is right/For dancin' in the streets." A radio reporter asks: "Isn't 'Dancin' in the Streets' a secret celebration of the riots in American cities?" Martha laughs—"My lord, it's a party song,"—but everybody prefers the riot answer. Rumors spread that young Black men play the song over PA's before they go out to loot and burn.

Gladys tells me Harlem CORE is broke. "The mayor's people got mad at us for making LBJ look bad in the stall-in. Pulled all the little city grants we were getting. Then we lost the white money after the riots. Now we're gonna have to shut down."

I write a story. "Harlem CORE, which has been in the forefront of the civil rights movement in New York City, is out of money and might have to shut down. And quote Gladys: "We're being punished for our activism.""

It's a soft exclusive, not an earthshaking revelation, but gets an outpouring of sympathy. Gladys calls me. "You saved us..." They've been contacted by foundations, funders, donors all over the country. The local pols have come back to the fold.

Gladys invites me for a "thank you dinner." I think it's going to be just the two of us, but when I get to her apartment the whole executive board of the Harlem chapter is there. We have fried chicken, Kraft Macaroni'n'Cheese and collard greens with sweet potato pie from the famous Better Pie Crust Bakery on Seventh Avenue. Gladys's slight sidelong smile tells me she knows I was hoping for something a little more intimate. "I've got another story for you," she says.

Harlem CORE is being pressured to repudiate Malcolm X. The Black Establishment is solidly and vocally against him. Judge Thurgood Marshall has condemned the Black Muslims as a "bunch of thugs organized in prisons" and called Malcolm, "a convicted pimp." Martin Luther King Jr. has said, "I wish Malcolm wouldn't talk about violence so much... He's doing our people a disservice..." Whitney Young of the Urban League: "Malcolm has never gotten a job or decent housing for anyone." Roy Wilkins of the NAACP: "We should recognize that a thug is a thug, white or black, and put him in his place..." James Farmer, head of National CORE: "Malcolm has done nothing but verbalize... There will come time when he'll have to chirp or get off the perch." But the local branches have refrained from criticism. "At the grassroots level they love the man," Gladys says.

"We know he's crazy," George says. "We can't even get a seat on a bus and he's talkin' about how we're gonna get ten states in the South. If the white man gave us Alabama and Mississippi, what do you think we'd be doin? Sharecroppin'..."

"It's costing us money, I know," Gladys says. "But we're on the street with angry people who have absolutely nothing going for them. They worship Malcolm. If we denounce him we'll lose all hope of reaching them. We need something to show them that they can do well in America..." She rubs her eyes with a tired sigh. "We need a victory..."

"THAT OTHER MOTHERFUCKER WAS GONNA GET US ALL KILLED"

November 1964

Joan Baez sings at an anti war protest in San Francisco. The cops count the crowd at five hundred. Organizers say it's more like two thousand. More guys burn their draft cards in Berkeley.

The Viet Cong launches a mortar barrage on a US air base at Bien Hoa, South Vietnam. Four Americans dead, seventy-two wounded. Five bombers destroyed. LBJ is described as "embarrassed" by this "brazen attack," but repeats his campaign promise "We are not about to send American boys nine or ten thousand miles away from home to do what Asian boys ought to be doing for themselves."

Barry Goldwater makes outrageous statements like: "You've got to forget about the civilian. Whenever you drop bombs, you're going to hit civilians..." When he's not scary he's a clown, saying, "If you don't mind smelling like peanut butter for a few days, peanut butter is darn good shaving cream..." He tells smutty, barroom jokes: "Any man in business would be foolish to fool around with his secretary. If it's somebody else's secretary, fine..." But then goes grim: "By one impulse act you could press a button and wipe out 300 million people before sundown." His campaign slogan is, "Extremism in defense of liberty is no vice." People wonder if he means it when he says, "I could turn North Vietnam into a mud puddle..."

Martin Luther King Jr., recently awarded the Nobel Peace Prize, campaigns tirelessly for LBJ, warning: "If Goldwater is elected there will be riots and violence the like of which this country has never seen."

Democrats run a scare ad. A little girl is counting the petals on a daisy, "one two, three five, six, eight…" A southern accent drowns her out. "Ten, nine, eight, seven, six…" There is a massive explosion. The little girl disappears in a mushroom cloud. LBJ's voice: "We must all love each other or die." Then an announcer: "Vote for Lyndon Johnson on Election Day. The stakes are too high not to…"

Election Day, I'm in Criminal Court covering the last day of the Lenny Bruce obscenity trial. In April, Bruce was dragged out of a packed house at the *Cafe au Gogo* on Bleecker Street by Vice Squad detectives. He was charged with violating Penal Code 1140-A, a 19th-century statute prohibiting "obscene, indecent and immoral drama which would tend to the corruption of the morals of youth and others…" The wording is so archaic it specifies a term of three years in the "workhouse," which no longer exists.

Bruce had risen out of the obscurity of suburban club dates to become the most controversial comedian in the country. His humor was startling, subversive, setting him apart from the new wave of comics like Nichols and May, Shelly Berman, Bob Newhart, Mort Sahl, who were hip and topical, but dealt with traditional themes— family problems, love trouble, conventional politics. He tore away the sitcom facade of the fifties. Talked about taboo subjects—sex in all its variations, drugs, racism, American hypocrisy. A meth head, he bopped around the stage in a tight-fitting Italian suit, popping his fingers like a jazz musician. His routines were riffs on a theme, like a jazz solo. He never repeated himself, running new variations on his classic routines. Made no concession to the audience. They either got his references or they didn't—if you'd never heard of Charlie Parker or Kraft-Ebbing he wasn't going to stop the flow to explain. He used Yiddish euphemisms, which no one, including most of his Jewish fans, could hope to understand. Talking about cunnilingus, he said, "Everybody *fresses* (eats) today, everybody is a *lecker* (a licker.) People gasped when he talked about *shtupping*, (screwing.) Or getting a *shmeckel* in the *tochus*... Or his mother saying his tattoo is a *"shandeh for the goyim,"* and will prevent his burial in a Jewish cemetery.

"There is only what is," Bruce said. "What should be is a dirty lie. We are all part of the same sick, hypocritical universe. We are in this together."

Bruce became a comedy *cause celebre*. Everyone leapt to his First Amendment defense. Steve Allen, host of the Tonight Show called him a "new voice in comedy," and booked him on prime time.

Local police had been raiding Bruce's shows and arresting him for obscenity and drug possession since 1960, but nobody really wanted to throw him in in jail. He was acquitted in Los Angeles, had his case dismissed in Chicago. Even the drug charges were dropped.

But then he went too far. His urge to "tell what is" trumped his instinct as a performer. After the assassination, everyone had commended Jackie Kennedy's courage in trying to help her fallen husband. Bruce came on stage with blow-ups of news photos of her climbing, dress bloodied, over the trunk of the car. "This story is bullshit," he said. "Does it look like she's trying to help him? She's hauling ass to save her ass. Every one of us would have done the same..."

Voice jagged with scorn Bruce did a savage takeoff of LBJ. "It's taken him six months to learn how to say to Negro... He portrayed LBJ's assistants coaching him. "It's easy, just say knee-grow..." while he struggles to get the word out. "Nigarow... Niggree... Goddamit I just can't say it..."

Did he misread the gasps? Had he gone too deep into the netherworld of druggies, hipsters and jazz musicians and lost touch with his audience? Jackie was our tragic heroine, standing alone with her two small children. That's how we wanted to see her. The Johnson riff was blunt, unsubtle. LBJ was a ruthless, vindictive Texas pol, but he was our champion against that lunatic warmonger Barry Goldwater. We needed to believe in him.

There were stories that Bobby Kennedy was after Bruce for what he said about Jackie. That the Catholic establishment, influential in law enforcement, was behind some of the arrests. That LBJ, protective of his liberal credentials, was infuriated at being portrayed as a racist.

The harassment became relentless. Bruce was set up by informers and drug dealers. Police officers took notes at every performance. He lost bookings, couldn't get back on network TV; only Hugh Hefner would book him on The Playboy Penthouse. In one year his income dropped from two hundred and fifty thousand to six thousand.

The same drugs that had made him manic and witty now plunged him into leaden depression. He saw himself as a legal expert. He lectured instead of performing. He was no longer funny.

In New York, an inspector from the State Liquor Authority sat in the Cafe au GoGo audience and transcribed phrases like "jack me off... nice tits... go come in your chicken..." and "lowest tit can..." The next night the cops barged past the line awaiting the ten o'clock show. Bruce and club owner Howard Solomon were cuffed, arraigned and held overnight. Bruce was quickly indicted and brought before a three-judge panel headed by Chief Administrative Judge John L. Murtagh, cold blue glare behind gold rims, nostrils pinched, finger over pursed lips, a pillar of the lay Catholic community.

I asked an Assistant DA why Bruce couldn't get a jury trial. "It's a statute violation," he said. "Take too long to explain to a jury..."

But the beat reporters knew better. "(Manhattan DA) Hogan wants his conviction fast," said Jim R... of the AP. "That's why he picked Murtagh. He doesn't want to give Bruce a chance to make a circus out of this..."

In a few short years Bruce has aged and deteriorated. No longer the Jewish pretty boy, he is puffy, slow moving, with bleary eyes over heavy pouches. Against the advice of his lawyers he has shown up in a bleached dungaree suit, work shirt, construction shoes.

"Looks like a jailbird already," somebody whispers.

Bruce's attorney Martin Garbus says the indictment is a vendetta straight from the White House. "Lenny Bruce is being prosecuted for his attacks on religion and public figures, not for his use of dirty words." His other attorney, Ephraim London, winner of nine First Amendment cases before the Supreme Court, enlists the cultural elite to testify that Bruce is not obscene, his language not "sexually arousing," and that it would be unthinkable for liberal city like New York to put a comic in jail for exercising his First Amendment rights. The judges sit stone faced as esteemed critics, famous writers, columnists, theater stars, right and left-wing celebrities parade to the stand. They call Bruce a "satirist," an "innovator." Someone on the Village Voice says he is the "art martyr" of our generation.

High praise, but Bruce can't stand it. He writhes in frustration and whispers vehemently to his attorneys. London puts a calming hand on his arm. Bruce turns away, shaking his head.

In the hall during recess, he runs up to the reporters. "They're making me look like a jerk... I never said any of those things... Lowest tit can, what does that mean? What kinda schmuck would say go come in your chicken? See what they're doing, they're destroying me as a comedian... My lawyers won't let me defend myself..."

Back in court, more muttering at the defense table. As a witness was stepping down Bruce jumps up.

"Your honor..."

Murtagh cuts him off. "You'll have your chance to speak, Mr. Bruce..."

In the corridor at the end of the day, Bruce announces: "My lawyer said if I tried to speak he would resign. I've dismissed him. I'm representing myself."

London confirms he is off the case, but will still come to court in an advisory capacity.

That night I visit Bruce in his room at the Hotel Marlton on Waverly Place. Law books are scattered everywhere, legal pads, journals. "Looks like a law library after a wind storm," I say. Bruce smiles sourly... "Funny..." He insists his lawyers are using the wrong strategy. "You gotta be able to read your audience, man. This celebrity civil liberties routine is dying. See how judges sit back every time another of these cats comes to the stand. That's boredom, man. You want your audience leaning forward, watching your every move."

"So what would you do?" I ask.

"Use the law, man. That's what these cats respect..." He brandishes a law book. "I've got twelve free speech cases, all decided for the defendant. This kid from NYU is helping me. I got precedent, man. Pornographers sending dirty movies through the mail, more serious than what I did and they got acquitted. Wait a second, I gotta take a shit..."

He shuffles into the little bathroom, locking the door. I hear the water running, something clattering... I shout a question, "Do you think they're after you because of what you said about Jackie?"

A strained reply. "Everywhere I go people holler, 'Hey Lenny, tell us what you think of those photos.' They love the bit..."

"They say Johnson's mad because you called him a bigot..."

A long silence. I realize he's shooting up in there. Finally that strained voice.

"Johnson doesn't have time for a *schmeckel* like me."

The lock clicks and the door opens. Bruce stumbles out, eyes glittering like the Bruce of old. "Hey man, wanna read some interesting cases?"

Morning in an empty courtroom. A few beat reporters, no big names. Bruce comes in late and counts the house. He looks disappointed, but what did he expect? Everybody is covering the election.

Murtagh pointedly ignores him and asks London, "Is the defense ready?"

"Mr. Bruce would like to make a statement, your honor," London says.

Bruce is up wielding a legal pad. "I would like to petition the court to reopen my case," he says and then launches into an incoherent rant about the legal system, show business, sexual practices of Catholics as opposed to Jews, I try to take it down, picking up little bits like, "Jews understand anal intercourse," (where did he get that idea?) and, "it was genuflecting, not masturbating..." Bruce claims he's been misunderstood. "I'd be just as upset as you would if my daughter brought home a Filipino..." He pleads for a chance to do his act for the court. "Let me testify," he says. "Let me tell you what my show is about. Don't lock up my words. Don't finish me in show business..."

Murtagh gavels. "We must conclude these proceedings now..." And the judges retire to consider their verdict.

I rush out the corridor to try to catch Bruce, but he's disappeared. Run to the bathroom. See his shoes behind a stall. No point in trying to talk to him now.

The judges are back. London and Garbus rise, loyally, next to Bruce.

"We find the defendant guilty as charged," Murtagh says. His act is "prurient" and "offensive to average person in the community." And it "lacks redeeming social importance."

Amazingly, Judge Creel dissents and votes to acquit. He was the Black liberal put on the panel to rubber stamp Murtagh, but has risen to defy him. "I find nothing offensive in Mr. Bruce's performance," he says. Surprise in the press row. "That guy's gonna be in Staten Island Traffic Court for the rest of his career..."

Sentencing is put off until next month. "He can get three years," someone says.

"They wouldn't do that," I say.

"They'll do what [DA] Hogan tells them after he talks to Bobby Kennedy..."

I run to a phone. "Bruce guilty," I tell Scaduto. "A book and a half," he says, which means a short story for the back pages.

"But this guy's being persecuted," I say. "He's a great artist and they're destroying him."

"He's a comic who made fun of the wrong people," Scaduto says. "Go out in the street and get some reactions to the election."

LBJ has beaten Goldwater by sixteen million votes with sixty-one percent of the popular vote. The world exhales. Even the Russians are relieved. Soviet Premier Kosygin congratulates the American electorate on choosing "a more moderate and sober policy." Magnanimous in victory, LBJ promises to provide "equal opportunity for all and special privileges for none." To "try to achieve peace in our time for our people." There are stories about how he has already begun secretly withdrawing troops from Vietnam.

Outside the courthouse I find a cop who shakes a thick finger and says, "This country will rue the day they didn't vote for Goldwater..."

In a vest pocket park behind the Hall of Records, the bench jockeys are passing a quart of Thunderbird. I tell them Johnson won by a landslide

"That's good," one of them says. "That other motherfucker woulda got us all killed."

IT CAN COME AT ANY TIME

December 1964

LBJ's honeymoon is aborted. Relief at his election turns quickly to disillusion as he sends troops back to Vietnam. It looks like the hardcore radicals were right. He was lying about "bringing peace." He was just waiting until after the election to increase the draft call.

Martin Luther King Jr. has been hospitalized for exhaustion, but checks out and flies to Oslo to accept the Nobel Peace Prize. "Nonviolence is the answer to the crucial moral and political question of our time," he says. This simple statement is seized upon to show his opposition to LBJ's military action in Vietnam. Not a popular position among civil rights leaders, leery of Johnson's wrath. A. Phillip Randolph says, "I am against plunging the civil rights movement into the controversy... The real front is the Alabama-Mississippi front..."

It's getting harder to beat the draft. Village kids with years of therapy are being told they will need evidence of incapacitating neurosis. Shrinks are balking at exaggerating symptoms for fear that they will be called to testify at the draft boards.

The drug ploy isn't automatic anymore. There has to be some proof in the form of hospital records or doctors' notes. A kid tells an army shrink he's taken so much LSD he has occasional "acid flashes" and can't tell what's real. "What if I think people are shooting at me?" The shrink smiles. "Duck," he says.

Merely admitting to homosexual urges had been a guaranteed ticket out. Now you have to prove you're queer in the form of a shrink note, job dismissal, school expulsion, even a police record. A Village kid uses the same line that's worked for him twice before. "I have feelings of sexual attraction for men. I'm afraid I'll be persecuted." The Army shrink smiles blandly. "It'll still be better than civilian life." And hands him back his form. "The barracks latrine will probably be a lot safer than the public toilet at Penn Station."

Investigative columnist Jack Anderson reports that draft calls are being doubled for 1965. Didn't Johnson say he wasn't going to send American boys to fight for Asian boys? What about those hints that he was withdrawing troops? That he wanted us to "love each other…" We think we're immune to propaganda, but we can be sold a lie we want to believe.

December 17

They haven't lost my file. The draft board hasn't burned down. They just took their time. Long enough to make me forget that they were even after me, so I am stunned to see that familiar envelope at my door. "You are hereby summoned to appear…"

Now, two days before my twenty-second birthday, I'm freezing in my underwear in a line of restive teenagers at Whitehall Street. I'm taking my third physical and I'm the oldest there. Everybody my age is either in or out.

Navy medics in sparkling white scrubs. A kid asks, "Will flat feet get you out?" and gets a snide, "This isn't the ballet, honey…"

The line moves sluggishly. Sergeants herd us along. No giggles at the hernia station. A big Black kid pushes the doctor's hand away. "Don't touch me faggot." MPs rush in and take him off the line. The "spread your cheeks" command at the hemorrhoid check usually gets snickers. Today we "spread' em" with sullen obedience.

A kid with stringy, long hair falling over his face. Boxer muscles, deep, livid scratches on his back, eye shadow, rouge and lipstick. He moves along the line, tossing his hair, hands on hips. Two medics tap him on the shoulder. "Follow us, sweetie."

A flabby kid in stained drawers. "He's been eating cookies and cake for three weeks, so he'd go over the two-fifty weight limit," his friend says.

"Two-fifty is nothin'. Look at all the fat bastards on this line."

In the urine room, a bouncy red-headed kid with billowing white boxers is offering tainted specimens. "Sugar piss, five dollars a dose, made by an old man with diabetes." Little baby arms, he looks like Cupid in a fountain, all he needs is a stream coming out of his dick. Vials are stuffed like cartridges in his drawers. "Guaranteed 4F. Refund if it doesn't work. "

As we turn a corner we see the Black kid pinned against the wall by four Marines. "I ain't seein' no fuckin psychiatrist…" He tries to break free. They push him back, talking calmly like cops trying to soothe a psycho. He throws a wild punch. This is what they've been waiting for. They grab his arms, the back of his shirt and drag him down the corridor, shouting: "You can't do nothin' to me. I ain't goin' in your motherfuckin' army and you can't make me…"

A door slams. Quiet…

The white kids talk. The Black kids stare straight ahead.

"If he didn't wanna take the physical he shouldn't have come…"

"You have to show up. It says on the letter if you don't report you're subject to five years imprisonment or a ten thousand dollar fine."

"How about that kid all made up like a girl?"

"Think he came on the subway like this?"

"See the guns on him? He can handle himself."

"Nobody's gonna fuck with a guy who looks like that anyway."

"It took balls to do what they did."

Yeah, but it was the only thing they could have done. They're street kids. Shrink notes and student exemptions, the conventional middle class avenues of escape, aren't available to them. There's only Direct Action, the individual confronting the state. And why not? The state offers them nothing but exploitation and subsistence and only if they slavishly conform. They have nothing to lose.

But I do. I've got a job to protect. I can't freak out at an army physical. They'll investigate me. The FBI will tell the *Post*. Davis will take me off important stories. Send me to toy shows and rodeos, slop page features that don't matter. Write me off. Force me to quit.

I'm a slave of the status quo. My sub-basement, my phony desperado existence are mere squeals of bourgeois petulance. Those kids are the true anarchists. I'm just a poseur.

Tripping down Barrow Street in the drizzly dawn. That familiar soggy envelope outside my door. "You have been classified 1A."

Marijuana merriment evaporates. I've been expecting this, but it's still a massive bring down. The next letter will tell me when I have to report for induction. It can come at any time

"JUST TO SAVE FACE"

We haven't had FDR's "day of infamy," Churchill's "we will fight them on the beaches." Ringing calls to arms that sent people running to the recruiting offices. Kennedy and Johnson vowed to resist "Communist aggression," but they never asked us to join their crusade. It was as if they knew they had a tough sell. Better to raise the draft call incrementally, let the war seep into the public consciousness until we woke up one morning and it was a fact of life.

In Washington Square Park, an old guy in a seersucker jacket, tired eyes behind rimless glasses, is handing out pamphlets. "Don't be a cog in the War Machine. Don't murder innocent children..." Brown blotches on his neck. Nails bitten down to the cuticles. He's always around, declaiming to indifferent passersby. But today he's drawing a crowd. "Make the Peace Testimony and register as a Conscientious Objector," he says.

A kid is dubious. "So all I have to do is say I object to the war and I'm out?"

"Not exactly. You'll have to do alternate service. Take care of patients in mental hospitals. Do gardening and public works... "

"How long do we have to stay?"

Bowtie looks away, his voice dropping. "CO's are contracted for five years."

"Five years? Army's only two." He walks away, laughing.

Bowtie takes a few hesitant steps after him. "Time well spent passes quickly..." Turns to the crowd. "We're at the Friends School on 14th street. We'll support your claim. If they don't accept it you can still refuse to serve as a pacifist."

"And get out the same way?"

"You'll have to go through a court proceeding, but more often than not they put you on probation…"

"Bullshit!"

A burly bench bum at the edge of the crowd. Red face peeling under a scraggly beard, cut off sleeves showing snake and dragon tattoos. "More often than not you'll spend five years gettin' fist fucked in Leavenworth…"

Everyone laughs and moves on. Bowtie chases the stragglers, waving a pamphlet. "This will explain everything much better than I could. There's some interesting background on what the American Friends did in Wars One and Two."

"Do Quakers object to all wars, or only this one?" the kid asks.

"All wars are equally evil," Bowtie says. "Only the pretext is different…"

"You call Hitler a pretext?" I say. "He was killing millions of people."

"Only once we entered the war…"

"Not true. He was already putting people in extermination camps…"

"Labor camps," Bowtie corrects. "I know, I was there… I was eighteen in 1917 when the US entered World War I. They were assigning Quakers to agricultural labor, replacing farmers who had gone into the army. My father refused to go, saying that would be supporting the war effort. They sent him to prison instead. He was beaten so badly he had to be hospitalized, but insisted on returning to the same cell bloc. After that he won the respect of the same inmates who had beaten him. They were men who understood violence and its consequences. Some became converts. He told me he experienced the joy Christ must have felt, watching young men flock to his cause. Urged me to join him, but I didn't want to give my witness in prison. I went overseas with the American Friends Service Committee. We organized ambulance services. Ferried wounded German prisoners to hospitals. After the war the world looted Germany of territory and resources. I saw German children starving on the streets. If we had been humane in victory we wouldn't have created the bitterness that led to Hitler. A little kindness might have spared the world the nightmare that was to come..."

"Would it have spared six million Jews?"

He moves closer, a trembly little guy, trying hard to win me over. "Look I understand this is a very emotional issue for Jewish people. But if America had refused to fight the German people might have been inspired by our example. We might have saved millions of lives. We face the same crisis now. If every individual acts out of his own conscience we can stop this war before it gets out of control. Once Johnson commits thousands of troops and starts taking American casualties it will be too late. He'll sacrifice a generation of young men. Just to save face."

"OR MORE"

February 6, 1965

North Vietnamese troops cross the border and attack Camp Holloway, a US helicopter base at Pleiku in the Central Highlands. They cut through an electrified fence and slaughter the South Vietnamese troops guarding the perimeter. Mortar the American barracks and attack the fleeing troops with AK-47s. Eight Americans are killed, more than a hundred wounded and twenty helicopters are destroyed.

This marks the first time North Vietnamese have attacked American troops. The next day LBJ orders a "retaliatory" attack on a North Vietnamese army camp at Dong Hoi. It's the first time the US has attacked targets in North Vietnam. Johnson goes on TV to assure the public there has been "no change in policy." The attacks have been "carefully limited to military areas" and are "appropriate and fitting" because "we seek no wider war."

But the media doesn't agree.

"It's time to call a spade a bloody shovel," James Reston writes in the *Times*. "This country is in an undeclared war in Vietnam."

The war is Page One every day.

Daily updates about Viet Cong tactics. A lot of rewrite lingo you can drop into a story without thinking. The Viet Cong always "melts into the jungle." They avoid "major battles," sending small units out on "hit and run" skirmishes. Lay in ambush for South Vietnamese patrols and their American "advisors," attacking with small arms, grenades, fifty-millimeter machine guns. Crouching in the tall grasses as US helicopters fly in reinforcements; "raking the landing zones" as the troops disembark.

We're told how brutal they are with their own people. Taking over villages and forcing the young men and women to fight for them. Torturing "traitors" with burning cigarettes, bamboo shoots under fingernails. Splaying flayed and mutilated bodies on stakes in rice paddies as a warning against dealing with the Americans.

The US is suffering frequent but minimal (if you're not one of them) casualties. Five dead in a place called Bin Ghia. Three when they bomb the US Information Agency office in Saigon. Another few killed when a firebase is overrun. The number inches up every day.

The troop count is inching up as well. The AP counts 23,000 service people on the ground some of them Marines with a clear combat mission. In his inaugural address LBJ had hinted at an even further escalation. "We can never again stand aside, prideful in isolation," he said. "If American lives must end, and American treasure be spilled, in countries that we barely know, then that is the price of our enduring covenant."

That's the party line: We are in Vietnam to protect these helpless people from the scourge of Communism. How could any decent American object to our mission?

But many "informed sources" are using their friends in the press to express discreet dissent. General Maxwell Taylor, Ambassador to Vietnam, is said to recommend bombing North Vietnamese supply routes into the south instead of engaging the Viet Cong on the ground. Senator Mike Mansfield of Montana, the acknowledged Asia expert in Congress, says that South Vietnam should be "neutralized" through negotiations with Hanoi. General Matthew Ridgeway, who as Army Chief of Staff, had opposed US intervention in 1953 when the French were driven out of Southeast Asia by Viet Minh Communist guerrillas, advises that nothing can be gained from US military involvement against the Viet Cong. General David Shoup, retired Commandant of the Marine Corps, is more emphatic:

"I believe that if we had and would keep our dirty, bloody, dollar-crooked fingers out of the business of these nations so full of depressed, exploited people, they will arrive at a solution of their own. That they design and want. That they fight and work for. Not one crammed down their throats by Americans."

A Marine battalion lands at Danang...

The pundits are checking wind direction. Lippmann, who had endorsed Johnson's early escalation, now says: "For this country to involve itself in such a war in Asia would be an act of supreme folly." He says the bombings cannot succeed because the Vietnamese "do not value their material possessions which are few, nor even their lives, which are short and unhappy, as do the people of a county [like the US] who have much to lose and much to live for." He is accused of racism, but says he was merely explaining why the US could never force a surrender by bombardment.

Reston, a Johnson confidant, decries the "crooked course" America is taking and warns that we are sinking into the "accustomed military rut." The *New Yotk Times,* which had supported Johnson, changes editorial course, declaring "the only sane way out is diplomatic... not military."

Another battalion of Marines lands at La Trang.

Johnson acknowledges that, "400 young [American] men... have ended their lives on Vietnam's steaming soil," but insists that, "Our objective is the independence of South Vietnam and its freedom from attack. We want nothing for ourselves..."

Which leads the *Omaha World-Herald* to editorialize, "Since the Cuban Missile Crisis no American can be sure that his government is giving him the whole story."

And two more Marine battalions land at Danang to protect an American air base from daily Viet Cong mortar attack.

This is the classic guerrilla war of attrition, we are told. The Viet Cong strategy is to kill as many Americans as it will take to turn the public against the war. But polls show support is growing. LBJ's approval rating has jumped thirty percent, more than any President since FDR. Three out of four Americans believe more troops should be sent to Vietnam.

Just as long as it isn't them. They're like the kid in the Phil Ochs lyric—*Someone's gotta go over there/And that someone isn't me.* Students are switching their major to education and taking the pedagogy exam because teachers have a higher draft number. Three kids from my old neighborhood are applying to the Police Academy on the unconfirmed rumor that cops get a possible deferment. But there is no guaranteed exemption. Draft boards can take any male under twenty-six to fill their quota. And their quotas have doubled.

A new group of radicals has landed in the city. White guys with no identifiable accent. Strong and intimidating, lock eyes, daring you to disagree. Most left-wing males look like one of the Marx Brothers. These guys are pure American—Gary Cooper, Montgomery Clift— always surrounded by vying females. Some are members of newly-formed Veterans Against the War. They talk about helicopters pouring fire into the jungles of Vietnam, strafing villages, killing anything that moves. Others wear college tees, but look too old to be students. They warn of a secret, plan to mobilize millions and occupy all of Southeast Asia. A guy in a Swarthmore tee says, "We reject electoral politics. Revolution is not possible from within the system."

An old lefty in the park warns: "Too good to be true, they're FBI."

There's a Southern clique, fair and lean with pale, faraway eyes, called the Fort Jackson Eight. The Bohos have come out of the hip bars—the San Remo, Lion's Head, Cedar Bar—to cultivate them. "We're gonna need a million real workers like this if we're ever gonna have a revolution," a Village Marxist says. David M. a novelist, wants to write their story. "Coal miner kids from West Virginia," he says. "They tried to organize a union during Basic Training. If you've ever been in the Army you know how recklessly brave that is."

I try to check their story. There are no clips on the "Fort Jackson

Eight." The AP never heard of them. I call Fort Jackson. The Public Information Officer laughs. "I don't know who these guys are, but anybody who tried to start a union down here would be thrown in the deepest, darkest dungeon the Army could find..."

A kid named Carl is handing out *The Manual for Draft-Age Immigrants to Canada*. "Canada and Sweden have announced that they will give political asylum to anyone resisting the draft," he says. "All you have to do is go to the embassy and renounce your citizenship and they'll make you a political refugee."

"But you'll be charged with desertion," I say.

"They can't get you. Political refugees are not covered by extradition treaties."

"But you'll be a man without a country..."

"Not for long. The war will be over in a coupla months, a year tops. Politicians will declare an amnesty. A million exiles who want to come home is a lot of votes from friends and family..."

"You think a million guys will go to Canada?"

"Or more..."

AND THREE GULLIBLE POTHEADS ARE GOING TO JAIL

February 17, 1965

Police Headquarters. Saboteurs on their way to blow up the Statue of Liberty have been arrested with a car full of dynamite.

Police Commissioner Michael Murphy, a cadre of thick, solemn guys in suits, behind him: "This morning, the New York Police Department in coordination with the FBI and RCMP foiled an attack on the symbols of our American democracy."

"Who the fuck is the RCMP?" somebody whispers. "Royal Canadian Mounted Police," he is told. "The guys in the red tunics with the St. Bernards with brandy around their necks."

Arrested were three Black Americans, "supporters of the Black Liberation Front," Murphy says, and a female French-Canadian TV talk show host named Michelle Duclos. Their plan was hatched after a visit to Cuba and a meeting with Che Guevara. Ringleader Robert Collier, a Black Liberation member, recruited the two others to "blow up that old bitch," as conspirator Walter B. called the statue. They traveled to Canada where they made contact with Duclos, a supporter of the Quebec separatist movement. Duclos secured thirty sticks of dynamite, three blasting caps and a few ounces of marijuana and smuggled them across the border. She stashed the dynamite laden car in a parking lot in the Bronx as the cell made last minute preparations.

Walter B. had the key to a locked passageway that leads from the head of the statue to its arm, Murphy says. They planned to plant the dynamite with a timing device and then drive away, watching the smoke from the decapitated Statue in their rearview mirror. Then, it was on to Philadelphia to blow up the Liberty Bell. And, while police were preoccupied with this second explosion, to D.C. to dynamite the Washington Monument.

But the plot never had a chance to succeed because their cell had been "penetrated" by a "courageous undercover police officer," says Murphy. This hero was still a cadet in the Police Academy when he made contact with the conspirators and was informed of their plans. He immediately informed the FBI and NYPD and was assigned to the PD's top-secret Bureau of Special Services, which monitors subversive activity in the city. He joined the plotters, "at great personal risk," and traveled with them to Canada to secure the explosives. Went with them on the day they planned to execute their plot. Participated in their arrest, subduing one of the men who was a black belt judo instructor.

"They might have accomplished their mission if he hadn't infiltrated their group," Murphy says. "We all owe this brave young policeman a debt of gratitude..."

The hero cop comes out of a side room like an actor taking a curtain call. A tall, Black guy...

SHIT! It's Ray W...

Murphy is presenting Ray with a gold shield. "In recognition of Detective W.'s services we are going to promote him to Detective First Class," he says.

Ray—Fuckin'—W., the fearless radical, screwing the adoring females, egging everybody on to resistance and sabotage.

A curly red-haired guy comes out of the side room. He was the cop who blackjacked Ray at the Plumbers Union demo. I wondered at the light blow. Now I know it was all a set up. That bust was staged to build up Ray's rep.

Flash bulbs are popping, cameramen jostling. I'm in the front, he can't miss me. "Hey Ray," I shout, "Does Naomi know you're a cop?"

Al B. police reporter for the *Times* turns to me. "You know this guy?"

So freaked, I'm about to blab it all. This guy didn't come out of the Academy, he's been inciting and entrapping for years. But then I realize: I've got a scoop.

"Can you get a picture of this guy?" I ask Barney Stein.

"I'll catch him on the corner of Broome and Center," he says.

I chase Ray through the building to the alley behind Headquarters. Barney crouches behind a parked car, clicking away. "Hey Ray," I call. He jumps into a gray Plymouth, the redhead at the wheel, and shoots me a baleful look as it rumbles away.

Run to a phone, the story clicking like a telex in my brain. "This whole thing is a set up," I tell Nathanson. "The cops have created a cover story to protect this guy. He's been agitating for years. I personally heard him tell some kids to throw a grenade at the Lincoln Memorial. He was making trouble at construction sites. I personally heard him tell people to resist arrest at the Plumbers Union. He was busted by a red-headed cop, who play jacked him a coupla times to make it look good. Finally found three schmucks to frame. Probably scored the dynamite and grass for them himself."

"See what the cops say about this," he says.

I call Captain Paul B. press officer for the NYPD. "You must have confused him with somebody else," he says." Detective W. has been on the force for less than a year. He learned of this plot and was put on the case under the supervision of the Bureau of Special Services…"

"The cops are lying," I tell Nathanson.

"Do we have a picture of the guy at one of those other events?" he asks.

I call Harry in the lab. In all the crowd scenes there is not one shot of Ray. "See how careful he is to avoid having his picture taken?" I tell Nathanson. "That should prove something."

"Yeah, that he wasn't there," he says.

The *Post* goes with the official version: A courageous young cop saved the country from a heinous act of sabotage. The editorial page uses a quote from Robert Collier, one of the plotters—"I wanted to draw attention to the condition of my race"—to warn that use of violence will turn the public against their worthy cause.

In a fever of indignation I bang out a lead:

"Was he an undercover hero? Or a police agitator? Did he uncover a plot to blow up the Statue of Liberty? Or foment one to entrap innocent people?"

Won't work. Without corroboration it's my word against the NYPD. I can see Bob F. handing the copy to George T. "Look at this masterpiece." And Trow spiking it with savage glee.

It's infuriating. This guy is taking bows. And three gullible potheads are going to jail.

"BUT NOT THIS WAY"

March 1965

Every night I check the doorway for the white envelope with my induction notice. No relief when it's not there. Only means the day of reckoning is that much closer.

"Book a bust," Benny says. "Get caught boosting a book or a record. It'll take six months for your case to come up, then they'll put you on probation, which'll push you even further to the back of the line."

"Is that what you did?" I ask.

"Nah, I'm puttin' in for the Marines."

My father has the solution: join the National Guard. It's an easy, legal way to duck the draft without the stigma. An eight-year commitment, but keeps you at home and working and spares you two years active duty. His Army buddy Warren F. is commander of a Signal Corps Company in Westchester. "There are only a few spots open and they keep them for the local kids," my father says, "but he'll fit you in..."

The Company is in an old Armory off the Saw Mill River Parkway. There's a bronze pillar showing the names of the founding members. An orange and white Signal Corps flag flutters over the doorway next to Old Glory.

Through a vestibule, photos of past commanders, old uniforms, rifles, helmets, sepia photos in glass cases. Into an empty hall, sun streaming through vaulted windows. A kid in fatigues is pushing a mop. The suspicious look you get in a strange neighborhood just before they jump you. I ask for Colonel F…" Yeah," he says and throws the mop clattering across the floor in an obscure threat.

I follow him down a corridor of empty offices. "This company is for guys from the area," he says without turning around. "We all grew up together. Some of our dads were in it, too."

Message received: It's a country club and you're not a member. He opens a door marked "Commander" and ushers me in with a snotty bow. Colonel F. is squat like a high school tackle, starched tunic, red face bulging at the sides, like a balloon ready to pop. He jumps up, hand out.

"Is this Bernie's boy?" Bone crushing grip. Testing me? Okay asshole… I squeeze back and see the tiniest wince around his eyes. "Tough like your old man. Can you drink like him? Bet you can, being a newspaper man. We'll put you to the test up here. A lot of the old timers show up for the July Fourth barbeque. Maybe we can talk Bernie into leaving Brooklyn for a few hours."

"It'll take more than burgers," I say.

"I know a dish that could get him up here in a heartbeat," he says, then catches himself. "Well, enough of that… We're a real military unit with a real tradition of service. You have some companies, in Westchester especially, we call them Champagne Clubs because they're just an excuse to dodge the draft without doing anything. We're soldiers here. Mandatory presence at monthly meetings and two weeks of summer camp. We drill and run and do calisthenics, self-defense, marksmanship. You'll be as sharp as any active-duty soldier. And you'll learn a technical specialty, from wire stringing to complex electronics. Your dad said you didn't want to be treated as a privileged character. Don't worry, we'll make good use of your talents. You can help publicize the events we hold in the hall. We have a monthly newsletter. You could edit it into a real professional publication…"

So I'll spend eight years with a bunch of guys who hate me. Write press releases about the Ladies Auxiliary Bake Sale. Obits for the "old timers" from the Soldiers and Sailors Home...

F. hands me a brochure, "The Signal Corps is the nerve center of the military," he says. "In charge of everything from field telephones to classified networks. Signal Corps counts five Medal of Honor winners. We're in the field setting up communications, often under fire. We saw action in World War I and II. We train to be ready in case we're mobilized. But don't worry we won't be. All active units would have to be committed and then they call up the Reserves before they get around to the Guard..." Leans forward and lowers his voice..." Confidentially, we'll be needed to protect the home front. We've had secret briefings about Communist agitators trying to incite sabotage, mass marches, attacks on recruiting centers..."

Great... When I'm not flacking cookies I'll be clubbing peace marchers.

"Come up for our meeting next week," F says. "It's only an hour. We'll go out for a beer after. You can get to know the guys..."

Outside I pass the mop boy dropping a slug in the Coke machine. He ignores me.

I tear up my enlistment forms. Skip the meeting...

"F. called me," my father says. "They missed you last week."

"Can't do it," I say. "Felt like a snotty rich guy getting special privileges..."

"It'll keep you out. Isn't that what you want?"

"Yeah. But not this way."

ONLY IN AMERICA

It's the Doomsday Solution: Marriage. Married men are not officially exempt, but they're given high draft numbers and so far no one's been taken.

I pitch a story about how more men are getting married to avoid the draft. "Prove it," Nathanson says.

I spend the morning at the Marriage License Bureau. My theory is that if draft calls have doubled, marriage licenses must have increased as well. Wrong, a clerk tells me. License applications are the lowest they've been in months.

Okay, I don't need stats for a feature, three good stories will suffice. I look for odd couples: Old-young, foreign-native, bohos, unmatched pairs who look like they came together in the peace movement. No one will say they're getting married to duck the draft. I appeal to a hippie couple. "It's important to tell this story." They exchange doubtful looks. "Sorry, We don't want the FBI breathing down our necks."

Why am I obsessed with this story? Will I feel better if I find others who are lying and conniving like me? This is a phony war, no one in my family supports it. So why are they trying to make me feel guilty?

My father and uncles have been conspicuously reminiscing about their wartime experiences. My mother is strangely silent on the subject, but she's already given me up to the Draft Board. My grandmother tells stories about Easter pogroms in the old country. Polish peasants spitting on her father's gaberdine. Her cousin Asher hiding in a potato cellar in Kishinev as the Cossacks impaled Jewish men on pitchforks, slit open pregnant women's bellies and dropped in live cats to eat the fetuses. (Who could think of that?) America was their only chance. They cried when they saw the Statue of Liberty. Grandpa Dave tells how he went back to Czernowitz for a visit and the cop who had thrown his father down a well stopped him on the street. "Big shot Chief of Police. I held up my American passport like to a vampire and he ran away."

Do I owe Lyndon Johnson two years of my life because America saved my grandparents?

My mother's cousin Willie was a "*shlammer*", a collector for the notorious Brooklyn bookie Harry Gross, who corrupted the entire Vice Squad. But he flew over forty missions as a bombardier and when he was jailed for sending porno books and movies through the mail my uncle flew to Fort Worth and dropped his war record on the judge's bench without a word. "Case dismissed," the judge said. "Release this man immediately." The story always ends with the same refrain: "Only in America would they have done this for a Jew."

My father had to put up with Jew haters in Officers Candidate School. They messed up his bunk and footlocker before inspection, jammed his rifle, spread rumors about him, complained to the officers. But they were washed out, while he graduated with highest honors and a commendation from the General.

Yeah, I know. Only in America.

"I CAN'T SUBJECTIVIZE THE SEX ACT RIGHT NOW"

August 1965

Reports out of San Francisco that demonstrators spat on soldiers coming off the troop ships. Attacked them with buckets of red paint at San Francisco Airport. The West Coast movement is considered more militant and the Village radicals want to catch up. There's talk about "splatting" the sailors when the fleet comes in. Vandalizing recruiting offices. Rocks through the windows...

"Fuck vandalizing," someone says. "Blow the fuckers up."

"Might hurt somebody..."

"Fuck'em. Anybody in there deserves to die."

"Soldiers are workers," I say.

Sneers. "Bullshit! They're mercenaries."

It's snobbery, class prejudice. Suburban college kids playing at Revolution. One of them is probably FBI. Probably the one who wanted to "blow the fuckers up."

I might be the only one who actually has friends in the military. Loyal friends, who protected me against the Jew-hating bullies in the schoolyard. I'm against the war, but I can't be in a movement that will spit on the troops.

Marriage is my last resort.

I become the real person in my made-up story. Table hopping in bars and coffeehouses. Doing the room at parties. Asking:

"Will you marry me to keep me out of the army?"

That's me getting the cold looks, the laughter, the mock

343

negotiations.

"Is this a come on?"

"Do we have to live together?"

"You're paying the rent, right? And the food?"

"I have two cats."

"Can my boyfriend live with us?"

I see Peggy, my bus buddy from the "I Have a Dream" March walking down Macdougal.

"Will you marry me?"

"God…" She laughs. "This is so sudden…"

"I have to get married right away before I get my draft notice."

"Guys keep proposing" she says. "I've never been so popular in my life. I'm rethinking my opposition to the war."

"We don't have to have sex…"

"I'm glad you made that clear. Are you a good provider?"

"I'll pay the rent, buy the food…"

"At least you could get on one knee," she says.

I drop down right in the middle of Bleecker Street and take her hand. "Will you marry me?"

A doting smile. "I'd love to," she says. "But I'm already spoken for. My friend Dominic from Immaculate Heart School. He was expelled from the Seminary in a big scandal and got his draft notice a few weeks later. It's strictly platonic," Peggy says. "He's gay."

"Then all he has to do is tell them," I say.

"He can't, it would kill his mother…" She pats my cheek. "'Poor baby, you should see your face. Don't worry my friend Pam will do it. She's looking to marry a white guy to make a political statement…"

Marry a Black girl? Make a political statement? All I want is to get out of the Army.

"Is there a problem because she's Black?"

"Of course not," I say. "No problem at all."

The next night. Pam is at a window table in the Figaro. The dark skinned girl from the demo at the construction site and the March on

Washington. Big glasses, serious Afro. Hiding her body in a floppy work shirt over baggy jeans. So engrossed in *The Second Sex* she doesn't look up.

"Can't put it down, huh?"

"Have you read it?" she asks.

"Couldn't pick it up," I say.

She doesn't laugh, but at least she knows it's a joke.

"I used to see De Beauvoir and Sartre at the La Coupole in Paris," I say.

"Did you talk to them?"

"Can a cabbage talk to a king?"

"Look at a king," she corrects.

She turns down a cigarette. "Am I gonna have to go outside to smoke when we're married?" I ask.

"Why are are you doing this?" she asks.

"To get out of the Army," I say.

"I got that. But why do you want to get out of the Army?"

Trick question, but I know the answer. "I resent being a pawn in Johnson's proxy war with Russia…"

"Johnson's racist war you mean. He could never get away with this if it were white people."

"I don't know. We fought the Germans twice…"

"We let them kill a million French and British before we got into World War I. Stood by while Hitler conquered Europe. People like Lindbergh and Henry Ford actually supported him. Only got into it when the Japanese attacked Pearl Harbor because Roosevelt could sell white America a war against the Yellow Peril."

"The facts are right, but the conclusion is wrong," I say. "Not everything is done primarily for racist reasons."

"That's where *you're* wrong," she says.

"We're having our first fight," I say.

She reaches across the table "Hold my hand," she says. I take it. Warm… She looks around. "Kiss me," she says.

I lean across the table and aim for her lips, but she turns away and I get cheek.

"It's too easy in the Village" she says. "Let's go into enemy territory…"

We walk down Macdougal. "Put your arm around me," she says.

Down the stairs to the West Fourth Street station. Ordinary people, black and white. Sidelong looks, pursed lips of disapproval.

"Kiss me," Pam says.

"People resent public displays of affection from anybody," I say.

She holds her arms out. "Scared?"

I swoop down and grab her. Plant one on her soft lips before she can move her head. She pushes me away. "Don't overdo it."

People walk by, deliberately looking away.

"Feel the tension?" she asks. "Racist guilt causes a revulsion deep in the white psyche."

On the train she rests her head on my shoulder, pretending to sleep. A white woman gets up and changes her seat.

"I'm feeling it now," I say.

We get off at forty-second and walk through Times Square, arms around each other. Past the pimps, the junkies, drag queens and tourists. Glares and comments. Two Black guys walk right at us. We have to separate to avoid a collision.

"Hypocrites," Pam says. "They'll call me a traitor to my race and then go panting after white girls like dogs in heat"

We turn up Eleventh Avenue to the Market Diner, an all night joint across from the central UPS garage. Guys in brown uniforms. Cabbies, truck drivers…

"Two drunks broke my cousin's leg out here in the parking lot," Pam says.

"Was he with a white girl?"

"No, he just wanted a cheeseburger. Cops told him he should have known better than to come here…"

"Why? It's a worker's hangout…"

"That's old left romanticism," Pam says. "The white working class is the most bigoted group in America."

No heads turn as we take a window table, but I catch a few looks in the counter mirror. The waitress stands at the register pointedly ignoring us.

"She won't come," Pam says. "She thinks I'm a hooker."

"But you don't look anything like...

"Any Black woman with a white man is automatically a hooker to them. We know because we had this discussion with the owners. They're not ashamed. They told us they don't want the Times Square element, they called it, hanging around in here."

I swipe some menus off the counter. "See? Nobody bothered me." "You're bigger than they are."

"Taller, not bigger. I'm not scaring anybody. Let's order. If they don't serve us, I'll show them my press card..."

"No, they'll just spit in the food." She gets up. "C'mon, we have one more stop..."

We walk the gauntlet down Times Square again. More dirty looks and remarks.

"You've made this trip before," I say.

"With two other boys. They changed their minds, but I don't hold it against them. In some ways their commitment has to be stronger than mine. I mean I'm stuck being Black. I have to fight or die..."

We go to the uptown IRT. Stand in a crowded platform, holding hands. "Move back behind the pillars in case somebody tries to push you onto the tracks, "Pam says.

After one-sixteenth, Columbia University, I'm the only white person in the car. The looks are more curious than hostile.

"This would make a good story," I say. "A mixed couple takes a subway ride town. White hostility. Black curiosity turning into indifference as we head toward the Bronx, because Hispanics are used to mixed couples... A short film, Candid Camera style..."

We get out at one forty-seventh and walk, arms around each

other, like lovers to one forty-fourth and Convent Ave. "I think I just got a smile," I say.

"You'll get hostility up here too, but not as often," Pam says.

To a basement apartment in a brownstone. A cluttered Boho pad. Posters, paperbacks, a stack of albums by a turntable. Music stand. "My sister plays cello," Pam says. "She must be at rehearsal, but she'll be home soon."

I plop down on a couch. "Whose house is this?

"My parents," Pam says. "My dad teaches at Howard."

"Will they approve of this?"

"You kidding? They want me to marry a nice colored boy and give them grandchildren. I'm sure your folks won't approve either."

"Actually, they might. They're old time Commies. Put the social over the personal every time. My mom'll love you. My father, too. He fought in Spain with the Lincoln Brigade."

Pam shows me a folder full of clippings. "Did you ever hear of the Loving couple?"

"That's what we'll be..."

"No. Richard and Mildred Loving..."

A photo of a white guy with a blonde crewcut kissing a Black woman.

"Two simple rural people, who grew up together in Virginia," Pam says. "Fell in love and wanted to get married. But interracial marriages are illegal in the great Commonwealth of Virginia, home of Thomas Jefferson, George Washington. They were arrested and had to leave the state. They've been denied by every court in Virginia."

"The Supreme Court will vindicate them."

Shakes her head with a pitying smile. "You have this immigrant faith in American institutions. Spend a few months a married to a Black woman, you'll have a different perspective."

"You'll keep me strong..."

"Wait a second." She slides down the sofa. "This will have to be a partnership, not a real marriage. Not even a casual affair. I can't subjectivize the sex act right now."

"YOU DON'T HAVE TO TAKE ME HOME"

I feel redeemed. This marriage will give meaning to what is essentially a selfish act of draft dodging. My parents will be proud. The *Post* will love it. I can see the headline: REPORT FROM THE REVOLUTION.

We meet in the Figaro to plan the wedding. Should it be a trip to the License Bureau, civil ceremony and then an announcement to parents and friends? Should we include a minister to mollify Pam's parents?

"My folks won't go for that," I say. "They get Jewish at the weirdest times."

"Then, we'll get a Rabbi to co officiate," Pam says.

"You mean one of those folkies, who play three chords on a guitar and sing *Havah Nagilah?* My grandmother will put a curse on me."

"Maybe we can get Martin Luther King Jr. to marry us," she says. "Then that Rabbi who was at the march could co officiate…"

"Joachim Prinz? We'll have to make it a Page One story to get them. Maybe get married in Mississippi. Go to a courthouse in a small town. Maybe where Schwerner, Goodman and Chaney were killed. Or Medgar Evers… They'll turn us away. We get a local lawyer to help us. Get King and Prinz into it. Reporters from all over the world…"

We're sitting close, arms touching. Her thigh is warm against mine.

"What if we get scared at the last minute?" she asks.

"Trick is to get so much publicity we have to do it."

The subway ride is easier. No hostile looks.

"People are getting used to us," I say.

She pats my hand with a smile. " It's you. You're getting used to that feeling of strangeness. That part of you that's always watching. You've become the Other."

She stops me at the door. There's a light on in the apartment. "My sister's home. She doesn't know about this…"

"Let me come in, I won't tell her…"

She pushes me back. "No, not yet…"

"I get it, you're keeping your options open. Don't want anybody to know so you can back out."

"I won't need an excuse," she says.

"Well whenever this happens you have to promise me a present on our wedding night. Just one present. If you don't want to give it again, that's fine."

Hands on my shoulders. Electric touch. "Typical male. You think if I let you do it once I'll be your sex slave forever"

"That is my plan," I say.

She laughs and hugs me for the first time. The hug lasts a few seconds longer than it has to.

August 24th

Weeks of excitement. Obstacles rising and being overcome. The Martin Luther King Jr. option is a "logistical impossibility," we're told. Both he and Prinz are booked solid for months. But people in Mississippi can get us a Black pastor. And there's a Reform Rabbi in Oxford, who might co officiate.

Sleepless, full of pent up expectation. We speak ten times a day. When I'm out on a story I rush to a phone booth to call Pam. She leaves a stack of messages at the city room.

"This can't be the way you feel before a regular marriage," I say.

"That's because we're marrying for a real cause, not the illusion of romantic love," she says.

Thinking about her constantly, rushing to meet, talking excitedly about the world, while being oblivious to it. Nuzzling, hugging... I dream of her rising above me, shedding her clothes, her gleaming black body emerging like a butterfly...

"Are you beginning to subjectivize?" I ask.

"'Fraid not," she says.

August 25th

Lyndon Johnson poops on our party. Working in secret, with no prior announcement, he cancels the marriage exemption. Sneaks the statement on a slow news Saturday morning.

Anyone married after August 26 will now be eligible for the draft. All married men under the age of 26 will re examined for eligibility.

Johnson lied about expanding the war. About not sending American boys to fight a war Asian boys should be fighting. He lied about not drafting married men.

The old radicals in Union Square aren't surprised.

"He needs bodies," says Ben, Naomi's grandpa. "Thinks he can win by force of arms like we did in World War II. Kill 'em until they say uncle..."

"We'll need a million troops to hold Vietnam. The country won't stand for it."

"Generals always fight the last war."

"They're fighting the Revolutionary War," says one of the anti-war vets. "Marching patrols down the road in plain sight. Movin' heavy weapons so everybody knows where we are. Don't know nothin' about jungle fightin'..."

"We beat the Japanese in the jungles..."

The vet sucks so hard on his cigarette I expect him to have a coughing fit. "We outshot 'em... Plus the people were with us. Different this time. They don't want us there. Little kids, old ladies are the eyes and ears of the Viet Cong. Everybody wants to see us get our asses kicked."

News footage of a Marine putting his Zippo lighter to an old woman's cottage in the village of Cam Ne as she pleads piteously for him to stop.

Union Square. Grandpa Ben is drawing crowds with his radical rhetoric. "A totalitarian state can remain in a permanent state of war, because its people are expendable," he says. "A democracy needs the consent of the oppressed. During World War Two we agreed to put the Revolution on hold while we beat the fascists. It took us five hundred thousand American casualties to do it. That won't happen again."

But the latest Gallup poll shows that 61 per cent of the American public supports the escalation.

"That number will go down with every battle we lose."

But we're not losing. We forced the Viet Cong to lift the siege of Pleiku. The Marines killed 600 Viet Cong in an assault and only lost 50.

The vet takes another sucking drag. "Fifty dead is like fifty thousand to us…"

Pam is waiting at the Figaro. It's a farewell meeting. No handholding. Snuggling seems superfluous. "We should write to that column, 'Can This Marriage Be Saved,'" I say

She winces at the joke. "We could go through with it anyway and then you could refuse to be inducted."

"They'll lock me up. Just gave a guy twenty-two months for burning his draft card."

"It would be the big story you always want," she says.

"For a day. And then I've got twenty-one months and twenty-nine days behind bars. I can do more good writing and reporting…"

"Safe on the sidelines of the struggle? No personal commitment."

Is she mocking me, showing her true feelings now that she knows it's over?

"I was willing to commit to this marriage," I say.

"Because there was something in it for you. The real test is taking direct action with no hope of personal gain. Try it. Overcome your fear. You might discover a courage you didn't know you had."

A hard core radical, she senses something soft and malleable in me. The horny kid, the goofy jokester. I'm expendable.

"Foot soldier of the revolution," I say. "You want to replace one coercive state with another."

"I want to stop a war that's being used as a distraction to stop the Black Revolution," Pam says.

"It's more than that," I say. "Johnson doesn't want to be the first US president to lose a war. He'll sacrifice a whole generation to save face. But not me. I won't be his bitch or anybody else's…"

"Anybody else's?" Anger flares in her eyes. "You think you're my white bitch?"

She gets up. "You don't have to take me home."

HAVEN'T DONE THAT YET

It finally comes the week before Thanksgiving. The oversized white envelope from Selective Service with the dreaded salutation:

"GREETINGS... You are to report for "induction" on February 7, 1966..."

It's my own fault. I could have stayed with the shrink. Could have played the queer card. Married sooner instead of waiting until it was the only option left. Gone to Canada. Become a Quaker. Shot myself in the foot like the Jews in the Old Country did to dodge twenty-five years in the Czar's army. Jumped off a fire escape like Rizzo's cousin. In my acid-addled brain I was convinced that in some Kafkesque scenario a clerk would drop my file behind a cabinet where it would sink in a pile of dust, rats nibbling it to invisibility. And I would live happily ever after in the screwball comedy that was my life.

But Kafka didn't write Hollywood endings. This isn't *Bringing Up Baby*, it's *I Am a Fugitive from a Chain Gang*.

My father has pulled more strings. My Godfather Nat L. works in the Alien Registration section of the Justice Department and has friends in the Pentagon. He'll call a General and get me assigned to the Pubic Information Office at NATO Headquarters in Versailles.

This could be a great deal. Weekends in Paris. I could contrive to bump into Colette. "You'll have to make it easy for Nat to recommend you," my father says. "Score high on all the tests. Pass a special French exam..."

"I can do that."

"Excel in Basic. No General will sponsor a mediocre soldier."

"I'll excel."

He wants me to go in. Can't brag about a draft dodging son. Then again he has been trying all along to make things easy for me. He's as conflicted about this as I am.

I run it by the Sandy, a Wall Street lush in the Page One. Blue pin stripes, red tie, slurping his Gin and Bitter Lemon. He was in the ski troops, ran sabotage missions behind German lines. "Never happen, laddie," he says. "They need gook-speakers for this war. They'll promise you Paris and ship you to Monterrey to learn Vietnamese." He pats my cheek with a clammy hand. "Bring your snorkel, son, you're headed for the shit."

Richard Nixon issues a statement saying we'll need 125,000 troops to win the war. It's rumored that LBJ and McNamara have put a cap of 195,000 on the number they feel they can commit without political damage.

Derision around the City Desk.

"Meaningless. Ten per cent, maybe twelve and a half will be combat stroops. The rest will be in support..."

"Even if we send a million guys over there and shoot every kid in black pajamas..."

"They've been fighting a thousand years. The Chinese, the Japanese, the French, each other. Now us... They've got more troops than we have bullets. And if they run out, the Chinese will chip in like they did in Korea..."

Seven US planes are shot down in one day.

The National Coordinating Committee To End the War in Vietnam organizes protests all over the country.

Stories that Australian kids are running to New Zealand to dodge their draft.

On Christmas Eve LBJ announces a halt to the US bombing of

North Vietnam and tries to arrange negotiations for a ceasefire. The North Vietnamese won't come to the table. A foreign journalist writes: "they feel they can grind the Americans down in a war of attrition…"

I move my stuff back to my parents' house. My mother is using my room for storage. Piles of old clothes, stacks of my father's ten inch record albums. Boxes overflowing with assorted crap—broken dishes, playing cards, board games, mangled books, sepia photos from the old country. I get a scratchy throat and stuffed nose from the dust. Run into the city to sleep at a girlfriend's house. Complain to her: "My parents don't want me around anymore, but if I don't call they get pissed off…"

The enormity of the war has crept up on me. What started as a way to avoid two wasted years of excruciating boredom has become a statement of protest. The shame of dodging the draft is replaced by the guilt that I'm taking the easy way out with a cushy job when I should be burning my draft card.

A Quaker named Norman Morrison burns his card the hard way. He puts it in his pocket and sets himself on fire in front of the Pentagon. That Quaker in Washington Square said we should act according to the dictates of our conscience.

The goal is not to kill any "little brown people."

Haven't done that yet.

"GOULD!"

February 7, 1966

Early this morning my mother gave me a bag of sandwiches. Cream cheese and cucumber with tomato, tuna, leftover meat loaf. "I won't need this much," I say, "it's an hour's ride to Dix."

"Keep 'em," my father says. "Always make sure you have something to eat."

He gives me a package of jockey shorts and a few pair of thick white socks, along with a pair of shower scuffs. "Keep 'em in your foot locker. Always make sure you have dry socks..."

A quick hug from my mother, eyes shining. A nod from Dad. They seem proud of a son who's going off to serve in a war they detest. They would have been equally proud if I had married a Black woman and gone to jail for protesting that war.

Whitehall Street. They're hustling us from station to station. "Arm's length. Focus on the back of the neck of the man in front of you."

No rebels in the ranks. Some are looking forward to the experience. The rest accept their fate.

Compared to my other physicals this is done with military precision. We know the drill. "Say ahhh... Drop your pants... Cough... Piss in this vial and drop in this dipstick... Show it to me, don't give it to me... Bend over and touch the wall. Now spread your cheeks... Check this list. Bed wetting, drug use, homosexual urges..." Nobody checks.

No line in front of the shrink's office. I may be the only artless dodger in the ranks. Sergeant hands out another list. "Put a check next to any organization you know or have been affiliated with."

Don't remember seeing this. They must save it for a last minute loyalty check. Looks like a compendium of every radical group that ever existed. Lincoln Brigade, Socialist Workers Party. Industrial Workers of the World, founded by Eugene Debs. They're all defunct.

I check off every organization I know. Hand it back to the sergeant. He doesn't even look.

Silent shuffling, everyone alone with their thoughts. The little kid who wanted to go into the Airborne has latched onto me, chattering excitedly.

"My brother was at Parris Island. Now he's in Vietnam, can't tell us where. I wanted to go with him, but my parents said you gotta sign up for four years. Then I wanted to enlist in the Army and they told me that's three years. Let 'em draft you, my father said. Two years, you'll see if you like it. You can always re up..."

They march us down a flight of stairs.

"Takin' us out the back so we don't run into the picket line," a kid says.

My little friend blows a spritz of indignation at the sergeant. "I'd like to fuckin' machine gun those cocksuckers."

"They are within their Constitutional rights," he says.

"Let 'em go fuckin' fight for the Communists if that's the way they feel..."

They bring us into a large classroom. Blackboard with an oath of allegiance written in green chalk, podium with an oversized Stars'n' Stripes looming. A sergeant pulls down a screen and turns on a projector. The oath appears in bold caps.

A side door is opened. Line of school buses parked along Battery Park.

"Take a piss call and get some candy," the sergeant says. "You got a long bus ride."

Another sergeant walks to the front. "Anyone here have any objection to swearing the oath of allegiance?"

Shrugs and mutters.

"After you take the oath you'll form a double line and march to the buses. Recruits at the head of the line will go to the last bus. Once on the bus you will take seats in the rear, moving up row by row until the bus is filled..."

A few more shuffles and mutters.

"Alright settle down," he says and waits for silence.

"Raise your right hand..."

"GOULD!"

There's a sergeant at the door with a folder in his hand. He calls again:

"GOULD!"

"RICE OR NOODLES?"

Following the sergeant down a sputtering fluorescent hallway. He knocks on an office door.

A young guy is alone at a metal desk in a bare room. One bar means lieutenant. "Schwartz" on his nameplate. Another Jewish pretty boy, looks like Tony Curtis. Doing it the right way. Good marks, good college, pre med... ROTC...

Takes the folder. "Thank you, Sergeant..."

"Buses are leaving in seventeen minutes, sir..."

"That's fine, thank you..." Squints like he thinks he knows me. "Heywood Gould..."

Looks at the list. "Lincoln Brigade went out of existence before you were born. So how could you be a member?"

"My father was a member," I say. "Fought in Spain..."

"Was he in the American Army as well?"

"Yes, he was a lieutenant..."

"Really? I wouldn't think they would give a commission to someone who fought in Spain."

Caught in a lie. Double down.

"He had a battlefield commission."

"Don't you want to follow in his footsteps?"

"I was ready to go. You pulled me off the line."

"We have to check. These are subversive groups. You might not be aware of the extent of their subversion... We've had people in here who refused to take the oath..." An indignant look. "Coordinated incidents where people lay down in front of the buses, while the inductees refused to get on. Would you do anything like that?"

"Don't have the guts," I say.

"To be a traitor? I hope not." Checks the list. "You're not really a member of the Socialist Workers Party, are you?"

"I was told to check off any group I was associated with or even knew about..."

"And how are you associated with the Socialist Worker's Party?"

"I've been to meetings. Know people in the party..."

"Know people in the Party," He writes it down "Okay... Committee to Free Ben Davis? Know who Ben Davis is?"

"Black Communist City Councilman framed for sedition."

"Framed? I don't think so..." Another look... "Vito Marcantonio Social Club, " he says.

"Labor Party City Councilman," I say. "An advocate for workers' rights."

"Also for the overthrow of the American government."

"Through the electoral process," I say.

"Industrial Workers of the World. They were bomb throwing anarchists."

"Most of the bombs were thrown by goons and Pinkertons," I say.

"Do you believe in their Marxist ideology?"

"I believe in the abolition of the wage system as the first step toward true equality."

"No wages? How are you going to get paid, in bananas?"

"All productive relationships will be restructured..."

Sounds pompous when I hear it said by others. But when I say it myself I feel conviction surging through me.

"Restructured by who?" he asks.

"By the workers. When their engagement in voluntary associations like unions and councils has created a new consciousness..."

"Oh please Mr. Gould, you don't really believe any of this will happen. You checked these organizations off because you knew that would get you out."

What does he mean, get me out?

"Where did you hear about this trick, at one of your Socialist Worker meetings?"

What trick?

He checks his watch. Only a few minutes before the bus leaves. "You're not a teacher, I hope. Subverting young minds."

"Reporter," I say. "I work for the *Post*."

'That's it, I knew I'd seen your name somewhere. You think the *Post* would want to know that one of its reporters is a Communist draft dodger? Because this will be reported to the FBI. They'll open a file on you, if they haven't already. They'll talk to friends and family. Interview your editors. Call you in for interrogation. This thing will haunt you the rest of your life. If you try to get a job or even a mortgage. If you want to run for office…"

"That'll never happen…"

"How do you know? Can you sit here and tell me what you'll be like twenty years from now?"

"I can tell you I won't want to run for office."

Smooths the list and puts it back in the folder. "You can go, Mr. Gould…"

Stunned… "You mean I'm not being inducted?"

"Don't think you're home free, this is just temporary… They'll check you out. Six months, maybe less. Probably clear you for service. That black mark will stay on your record. You'll regret what you did today."

Is this what got me out? Was the Army was so afraid of a bunch of dead radicals that they passed on a prime piece of cannon fodder, who could also type and write press releases?

Out in the hall. The sergeant is smoking a cigarette a few doors down. A knowing smile. Doesn't seem to hate me. Gives me a green ticket. "Here, you got a meal comin'…"

Upstairs to the commissary on the first floor. The two sergeants who beat up the pony tailed vet in the morning are eating apple pie a la mode. A Black guy in whites with a chef's toque is behind the counter. I hand him the ticket. He smiles—"uh huh"—like he knows what I did, too and holds up a plate.

"Goulash today… Rice or noodles…"

"Be right back…"

Call the paper. Get Bott, the City Editor. "They kicked you out, huh?" he says. "Probably found a condition they missed the first time around. Remember when you fainted at that fire in Brooklyn?"

I did not fucking faint! I thought the fire was under control and ran into the building. Got disoriented in a gust of wet smoke and bumped into a wall. Blacked out for a second, tops. Putz from the *News* got a shot of the firemen dragging me out by the collar. Made me the joke of the week.

"Lieberman's sick," Bott says. "Cover Brooklyn Police Headquarters tomorrow morning…"

Back to Square One. To *chicharrones* and floaters in Brownsville. They thought I was gone so they gave away my Criminal Court beat. There's a good murder trial in the Bronx, but somebody else has it. I was set for the 4 to 12 shift. Covering all the important stories alone. Now I'll be taking pizzeria stick ups off the ticker on Bergen Street.

I'll have to work my way back to the better stories. Maybe I can get them to send me cover the war. Nah, they'll make a joke out of it. "If the Army wouldn't send you to the Vietnam why should we?"

Call home. My mother is worried. "Did they say anything about your lungs?"

"No, why should they?"

"Nothing… We'll just have to get you a full check up. You've never really had one."

What's she been hiding from me? What's wrong with my lungs? They used to give me hot mustard plasters on my back when I was sick.

My grandmother poking me. "He's all bones." The doctor tapping my back with hard fingers. "Have you ever given him the skin test?" And my mother, "no, he's fine since he had his tonsils out."

Shit, do I have TB? All the reefer I've smoked, the hash... Packs of reds... Am I going to die spitting blood like Kafka or Orwell? But with no body of work to show for it.

Call my father in his office.

"I had a feeling you'd be back," he says. "What did you do, refuse the oath?"

"Checked off a list of subversive organizations. Lincoln Brigade, Socialist Workers... Will that get you into trouble?"

"Not me, you're the dangerous radical in the family now... What did they say?"

"They said the FBI would call me in for an interview and probably clear me for service."

"They won't give up, they need civilian talent. Might try to recruit you."

"For what?"

"To spy on the anti war movement. You have a perfect cover as a reporter. They'll offer you a monthly stipend to go to all the meetings. They probably have people doing it already."

He seems so sure of this. How does he know? Did they recruit him? My mother always said half the Bronx Communist Party were FBI informers. Was he one of them?

"Does the *Post* know what you did?" he asks.

"No, they think it's a medical issue..."

"Don't tell anybody," he says. "Not even your mother."

The buses are gone. All those kids, anxious, apprehensive about their new experience. I want to share it with them. I want to be everywhere. Travel all the roads at once. But I don't want to be part of this war.

Outside, picketers, chanting "Hell no/we won't go..." People running across the street to join them. Some of them are true believers like Peggy and Pam and the kid who got his ass kicked by the hardhats. Like Martin Luther King Jr. and Benjamin Spock. Like Gladys. Some just join the protest, pick up a sign, shout a slogan. Feel great. Be accepted. Some of them are FBI stoolies. What do they believe?

The kids on the bus have bought into the program. They're the guys who fall on the grenade. Others are just going with the flow. Doing their bit, then returning to their lives. Obedient, accepting their fate, whatever it might be. Good kids, we could have been friends. Like in an old war movie, I felt the camaraderie on the line. Would I have learned to make my bed?

Into the cold. Protesters call to me from behind the police barricade. "Right on, brother... Fight the power..." They see me as a hero who resisted at the last second. "C'mon brother, join us..."

Cops push them back. One young cop, trying to stare me down. Forget it, pal, I know your secret. You only joined the force for the deferment. You took the safe route, now you're acting like Captain America.

Icy wind cuts through me. I shiver and cringe. Why am I cold? Is it the guilt?

No, schmuck, you left your jacket in the commissary.

Run back up the stairs into the building. Cop at the door tries to block me—"where do you think you're going?" I jab step to the left and do a spin move around him.

Is that cop chasing me down the corridor? No, it's my own footsteps. Stop a few feet before the door and lean against the wall, to catch my breath so I can stroll in.

I had put my stuff on a chair when I went to the counter. But now it's gone!

Sneaky looks from the sergeants. Fuck this draft dodger, they said, let's dump his shit. Don't give them the satisfaction of asking. Just turn around and walk out.

"Hey buddy, this yours?"

The cook's got it. "You don't wanna leave stuff around here," he says.

The sergeants smile at my relief. They don't hate me. They don't care.

The cook hands me my black leather jacket, little gym bag with my mom's sandwiches and dad's brand new scuffs. "Thanks man, "I say, "I thought I lost it."

"Uh huh…" Twirls a spoon. "Rice or noodles?

THE END

ABOUT THE AUTHOR

Born and raised in Brooklyn, Heywood Gould got his start as a reporter for the New York Post, when it was still known as a pinko rag. Later he financed years of literary rejection with the usual colorful jobs—cabdriver, mortician's assistant, industrial floor waxer, bartender and writing screenplays.

Gould is the author of nine novels, among them *Cocktail, Fort Apache, The Bronx, Double Bang, Serial Killer's Daughter, Leading Lady*—a Hammett Award finalist and *Green Light for Murder*.

He has written nine movies, including *Cocktail, Boys From Brazil, Fort Apache, The Bronx* and *Rolling Thunder*. And has directed four features films. *One Good Cop*, starring Michael Keaton *Trial by Jury* with William Hurt, *Double Bang*, with William Baldwin and *Mistrial*, starring Bill Pullman. He currently lives in New York City.

Read more Heywood Gould stories at
tolmitchebooks.com
For more about the author visit his website
Heywoodgould.com

CPSIA information can be obtained
at www.ICGtesting.com
Printed in the USA
BVHW090852140621
609525BV00010B/333/J